GORDON CHILDE
Revolutions in Archaeology

Bruce G. Trigger

Gordon Childe
REVOLUTIONS IN ARCHÆOLOGY

COLUMBIA UNIVERSITY PRESS   NEW YORK   1980

Published in 1980 in the United States of America by
Columbia University Press

Library of Congress Cataloging in Publication Data

Trigger, Bruce G
  Gordon Childe, revolutions in archaeology.

  Bibliography: p.
  1. Childe, Vere Gordon, 1892–1957. 2. Man,
Prehistoric. 3. Archaeologists—Great Britain—
Biography. I. Title.
CC15.C45T74   1980   930'.1'0924 [B]   79-26410
ISBN 0-231-05038-0

Printed in the United States of America

Contents

Preface

IN RECENT YEARS there has been much renewed interest in the life and writings of Gordon Childe. While various articles have examined particular facets of his work, this is the first attempt to survey the development of his thought over his entire career, though a complete analysis of his life and works could fill many volumes. My book does not provide a detailed personal biography, nor relate the archaeologically less relevant aspects of his thought to the academic and social milieu in which he lived and worked. A lack of knowledge of eastern European languages, and of the intricacies of the history of Marxist philosophy, precludes an in-depth study of the relationship of Childe's ideas to Soviet archaeology and Marxism. The aim of this book is to relate the main lines of his thinking to the development of archaeological theory and practice in western Europe and the English-speaking world during the twentieth century. It seeks to demonstrate how his ideas grew out of an established tradition of archaeological analysis that was much influenced by the social attitudes of its time, and how he later contributed to the development of that tradition. It also shows how the originality and vitality of Childe's thought ensured that to this day his work contains much that has more than historical interest.

I wish to thank Sally Green, Peter Gathercole and George Munster for supplying me with information about various aspects of Childe's work, and for the opportunity to discuss Childe with them. All three are engaged in research on various aspects of his career. George Munster has also supplied me with copies of letters written by Childe that otherwise would not have come to my attention. Professor Robert J. Braidwood has kindly provided me with copies of all his correspondence with Childe. As will be evident from my notes, this has greatly assisted my understanding of him.

I would also like to thank Professor Grahame Clark, who is Childe's literary executor, and the Institute of Archaeology, for permission to reproduce this material.

I am indebted to Professor Robert McC. Adams, Professor Grahame Clark, Professor Glyn Daniel, Mr H. Kilbride-Jones,

7

Professor George Eogan, Professor Stuart Piggott, Dr Roger Summers, and Mr A. R. Turnbull for discussing various aspects of Childe's work with me. Chapter III has benefited from discussion following a presentation of its substance at Cambridge University, 9 May 1977. The substance of Chapter VI and Chapters VII–IX was presented as two lectures to the Anthropology Students' Association of McGill University in the spring term of 1978. Those who have provided pictures are duly acknowledged. The manuscript was typed by Victoria Fox and Alison McMaster.

The research was carried out in England in 1977 while I was on sabbatical leave from McGill University, and also held a Canada Council Leave Fellowship. The completion of the manuscript was further supported by a research grant from the Faculty of Graduate Studies and Research of McGill University.

It is appropriate that I dedicate this book to my mother. It was she who in 1946 presented her nine-year-old son with his first (and still treasured) copy of Childe's *What Happened in History*.

BRUCE G. TRIGGER

McGill University
1978

CHAPTER I

Man and Myth

VERE GORDON CHILDE died in 1957 at the age of sixty-five, yet his legacy still cannot be summarized in the conventional paragraphs that archaeological textbooks assign to scholars whose work truly belongs to the past. Many colleagues who knew Childe continue to regard him either as an inspiration or as a troublesome spirit whose thoughts require polite exorcism. Among a younger generation of British archaeologists, he has become both a potent father-figure to be rebelled against and the guru for a newly-fledged Marxist archaeology.[1] His voluminous and erudite writings are characterized by major shifts in emphasis and orientation and, for various reasons, were neither wholly understood nor accepted by other archaeologists during his lifetime. Controversies about the meaning of his work, especially in recent years, have proliferated. Although we are still too close in time to evaluate Childe's work wholly dispassionately, we can perhaps begin to examine the theoretical underpinnings that gave it world-wide importance and lasting interest.

Childe was born in Sydney, Australia, on 14 April 1892. After graduating from Sydney University he began to study at Oxford in 1914 where, under the influence of Sir Arthur Evans and Sir John Myres, his interests shifted from Classical philology to prehistoric archaeology. He returned to Australia two years later. There he became involved in left-wing political activities and worked for a time as private secretary to the premier of New South Wales. By 1922 he had become disenchanted with the politics of his native country and returned to England. He earned money as a translator, part-time lecturer, and working in the library at the Royal Anthropological Institute. Most of his energies, however, were devoted to studying the prehistory of south-eastern Europe. In 1925, he published *The Dawn of European Civilization* which was to go through six editions in his lifetime. The following year a companion book, *The Aryans*, appeared.

In 1927 Childe accepted the newly founded Abercromby Chair of Archaeology at the University of Edinburgh. Thus he became one of the few professional archaeologists in Britain at that time. In quick succession he published a series of books that confirmed his reputation as an expert on the prehistory of Europe and the Near East. These included *The Most Ancient East* (1928), *The Danube in Prehistory* (1929), *The Bronze Age* (1930), and the first of several revised editions of *The Most Ancient East* entitled *New Light on the Most Ancient East* (1934). Childe also excavated after 1927 in various parts of Scotland and published many studies in an effort to improve the understanding of the prehistory of his adopted land, including *The Prehistory of Scotland* (1935).

In the 1930s Childe became increasingly interested in the study of cultural evolution. This concern found expression in his two most widely read books, *Man Makes Himself* (1936) and *What Happened in History* (1942), as well as in his more specialized *Progress and Archaeology* (1944) and *Scotland Before the Scots* (1946). In these books he sought to delineate regularities in the development of cultures. He hoped that this might help to provide a more balanced understanding of the bleak period through which Europe was then passing.

In 1946 Childe left Edinburgh to become Professor of European Archaeology and Director of the Institute of Archaeology at the University of London. After the war he turned his attention increasingly to conceptual problems in archaeology, a trend reflected in his major publications: *History* (1947), *Social Evolution* (1951), *Piecing Together the Past* (1956), and *Society and Knowledge* (1956). Childe brought these new insights to bear on his interpretation of the prehistory of Europe and the Near East in his final book, *The Prehistory of European Society* (1958).

Childe retired from the Institute of Archaeology in 1956 and the following spring returned to Australia for his first visit in thirty-five years. While hiking in October of that year, he fell to his death in the Blue Mountains, near Sydney.

CHILDE'S REPUTATION

During the 1920s Childe established his professional status on the basis of his systematic study of European prehistory, especially for the second and third millennia BC. His syntheses of this material pioneered a way of viewing it for a generation or more of European archaeologists.[2] Prior to the publication of *Man Makes Himself*, knowledge of Childe's work was confined principally to European archaeologists. Afterwards he acquired a more controversial and world-wide reputation for his evolutionary interpretations of the development of civilization in the Near East from a materialist or rational-utilitarian point of view. In the United States, where his work on European prehistory never became well known, Childe tended to be regarded as a specialist on the Near East, which he asserted he was not.[3] American anthropologists also regarded him, along with their own Julian Steward and Leslie White, as being one of the founding fathers of 'Neo-evolutionism'.[4]

Contemporary archaeologists were especially impressed by Childe's detailed knowledge of the archaeological record for Europe and the Near East. To acquire this information he travelled regularly throughout Europe, visiting museums and excavations and cultivating professional acquaintances. He had an acute visual memory, allowing him to spot similarities among artefacts in far distant regions that went unnoticed by regional specialists.[5] He also read many European languages, and was famous for his industry in tracking down material in obscure journals and citing it in the various editions of his book, *The Dawn of European Civilization*. European archaeologists were aware of this, and sent him copies of their own books. Professor Stuart Piggott claims that Childe eventually came to view this 'less as a compliment than as a right, a due paid to his eminence as a scholar'.[6]

Throughout his career Childe provided archaeologists in different parts of the world with ideas that they found relevant to the analysis of their own data. It is therefore not surprising that his death occasioned a spate of tributes and memorials unprecedented in the field of archaeology. Prominent American archaeologists praised him as 'the leading prehistoric archaeologist of our time'[7] and 'one of archaeology's few very great synthesizers'.[8] In Britain Piggott, overcoming British modesty, described Childe as 'the greatest prehistorian in Britain and probably in the world',[9] while Sir Mortimer Wheeler, a die-hard humanist, stated that Childe had 'made the study of man as nearly a science as perhaps that wayward subject admits'.[10] In his native Australia Childe was described as 'probably the most prolific and the most translated Australian author'.[11] His books had indeed been translated into Chinese, Czech, Dutch, French, German, Hungarian, Italian, Japanese, Polish, Russian, Spanish, Swedish and Turkish.

Several articles have recently been published that have begun the task of examining various aspects of Childe's work from an historical perspective.[12] This has become necessary for understanding him, as the time lapse since his death has precluded most archaeologists today from automatically perceiving his writings in their original context. Instead there is a tendency for his ideas to be invoked or condemned piecemeal, as they relate to current controversies. Peter Gathercole has reminded us that such a procedure 'runs the danger of treating ...

history merely as myth, alternatively accepted or derided . . . in order to justify fashionable attitudes'.[13]

The present study will focus, not on Childe's interpretations of specific archaeological data, but on the ideas that shaped these interpretations. Successive phases of his thinking exerted a marked influence on the development of archaeology. Nevertheless there was sufficient continuity in the evolution of Childe's ideas that, for understanding his life's work, any adherence to a rigid sequence of stages would be highly arbitrary. Nothing can be gained from interpreting his thought as a series of paradigms that replaced one another, which, according to T. S. Kuhn, characterizes the development of a scientific discipline.[14]

The complexity of the influences that shape the thinking of a social scientist ensures that the development of archaeological theory, at least in the short run, is not a unilinear process. Many ideas that seem important or attractive at a particular point in time may prove false or worthless in the long run. Yet the origin of ideas can no more shape the long-term development of archaeological theory than mutation alone determines the development of a biological species. Members of the archaeological profession ultimately judge ideas according to how well they explain an ever-expanding body of archaeological data. This process of selection helps them to overcome the errors and fads of the moment, and to develop a cumulative body of theory that permits an improved and expanded understanding of the past. The frequent convergence of theory in separate archaeological traditions bears witness to the strength and inexorability of this process. Any evaluation of Childe's thought must consider to what degree his ability to modify and expand his understanding of archaeological data kept abreast or ran ahead of the general developments of his time. Such an analysis must take account of the growing corpus of data that was available to him and his awareness of methods for recovering and analysing it.

We will begin by examining the sources of Childe's ideas and how these ideas were modified by him and shaped into broader theoretical formulations that had the power to persuade and inspire contemporary archaeologists. By far the most important source, especially in the early stages of his career, was the highly developed tradition of western European archaeology, which had been established as a scientific discipline for over a century. His research and publications took the form mainly of contributions to the development of that tradition. His thinking was also influenced, however, by ideas that he derived from Soviet archaeology and American anthropology as well as from more remote disciplines. He had a subsidiary interest in philosophy and politics, and was more concerned than were most archaeologists of his time with justifying the social value of archaeology. His thought processes were also demonstrably influenced by his personal responses to the social and economic problems of his day.

CONTROVERSIES

Archaeologists have disagreed about the relative importance of different aspects of Childe's work. Many British archaeologists have chosen to view his theories as having little significance except as scaffolding for what they believe was his main work, the interpretation of European prehistory. Piggott described him as 'a great synthesist and systematizer who, for the first and perhaps for the last time, brought the whole field of European prehistory ... within the grasp of a single scholar's mind'.[15] Elsewhere Piggott stated that to the professional archaeologist Childe was 'above all the ... unwearied constructor of chronological schemes, the man who could survey the European scene with scholarly detachment and always distinguish the prehistoric woods amid the close-set trees of archaeological detail'.[16] Such views are in line with those of traditional historians like Leopold von Ranke, who conceived of facts as constituting the hard core of their discipline, while interpretations were regarded as little different from personal opinion. Other commentators, such as Alison Ravetz[17] and Peter Gathercole,[18] have agreed with Childe's own conclusion, expressed at the close of his career, that his most useful contributions to prehistory were 'interpretative concepts and methods of explanation'.[19] Colin Renfrew occupies a middle position. He has praised Childe for having 'replaced the squabbling contradictions of limited nationalist studies with a grand survey, based both on a detailed study of the actual cultural assemblages in each area and on an admirably explicit methodology'.[20] Renfrew's sustained effort to reinterpret Childe's findings is itself a testimonial to the continuing significance of Childe's work.

In accord with their view that Childe's syntheses of regional prehistory constitute the core of his life's work, some British archaeologists have divided his writings into technical works, aimed at fellow scholars, and other less important speculative writings, intended for the public at large. For the most part the technical works are equated with his regional syntheses, for which *The Dawn of European Civilization* stands as the prototype. Childe helped to foster such a view

13

by stating that *Man Makes Himself* was not a manual of archaeology, but a book written for the general reader.[21] This interpretation fails to take account of Childe's statement that one of his most important regional syntheses, *The Prehistory of Scotland*, had been written in order to stimulate an interest in archaeology among the 'mass of the Scottish people'.[22] *The Most Ancient East* was likewise intended both as a textbook for students and as a summary of Near Eastern archaeology for 'the man in the street'.[23]

There is also disagreement about which books belong to the popular category. Most archaeologists agree that *Man Makes Himself* and *What Happened in History* do; Glyn Daniel adds *Social Evolution*,[24] and Piggott *Progress and Archaeology*, *History* and *The Prehistory of European Society*.[25] Ravetz is certainly correct when she argues that Childe's 'little' books are not popularizations of his regional syntheses, but express another dimension of his scholarship.[26] Daniel recognized this when he described *Man Makes Himself*, *What Happened in History* and *Social Evolution* as 'the most important works of [broad] prehistoric synthesis so far attempted this century'.[27] Childe's work cannot be understood without taking account of both genres.

American archaeologists have alleged a related dichotomy in Childe's thinking. Robert J. Braidwood stated that 'to begin to understand the man, it seems necessary to stress Childe's early training in the humanities, as well as his early commitment to historical materialism'.[28] Irving Rouse argued that there was 'a sharp and conflicting dichotomy in Childe's interests and academic approach, which was to persist throughout most of his career'.[29] He maintained that on the one hand Childe was a humanist who, better than any other scholar of his generation, inductively synthesized archaeological data from an historical point of view; on the other hand, as a socialist, he was strongly influenced by Marxist theories of cultural evolution. This led him to write theoretical works in which he interpreted such data in terms of dialectical materialism. Rouse asserted that in the latter studies Childe adopted a deductive approach, which involved assuming certain theories to be true and selecting archaeological data to illustrate them. He took the view that in the application of this approach Childe ignored facts that were contrary to his theories.

To his fellow archaeologists in Britain 'the great puzzle of Childe at all times was to what extent he was a Marxist'.[30] Even in the Soviet Union, divergent opinions were expressed about his work. While *The Great Soviet Encyclopedia* praised him as 'the most eminent archaeologist of the twentieth century',[31] the archaeologist Alexander Mongait, in his declamation on 'The Crisis in Bourgeois Archaeology', maintained that Childe had not succeeded 'in overcoming many of the errors of bourgeois science', even though 'he understands that scientific truth is in the socialist camp and is not ashamed to call himself a pupil of Soviet archaeologists'.[32] In effect Mongait classified Childe among the despised bourgeois empiricists. Ravetz suggests that when the British Marxist and Classicist George Thomson protested that Childe failed to treat class conflict as a basic factor in social evolution, he was expressing the opinion of many western Marxist intellectuals who believed that Childe had not achieved 'the expected results because in some perverse way he did not try hard enough'.[33] However, John Morris, the editor of *Past and Present*, affirmed that in his archaeological work Childe had sought, perhaps not in vain, 'to shape Marxist philosophy'.[34] Childe's close friend from Oxford days, R. Palme Dutt, stated that Childe remained 'heart and soul with the Marxist movement', and argued that it was Childe's understanding of Marxism that had made him the leading archaeologist of his day.[35]

Gathercole agrees with Dutt that Marxism was 'a persistent intellectual force' from Childe's first book and that it made a logical whole of his work.[36] Nevertheless he believes that, while Childe's comprehension of Marxism grew more refined, he used this understanding as a tool for interpreting the prehistory of Europe in a disappointingly limited manner.[37] In particular Gathercole argues that, by stressing the objective function of scientific knowledge in his later works, Childe was moving away from the more flexible Marxist concept of a dialectical interaction between the means and the relations of production. Marx never made himself clear on the relationship between technology and the patterns of social interaction by which any society produces what its members require for their survival. Yet he saw the 'relations of production' as ultimately determining the form that political, legal and religious expressions of 'social consciousness' assumed in each society. Ravetz draws a distinction between Childe's Marxism of the 1930s, which she characterizes as naive, optimistic and mechanically understood, and the Marxism of his later years that was more subtle and creative. She argues that in the work of that time Childe realized that it was not permissible to apply Marxist theory to archaeological data ready-made, and that he attempted to initiate a more productive dialogue between Marxist theories and archaeological facts. Ravetz sees this as constituting a significant contribution to Marxist philosophy, the importance of which has not been recognized by British Marxists.[38] Ravetz appears to view Childe's work as an early manifestation of the more liberal Marxism now prevalent among Western intellectuals.

Most British archaeologists who knew Childe have tended to discount the importance of Marxism for his work. Wheeler stated that it coloured, rather than shaped Childe's interpretations.[39] Piggott has suggested that Childe experimented with Marxist theories of social development from time to time, and saw in them a model of the past that perhaps might prove useful for understanding archaeological data. He also suggested that the 'shy, idealistic, awkward' young Australian might have seen in Communism the blueprint of a society in which the intellectual enjoyed a more honoured status, and in which an 'Outsider' would be more easily admitted to privilege. In spite of this, Piggott interpreted much of Childe's professed interest in Marxism as a 'convoluted intellectual joke'.[40] Glyn Daniel allowed that Childe had ventured both sentimentally and seriously into Marxism in search of answers to archaeological problems. He also noted, however, that towards the end of his life Childe grew more critical of Soviet archaeological scholarship, and interpreted this to mean that he had also tired of Marxism.[41] Daniel cautioned that it is a mistake to suppose because Childe was a Marxist in politics, he was necessarily a Marxist in his archaeology.[42]

Grahame Clark has a less nuanced view of Childe's commitment to Marxism, and offers a strongly negative assessment of the influence it had on his work. He asserts that Marxism, having propelled Childe into archaeology, crippled the scholarship of his middle years. Only at the end of his life did Childe realize that 'his prophet had played him false' and that Marxism failed to explain cultural processes.[43] Yet the passages that Clark interprets as indicating Childe's disillusionment with Marxism in fact refer to the doctrines of the Soviet linguist and prehistorian, Nicholai Yakovlevich Marr, which Stalin himself denounced in 1950.[44]

There are many differences of opinion about when Childe did his best work. Rouse evidently viewed him as being at the height of his powers at the time of his death,[45] and Ravetz saw the work of his final years as highly creative, if not successful in all respects.[46] Clark stated that Childe's creative period was over by 1930, his further studies being blighted by his deepening involvement with Marxism. D. J. Mulvaney dismissed Childe's publications after 1936 as largely modifying or elaborating old themes,[47] while Gathercole sees his work after 1950 as flawed by his refusal to consider large areas of archaeological and ethnographic information that he might have used to test his hypotheses.[48]

Although Childe was a prolific writer, he is not an easy subject for biographical study. His marked reticence and reluctance to reveal his personal opinions and reactions create problems even for an assessment of his career in which biographical matters are of secondary concern. Childe published only two short evaluations of his work that, as Gathercole observed, 'are too brief to give the reader more than a passing glimpse of . . . his mind, and that very near the end of his life'.[49] The impersonal nature of his books and papers and much of his archaeological correspondence gives special importance to the rare expressions of personal opinion that occur in them, as do the dramatic – often delphic – punch lines in his books. These suggest that, however little we know about his personal beliefs and feelings, it is an error to view Childe as simply the embodiment of his work.[50]

Much has been written about Childe's alleged shyness, social awkwardness and lack of close friends. Stuart Piggott attributed a good deal of this to his physical appearance, which Childe himself deprecated, and Max Mallowan unkindly described him as being so ugly that he was painful to look at.[51] The Australian author Jack Lindsay found his appearance 'odd though likeable', and also suggested that it might account for Childe's reticence.[52] Grahame Clark, however, is sceptical about such speculation, noting that Childe 'was at least as willing as the next man to be photographed'.[53] Piggott has suggested that Childe's personal and professional relationships were complicated by the fact that, as an Australian, he was an outsider in Britain.[54] Clark and Gathercole interpret his academic and emotional involvement with Europe as a reaction against his Australian origins.[55] Yet Lindsay's description of Childe, as he knew him in 1921, suggests that his personality was formed well before his departure from Australia.[56] We shall later argue that the Eurocentrism Childe expressed in his publications may have been derived from the archaeological tradition to which he was exposed as a student at Oxford.

Glyn Daniel recently provided a timely corrective to the view of Childe as an awkward and friendless individual when he stated that he 'was the kindest of men, good company, enjoyed good living and the friendship of very many acquaintances and the devotion of many colleagues and pupils'.[57] Sir Mortimer Wheeler likewise commented on his frequent and kind hospitality.[58] Although Childe was often judged not to be a particularly effective lecturer, he gave generously of his time to undergraduates who sought him out, and he inspired great affection among graduate students at the Institute of Archaeology. In Scotland his archaeological surveys and excavations brought him into contact with a wide cross-section of the population. During his travels abroad he sought out and befriended foreign colleagues. His severest critics admit that he made himself agreeable at parties and delighted in his membership of the Athenaeum. He enjoyed plays, concerts and playing bridge, as well as hiking and motoring in the company of friends and students. Although Childe kept out of the political limelight, he served unobtrusively on the committees of various journals and associations. While he may have avoided the entanglements of close personal friendships, he was clearly not misanthropic nor insensitive to social pleasures and responsibilities.

Although Childe was well aware of the eminence that he had achieved as a scholar, most people who knew him were impressed by his unaffected modesty. This trait may explain his unwillingness to impose himself and his ideas too strongly upon other people, and his notorious lack of concern with appearance. Yet Childe compensated for his modesty with a pervasive sense of humour that ranged from the subtle to the burlesque. He seems to have revelled in the shabby and eccentric clothes that he wore, outraging the Scots with his shorts, and astonishing Chicago bus drivers with his broad-brimmed Australian hat and flowing cape. He once informed Braidwood that he had purchased the shabby trousers he was wearing when he had visited Belgrade twenty-five years before and demanded to know if they were not still in fine condition.[59] Childe was equally indifferent to his lodgings. He was evidently attracted to the dismal Hotel de Vere in Edinburgh because of its name, and in London he chose to live for a time in an apartment building called Moscow Mansions. During the years he worked in Scotland, from 1927 to 1946, Childe went out of his way to write as if he were a native Scot; in part no doubt to annoy those who resented the appointment of a foreigner to the Edinburgh chair of archaeology. He also flaunted his left-wing interests; signing letters in Cyrillic script, demanding copies of the *Daily Worker* at smart hotels, displaying that newspaper in his office, and injecting quotations from Stalin into his public speeches. Such activities have generally been interpreted as a playful effort to shock middle-class friends and audiences,[60] but it has been suggested that they may also have been a conscious attempt to disguise the seriousness of Childe's commitment to Marxism and avoid the attendant social penalties.[61] More likely this behaviour was merely an honest reflection of the essentially non-political (and hence 'harmless') nature of his academic commitment to Marxism.

Childe's contemporaries have raised the issue of how far he extended such 'naughtiness' to his archaeological writings. It has been suggested that the overt Marxism of *Scotland Before the Scots* was designed both to scandalize the audience of the Society of Antiquaries of Scotland and as a parting insult to the Scots. Piggott argues that Childe regarded such activities as a stimulating intellectual game, but that it was one that was apt to confuse those who did not recognize it for what it was.[62]

Childe clearly did not take all of his ideas equally seriously. He was devoted to some, tried others on for size, and may have regarded still others as jokes or bits of whimsy. Yet even today archaeologists cannot agree which of his ideas fall into which category. While it would be a mistake to treat Childe more seriously than he took himself, there is also danger in assuming that he did not treat seriously ideas with which we may not agree. A more objective procedure is to determine which of his ideas continued to enjoy his favour over long periods and which were of ephemeral importance in his writings. In the following chapters my endeavour has been to trace how Childe's more important ideas developed during his scholarly career, and on this basis to determine the long-term significance of these ideas as well as their relationship to one another at different periods.

Finally I have tried to assess the substantial contributions that Childe's work still can make to the development of archaeology. This has required a careful clarification of the principles that guided Childe's thinking in its final and what I regard as its most mature state. The lack of a detailed application of his later ideas to specific problems of European prehistory has obscured the importance of this work. Yet at this time Childe evolved a set of well-integrated concepts that in many important respects anticipated the tenets of the New Archaeology, which has flourished in the United States since the early 1960s. It is also evident, however, that his understanding of Marxist philosophy (which is not to be confused with a blind commitment to any political dogma) led him to take certain stands that are directly opposed to the New Archaeology, and which have a strong bearing on what archaeology is or should be about. It is in this still unexplored area of controversy that Childe's thought continues to constitute an important challenge to archaeology.

CHAPTER II

Archaeology before Childe

THE TRADITION OF scientific archaeology on which Childe's work was based was a product of the Enlightenment. Its development, which began early in the nineteenth century, was nurtured by the fascination with technological progress that the Industrial Revolution had aroused among the expanding middle classes of western Europe. Scientific archaeology grew out of an antiquarianism that in turn had commenced in northern Europe in the sixteenth century. The development of the latter was associated with the early stirrings of nationalism and hence to some degree with the Reformation. It also provided less affluent savants with an acceptable substitute for the collection and study of Greek and Roman antiquities, which in general remained a prerogative of the nobility. At first these antiquaries were concerned with recording local standing monuments of historic and prehistoric times. Gradually, however, their interest extended to smaller artefacts, especially as ethnographic material arriving from the New World demonstrated beyond doubt the human origin of chipped and polished stone tools. The antiquaries failed, however, to derive an acceptable chronology for prehistoric times from the monuments alone. Their findings had to be interpreted, if at all, in terms of written records. Indeed their discoveries were generally regarded as illustrations of what was recounted in early written records. The widespread belief in Archbishop Ussher's theory that the world had been created about 4004 BC dulled concern with prehistoric culture change. The prehistoric remains of a region generally were 'explained' by attributing them to its protohistoric inhabitants.[1]

EVOLUTIONARY ARCHAEOLOGY

The philosophers of the Enlightenment were the first in modern times to stress the desirability or inevitability of cultural progress. They also emphasized the doctrine of psychic unity, which maintained that human nature and abilities were everywhere very similar; hence all societies tended of their own accord to evolve in a unilinear fashion. Anne Robert Turgot, Marie-Jean Condorcet, Baron de Montesquieu and Voltaire in France, and Adam Ferguson, John Millar and William Robertson in Scotland proposed various hypothetical schemes that traced human progress from savagery to civilization by naturalistic processes involving the exercise of human reason to better the human condition. Most of these philosophers relied upon ethnographic data to illustrate their sequences, although on rare occasions references were made to archaeological data.[2]

This approach, coupled with a growing awareness among antiquaries that there had probably been a time in the past when there had been stone but no metal tools, prompted a young Dane named Christian Thomsen to see if the antiquities of his country could be organized in terms of three successive ages of Stone, Bronze and Iron. As a hypothetical scheme, these Three Ages dated back to the Roman poet Lucretius. Early in the nineteenth century they had been popularized in Denmark by the historian L. S. Vedel-Simonsen. By applying a knowledge of typology derived from his earlier studies of numismatics to groups of artefacts recovered from single burials or from other contexts suggesting close proximity in time, Thomsen worked out between 1816 and 1819 a convincing stylistic sequence that established the Three Age system for Denmark. Thus he was able to distinguish bronze work of the Iron Age from that of the preceding Bronze Age.[3] His success not only vindicated his technological model as a means for working out a sequence of cultural development for northern Europe, but also demonstrated that archaeological data could be chronologically ordered and explained without reference to written records or oral traditions. In this manner a scientific prehistoric archaeology was born out of antiquarianism.

Thomsen's Three Age chronology was validated by the strati-graphic excavations that his pupil, J. J. A. Worsaae, carried out in the Danish bogs.[4] The Swedish zoologist, Sven Nilsson, amplified Thomsen's research by systematically comparing prehistoric tools with ethnographic specimens in an effort to determine the use of the former. Nilsson modelled his approach to data on that of the palaeontologist Georges Cuvier. He placed strong emphasis on the concept of uniformitarianism, the assumption that the products of processes that went on in the past can be interpreted in terms of processes that can be observed in action at the present time, and on the doctrine of psychic unity. Yet Nilsson also studied the use-marks on prehistoric tools in order to confirm his interpretations.[5]

Worsaae's *Primeval Antiquities of Denmark* appeared in an English translation in 1849, only two years before Daniel Wilson published his *Archaeology and Prehistoric Annals of Scotland*.[6] The latter book was the first substantial effort to analyse British archaeological data in terms of the Three Age system, and it marked the beginning of the modern phase of archaeology in Britain. Further public interest in archaeology was aroused by the discovery, beginning in 1854, of the prehistoric 'Lake Dwellings' in Switzerland. These sites, in what was already an important centre of European tourism, yielded not simply stone artefacts, but celts and other tools mounted in their original wooden handles, together with a wealth of organic remains not hitherto noted in archaeological sites. These finds helped to establish the reality of prehistoric cultural evolution in the minds of the educated public and enhanced the prestige of archaeology.[7]

The great attraction of archaeology at this time was its seeming proof that the progress then valued by the middle class was characteristic, not only of the present, but of all human history. Yet while archaeologists were convinced that the archaeological record, taken as a whole, demonstrated the fact of cultural evolution, they also saw diffusion and, more importantly, migration as major forces shaping that record. Worsaae believed that the transitions between the Three Ages in Denmark had been abrupt, attributing the introduction of bronze and then iron to new races of people 'possessing a higher degree of cultivation than the earlier inhabitants'.[8] At the same time the sparseness of stratified sites in central and northern Europe encouraged archaeologists to use typological comparison as their primary means of deriving relative chronologies.[9]

In 1859 the publication of Charles Darwin's *On the Origin of Species* and the verification of the antiquity of the stone tools that Jacques Boucher de Perthes was finding in the Somme Valley opened a new dimension for archaeological research. Prior to that date few archaeologists had found cause to question the biblical chronology and account of human origins. After 1859 archaeological evidence became crucial for solving the burning questions of how and when mankind had originated. The efforts of those who supported the theory of evolution to establish the antiquity of man spurred the development of Palaeolithic archaeology, and led to close co-operation among archaeologists, palaeontologists and historical geologists. In western Europe the extension and refinement of Thomsen's Three Age system was accomplished by subdividing his ages into a number of successive epochs, each distinguished by specific types of artefacts. The French archaeologist, Gabriel de Mortillet, viewed his particular series as constituting a continuation of the geological epochs. In his more doctrinaire pronouncements, he suggested that it represented a universal sequence that humanity passed through everywhere, but at different rates and hence at different times. Their association with geologists and palaeontologists also encouraged archaeologists to view artefacts, not as evidence for past human behaviour but as 'index fossils' suitable for assigning archaeological assemblages to specific stages of cultural development. As a result many types of artefacts that were not useful for this purpose were ignored, and no reason was seen to record the context in which artefacts were found more specifically than by associating them with a particular stratum.[10]

Although many archaeologists realized that this sort of approach could only be applied within a specific geographical region, it nevertheless reinforced the faith that archaeologists had in psychic unity and in the likelihood of parallel unilinear development occurring in the absence of historical contact. It also encouraged archaeologists to treat technologically less advanced peoples as arrested examples of the stages through which more advanced cultures had developed. The findings of archaeologists stimulated a major resurgence of interest in unilinear evolution among ethnologists between 1860 and 1890.[11] The belief that archaeologists could learn all they wished about prehistoric societies by studying modern ones at the same level of development diminished interest in Nilsson's functional studies of prehistoric tools. It limited concern to artefacts that served as indices of particular stages of development. While unilinear evolution bound archaeology and ethnology together, the alliance inhibited archaeologists from playing a significant role in attempting to understand human behaviour. The main use that was made of archaeological evidence was to determine when a particular region was at a certain stage of development. To understand that stage archaeologists and ethnologists alike turned to ethnographic data.

While enthusiasm for technological development remained widespread during most of the nineteenth century, the same century witnessed the erosion of the Enlightenment principles that had given birth to this enthusiasm. The Napoleonic conquests encouraged the development of nationalistic sentiments throughout Europe. This led to the glorification of traits that were believed to be innate in people as members of ethnic groups in place of a belief in reason and psychic unity. By mid-century these sentiments had helped to produce a new, intellectualized and explicit form of racism. Darwinian thought dealt a further blow to the idea of psychic unity by suggesting that, as a result of natural selection, peoples at different levels of cultural development had acquired unequal mental endowments, the most developed groups being the most intelligent. The ideals of the Enlightenment were held tenaciously by those who hoped for revolutionary social change, and therefore valued the plasticity of human nature. Conservatives and liberals, on the other hand, tended to find comfort in the view that human nature was unchangeable and attuned to traditional values.

This new and more pessimistic view of man was introduced into archaeology after 1865 by scholars such as John Lubbock.[12] In his desire to demonstrate that cultural progress had indeed transformed every aspect of human behaviour, Lubbock went out of his way to portray less developed peoples as savages. So-called primitive groups came to be viewed as uncreative, to the degree that modern primitives often were thought to be biologically incapable of being civilized. Change in the archaeological record was attributed almost exclusively to migration and diffusion, rather than to independent invention. A. Pitt-Rivers spoke of sequence rather than progress as constituting the basis of typology and, by increasingly invoking diffusion, he ceased to view evolution in a strictly unilinear fashion.[13] The decline of unilinear evolution encouraged a renewed interest in the function of artefacts and in the historical and ethnic interpretation of archaeological data.

ETHNIC PREHISTORY

Towards the end of the nineteenth century, increasing economic and social conflict in Europe produced dramatic disillusionment with the Industrial Revolution. According to G. M. Trevelyan, John Ruskin inspired a rising generation of writers and thinkers 'with disgust at the industrial civilization that had filled their fathers with such pride'.[14] In his Romanes lecture of 1893 Thomas Huxley concluded that the theory of evolution offered no basis to hope for a millennium.[15] In all of the social sciences grand evolutionary schemes were being criticized as unsound and abandoned in favour of particularistic, inductive approaches. Historians emphasized the importance of the dispassionate collection of facts, and regarded interpretation as little more than irrelevant personal opinion; anthropologists became preoccupied with the endless minutiae of cultural diffusion, and geographers vacillated between deterministic and probabilistic approaches. The complexity of human behaviour was emphasized, and accident, idiosyncratic choice and idealistic factors were assigned important roles in explaining cultural change. Many social scientists doubted that human nature could be explained at all. They argued that the wayward thoughts of man were a law to themselves and not subject to the laws of nature.[16]

At the same time concepts of racial and national identity were being invoked with increasing fervour by scholars and politicians alike, in order to counteract growing class conflicts and promote a sense of national unity. These qualities were romanticized by attributing maximum antiquity to them. Human beings were idealized as being naturally resistant to change and cultures as being expressions of the innate qualities of particular peoples. Cultural change was identified with ethnic change.

Archaeologists responded to this post-Enlightenment view of man by trying to explain the changes that were apparent in the archaeological record almost exclusively in terms of migration and diffusion. Sir John Myres was simply expressing the conventional belief of his day when he wrote that among savages innovators are hated and suppressed.[17] This view acquired extreme expression in W. M. F. Petrie's interpretation of Predynastic Egypt, where he attributed all cultural innovation to the arrival of new ethnic groups,[18] and in George Reisner's interpretation of Nubian prehistory, which explained successive cultures as resulting from the replacement of one ethnic group by another.[19] The same theme was expressed more moderately in the work of Oscar Montelius, who sought to explain the development of European culture in terms of the diffusion of ideas from the Near East where civilization was believed to have developed at an earlier date. This position came to be labelled *ex oriente lux*.[20] Montelius used the typological method to extend a minutely subdivided version of the Three Age system across Europe. By cross-dating this sequence to historical cultures in the Near East, he was able to suggest absolute dates for the latter part of it. By assuming that Europeans were able to profit from ideas that reached them from the Near East, Montelius espoused a more optimistic view of human nature than did many contemporary archaeologists.

The adulation of German culture was expressed in the work of Gustaf Kossinna, a philologist who turned to archaeology in order to demonstrate that the original homeland of the Indo-Europeans, and of the supposedly related Finns and Sumerians, had been in the recently annexed territories of Schleswig and Holstein in northern Germany. By inflating the German chronology relative to that of other regions, Kossinna sought to prove that German culture was the most innovative in the world and that, even in prehistoric times, it had borne witness to the superiority of the German people. Kossinna saw civilization elsewhere as resulting from invasions and conquests by Germans or Indo-Europeans, even when no proof of these had been forthcoming. He regarded the Germans as the Indo-Europeans who had been least contaminated by other peoples or cultures, since they alone had remained in the Indo-European homeland. They were also the most talented and the most creative of the Indo-Europeans because of this lack of contamination. After 1912 Kossinna came to view the superiority of the Germans increasingly in terms of racial theories that were already popular in Germany.[21] Although racial interpretations of history were no less common in Britain prior to World War II, Kossinna's theories were not popular there. This was not only because his ideas were German. The British were fully aware, from historical records, of the ethnic complexity of their own past, and tended to stress the benefits of racial and cultural mixture – at least among the White race. Hence they, unlike the Germans, had no interest in attributing success to racial or cultural purity.[22]

Beginning in 1911 a non-racial but still more negative view of human creativity was eloquently expounded in the hyperdiffusionist works of Grafton Elliot Smith and his disciple William J. Perry.[23] Neither was an archaeologist. Perry was an anthropologist and Smith an anatomist who had worked as a physical anthropologist for the Archaeological Survey of Nubia, and had become obsessed with the primacy of the culture of ancient Egypt. Although Smith's later writings, and those of Perry, were ethnological rather than archaeological in character, the historical cast that they gave to their arguments caused their work to impinge on prehistoric archaeology. Smith and Perry did not deny that technological evolution had taken place, but they argued that this development was unnatural and contradictory to human nature. The condition to which man was naturally suited was that of a hunter and gatherer. They argued that the invention of agriculture and the subsequent rise of civilization had resulted from a series of accidents that had taken place in Egypt, just as the Industrial Revolution had occurred as the result of a series of accidents in western Europe. They claimed that Egyptian culture had been spread throughout the world by Egyptian traders and prospectors looking for ore, precious stones and other materials valued for their supposed magical qualities, Givers of Life, that were believed to confer health and long life on those who possessed them. Thus religion was accorded a major role as a factor promoting cultural development. Foreign peoples often adopted only a few traits of Egyptian civilization, and the secondary civilizations that sprang up as far away as Mexico and Peru generally tended to disintegrate once they became isolated from continuing Egyptian influence. All civilizations were in any case inherently unstable. Most of them, after a few centuries, lapsed into political chaos from which they did not recover. Thus the concept of degeneration, which the unilinear evolutionists had been anxious to put down, was once again espoused as a major factor in human history. While few archaeologists were impressed by Smith's overall explanation of variations in the archaeological record, his pessimism about human creativity was sufficiently in accord with the spirit of the times for aspects of his writings to influence the thinking of most British archaeologists in the 1920s.

As European archaeologists compared increasing amounts of data about particular regions, it became clear that there was significant geographical variation in the archaeological record that could not be explained in terms of unilinear evolution. As early as 1851 Daniel Wilson had noted marked differences between the artefacts associated with the late Iron Age in Scotland and in Scandinavia, and he had attributed these differences to different cultural traditions.[24] Only seven years later Worsaae suggested that Bronze Age Europe would have to be studied in terms of regional variation. This proposal was put into effect by Ernest Chantre in his *Age du Bronze*, published 1875–76, where the evidence was discussed in terms of three archaeological provinces: Uralian, Danubian and Mediterranean.[25]

Late in the nineteenth century geographical variations came to be interpreted as expressions of different prehistoric peoples. This revived an interest in trying to trace the prehistoric development of known peoples in the archaeological record that had been strong among antiquaries prior to the development of evolutionary archaeology, and had never disappeared in Classical archaeology. The French excavations at Alesia (Mont Auxois) between 1862 and 1865 clearly illustrated the remains of Celtic culture at the time of the Roman conquest. This enabled archaeologists to recognize a collection of iron tools from La Tène, on Lake Neuchâtel, as similar and therefore putatively Celtic, while in 1871 the unilinear evolutionist, de Mortillet, attributed still other similar weapons in northern Italy to a Celtic invasion.[26] In 1874 Boyd Dawkins suggested that some of the differences between de Mortillet's Palaeolithic epochs might be ethnic ones rather than different stages in an evolutionary sequence.[27] By 1890 Arthur Evans had no difficulty in attributing the late Celtic urnfield at Aylesford in Kent to Belgic invaders; in 1898 Sophus Müller interpreted the 'separate graves' and megaliths of Denmark as the work of two contemporary, but culturally different groups, and in 1901 John Abercromby identified the Beaker-folk as a significant element in British prehistory.[28] In the eastern Mediterranean archaeologists trained in the Classical tradition applied geographical and mythical labels such as Mycenaean, Minoan and Cycladic to a variety of coeval prehistoric cultural sequences.[29]

By the beginning of the twentieth century German and Czech archaeologists were delineating local geographical variations beginning as early as the Neolithic period in central Europe. They called these units 'cultures' and, for the most part, named them after characteristic pottery types. The term culture had been used in Germany since the eighteenth century to designate the customs of individual societies. It was also in Germany that the ethnological concept of cultures and culture areas had been developed and popularized by the geographer Friedrich Ratzel, beginning in the 1880s.[30]

The concept of the archaeological culture was used by Kossinna to organize archaeological data for much of central Europe. He equated archaeological cultures with specific tribes such as the Saxons, and provinces, or complexes of related cultures, with broader ethnic categories such as the Germans. The equation of *Kultur* and *Volk* was so important to Kossinna that he preferred the expression *Kulturgruppe* to *Kultur* because it emphasized the explicitly ethnic nature of his units. By applying the direct historical approach, which involved tracing the archaeological antecedents of historic cultures of known ethnic identity into the ever more remote past, Kossinna sought to demonstrate the autochthonous origins of the German people.[31]

Through the work of Kossinna, the archaeological culture was established as an important concept. Because each culture was defined in terms of traits associated with sites in a particular area at a particular time, rather than by subdividing an age or an epoch, it existed independently from the Three Age system, although it did not in any way rule out a concern with Thomsen's scheme of technological development. Yet Kossinna, like many other archaeologists of that period, was no longer interested in general schemes of cultural development; instead he sought to use archaeological data to trace the history of specific regions or ethnic groups prior to the availability of written records. This particularistic, historical approach generated a renewed interest in the ways of life of prehistoric peoples. To satisfy this interest, Kossinna sought to describe cultures in terms of all criteria, not merely to define them, as epochs had been defined, in terms of a few index fossils.

The new historicism encouraged efforts to elicit more information from archaeological data. There was a growing interest in prehistoric environments and human adjustments to these environments. J. J. A. Worsaae had demonstrated a succession of vegetation types in the Danish bogs, and had roughly correlated these with his sequence of cultural change, while Edouard Lartet had based his classification of still earlier Palaeolithic material on palaeontological criteria.[32] In 1898 Robert Gradmann noted a correlation between the distribution of Neolithic settlements and loess soils in central Europe, and attempted to explain this correlation by assuming that early farmers had been unable to clear land, and therefore had settled in areas that were lightly forested, if at all. Gradmann's theory was eagerly espoused by many central European archaeologists and was soon well known throughout Europe.[33]

F. J. Haverfield demonstrated the correlation between the extent of Roman occupation and the geography of Britain, while John Myres drew upon the geographical tradition of H. J. Mackinder and Edwin Guest to preach the value of a geographical approach to archaeological data.[34] O. G. S. Crawford was inspired by his Oxford training to devote much time to studying prehistory in relation to the geographical environment. Through his work with the Ordnance Survey, early mapping of artefact distributions led to detailed studies of specific culture periods from a geographical point of view, with special emphasis on the reconstruction of original patterns of vegetation. W. G. Clarke, J. P. Williams-Freeman, Herbert Fleure, W. E. Whitehouse and Cyril Fox also undertook studies of the relationship of prehistoric settlement in various regions of Britain to vegetation covers. In *The Personality of Britain*, published in 1932, Fox combined the ecological-distributional approach of Gradmann and Crawford with the positional geography of Mackinder and the possibilism of French geographers to produce what Glyn Daniel has called a 'startlingly new approach to the facts of prehistory'.[35]

In 1908, in the publication of his excavations at Anau, near Ashkhabad in what is now the Turkmen Soviet Socialist Republic, the American archaeologist, R. Pumpelly, proposed the desiccation or oasis theory of agricultural origins.[36] This theory, which was to become widely popular among Old World archaeologists in succeeding decades, suggested that as the Near East became drier following the last ice age, men were compelled to gather around surviving sources of water, and to 'conquer new means of support' by domesticating wild animals and grasses.

Early memoirs on the flora and fauna of the Swiss lake dwellings had demonstrated that specialized scientific studies could yield data of value for the better understanding of prehistory. In 1878 Pitt-Rivers recognized the significance of post holes for tracing the ground plans of vanished wooden structures in Sussex and, between 1892 and 1902, the Roman-German Boundary Commission systematically extended the study of post holes to a wide variety of soils. Growing interest in prehistoric social organization also led to the excavation of whole sites, such as Phylakopi on Melos between 1899 and 1901 and Glastonbury in 1911.[37]

In the later nineteenth century much interest was aroused by Heinrich Schliemann's excavations at Troy, Mycenae and elsewhere in the Aegean area. His newly discovered Mycenaean civilization became an important focus for disputes about the origins of European civilization. Some archaeologists, especially German ones, regarded Mycenaean civilization as the creation of Aryan invaders from the north. In his *Le Mirage Oriental*, published in 1893, Salomon Reinach declared that eastern elements had been grossly overrated, and that the Mycenaean culture, like other European ones, was essentially of native origin. Oscar Montelius and the supporters of his *ex oriente lux* position argued that European civilization, on the contrary, was 'for long only a pale reflection of Oriental culture'.[38]

The two British scholars who became most involved in these debates about the prehistory of the eastern Mediterranean were Arthur Evans and John Myres, both at Oxford. As Glyn Daniel has pointed out, these men did not view the theories of Montelius and Reinach as being mutually exclusive.[39] Evans believed Aegean civilization to be a local manifestation within a broader Anatolian-Danubian province that owed something to both Europe and the Near East. Myres argued that the European capacity for assimilation had preserved an independent European element in the Aegean, in spite of substantial borrowing of concepts from the Near East.[40] One of the two main themes of Myres' *The Dawn of History*, published in 1911, was the spread of civilization from Egypt and Mesopotamia to the eastern Mediterranean, and successively later to Italy, central and northern Europe. His second theme was that political societies arose when the grasslands peoples of Asia or Arabia were forced by drought to conquer peoples living nearer the Mediterranean. Myres believed that the Indo-Europeans were one example of such peoples. According to Myres, they were skilful at imposing their language, beliefs and social practices on conquered peoples, while adopting the latter's material culture. Out of the encounter between Near Eastern cultural influences and the Indo-European peoples, a vital and distinctive European culture was created. Like many other Englishmen, Myres viewed trade and ethnic contact as important factors in cultural development.[41]

Throughout the nineteenth century archaeologists wrestled with an increasing body of archaeological data. Their interpretations of these data were influenced by different national traditions and by changing social attitudes, especially a growing pessimism about human inventiveness, and an increasing preoccupation with biologically based ethnic characteristics. German archaeologists, confronted by no obvious signs of ethnic change in the history or archaeological record of their homeland, joined in the frenzied adulation of all things German that characterized intellectual life in their country after 1870. They equated cultural greatness with their imagined racial and cultural purity. The British, proud of their mixed origins, espoused a different view of their past and, on that basis, their archaeologists interpreted cultural heterogeneity and contact as major sources of innovation and progress. The latter view, especially as expounded by Evans and Myres, was a major component of the archaeological tradition into which Gordon Childe was initiated.

CHAPTER III

The Dawn and *The Aryans*

GORDON CHILDE GREW UP in Australia in the decades that witnessed the rise of the Australian labour parties and their electoral successes in New South Wales, Queensland, and later in federal politics. Republicanism was strong at this time, and radical movements, including utopian and Marxist-style ones, flourished. He was the son of the Reverend Stephen Henry Childe and his second wife, Harriet Eliza Gordon, both of whom had come to Australia from England. The Reverend Childe, who already had several children by his first marriage, was rector of St Thomas's, the largest Anglican church in North Sydney. He has been described as a man of 'strict and narrow views'. Piggott states that in later life Childe talked 'occasionally, and with reluctance, of a boyhood during which the natural rebel in him was irritated by the complacent late nineteenth-century atmosphere in which he found himself'.[1] There was evidently a strong contrast between Childe's conservative home environment and the politically radical ferment at work in some segments of Australian society.

EARLY LIFE

Childe studied at the Sydney Church of England Grammar School, and obtained a first class honours degree in Latin, Greek and Philosophy from Sydney University. He was awarded a graduate scholarship to Queen's College, Oxford, in 1914, and entered the university at a time when many students were enlisting for World War I. He received little formal instruction in archaeology. He later observed, 'My Oxford training was in the Classical tradition to which bronzes, terracottas and pottery (at least if painted) were respectable while stone and bone tools were banausic'.[2] Yet Grahame Clark has argued that the training in the formal analysis of pottery that Childe received from John Beazley in the course for the diploma in Classical archaeology stood him in good stead for the rest of his life.[3]

Childe's broader view of prehistory was shaped by his contacts with Evans and Myres, and he received a B. Litt. for a study on an Indo-

1 Gordon Childe, Edinburgh, 1927

MEN WHO INFLUENCED
GORDON CHILDE

2 The Right Honourable John,
Fifth Baron Abercromby of
Aboukir and Tullibody,
1841–1924

3 Oscar Montelius, 1843–1921

4 Gustaf Kossinna, 1858–1931. Photograph taken at a meeting of the Society for German Prehistory, Königsberg, 1930. Kossinna is in the centre, holding an umbrella

6 Sir John Myres, 1869–1954

5 Sir Arthur Evans, 1851–1941

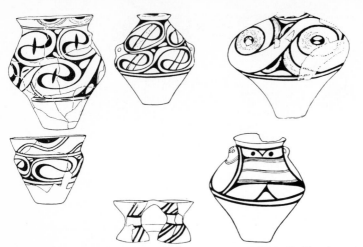

7 Painted pottery of the Tripolje culture, from Childe's *Prehistoric Migrations in Europe*, 1950

8, 9 Metal-workers as portrayed in Egypt in the tomb of Petosiris and on a Greek black-figured vase. From Childe's 'Archaeological Ages as Technological Stages', 1944

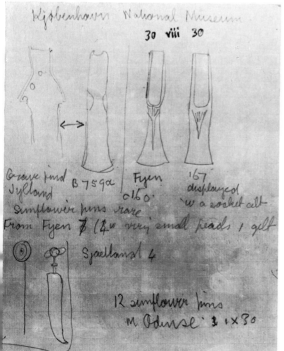

10 (*above*) Profile of the stratigraphy at Vinča, visited by Childe in the summer of 1926

11 Sketches by Childe of artefacts in Danish museums, 30 August and 1 September 1930, from his Notebook No. 50, preserved at the Institute of Archaeology, London

12 Skara Brae, Orkney

13 Childe at Skara Brae, Orkney. The photograph shows Hut 4, Door and Cell 2

14 Childe with a group of workmen at Skara Brae, Orkney

15 Rinyo, Rousay, Orkney. The photograph shows Chamber B, Hearth and Door AB

Braes of Rinyo on farm of Bigland
Room C

4. vi 38 S of H Torsein had found a clay oven becked against
S kerbs walls 9½ – 4½" thick – 1'3" x 1'3" inside
in E wall ?2 slabs on end innermost 9½" h from
floor slab in W corners walls E 5½" W 4½" h. oven's
base a flat slab extends beyond walls on S & W in
middle of W wall trace of gap: wall slops 1½" above
floor slab: width . 4"

in the red ash of hearth was a hole filled
with looser earth 9½" w × 8½" deep. At its
left lay a pot lid 7½ x 6½" in diameter

June 10 On removing the clay oven the slab on which it stood
was seen to bear the exact outline of the clay walls:
a skin only a couple of mm deep had been removed
over the whole area not under the clay, as if cut out
Unfortunately the slab fell to pieces on lifting

10 Under edge of rear wall a flint scraper
12 direct under front stone of hearth Hc 2 large pot.
11 polished haematite w pot found just outside door of F
opp. door of A.

13 flint knife trimmed along
one edge
14 flake of flint trimmed on
both edges
15 pot sherds
H 16 sherds of one pot
17 edge of pol. flint axe

June 11 Under Hc ashes containing a few flints & sherds
extend down to about 12.10 then there is a thin bed of
white clay Nearly on this lay 13 & 14
Seaweed is Ascophyllum nodosum one of the Fucaceae NYO
charcoal from below clay in flint under Hc-d is BIRCH MYO
20 under bed slab behind Hc 6 richly decorated sherds

16 Notes by Childe on his excavations at Rinyo, Orkney, 1938

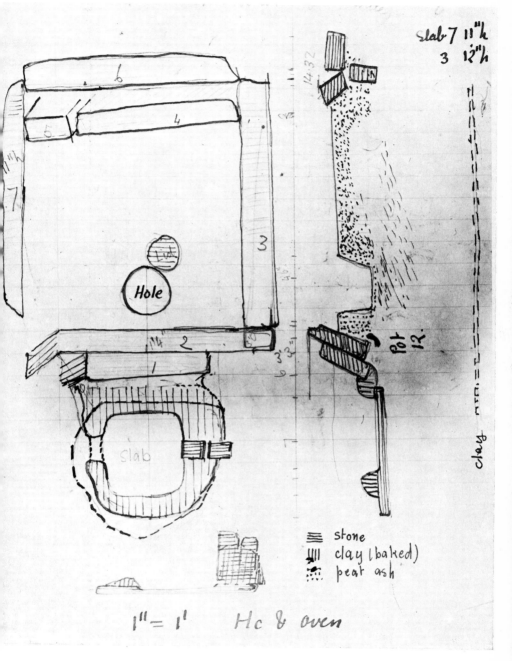

Slab 7 11"h
3 12"h

14.32

Hole

3

4

6

5

7

2

1

slab

Pot 12

clay ≡≡≡≡

≡ stone
⫴ clay (baked)
⋮⋮ peat ash

1" = 1'   Hc & oven

17 Diagram from Childe's notes on his excavations at Rinyo, Orkney, 1938

18 Rahoy Argyll; experiment at duplicating vitrified fortifications. *Left*, model wall completed; *below*, model wall after burning

(21)

FROM PROFESSOR V. G. CHILDE
DEPARTMENT OF
PREHISTORIC ARCHAEOLOGY
22. November 1945

My dear Braidwood   I waited to answer yours of 8th till Hassuna proofs turned up as they did today. Many thanks for both. I have promised to do a note on it for *Antiquity* but must wait for the pictures. On the stone implements the list is admittedly inadequate: they don't even distinguish between ax axe & an adze. I hope the pictures may fill out this blank. On the whole we haven't yet got as clear a picture of "neolithic" life in the Tigris valley as from Sialk in Iran but it is clearing up a bit at least — granaries, ovens, houseplans at last. I hope the grains & charcoal will eventually be studied.

Tell Malaf I have not yet seen the just received Arne's finally report on Shah Tepé: it doesn't add much that was not given in *Acta Arch.*, save a mould from III. This I believe was for casting a shaft hole adze like the one from Hissar III so it would be quite in order. Horse & camel are both attested well in II & probably in III: this early use of camel is very interesting.

As to Russian books I know no way of ensuring that one gets them. Booksellers are quite useless. One must get to the Academy, Hermitage etc: but this is curiously difficult. One must rely on exchanges but they don't work so smoothly. In theory the Soviets think one should work these through either VOKS (ВОКС) or Lenin Library (Библиотека им. Ленина) but VOKS is very stupid. Last week they sent me four childrens books & 2 books of poems! & a number of things I sent through them never reached their addresses. Curiously enough citing Myself in Moscow came off worst although VOKS is in Moscow. The things I've sent to Институт Institut

19 First page of a letter from Gordon Childe to Professor R.J.Braidwood, 22 November 1945. The letter discusses problems Childe experienced in obtaining archaeological publications from the Soviet Union

21 Childe in Ankara, 1947

20 Childe visiting Stuart Piggott's excavations at Dorchester-on-Thames in 1946, the year that Piggott succeeded him as Abercromby Professor in Edinburgh

22 Childe in Czecho-slovakia, 1949. On the left, Professor F. Kalousek, a Slavonic archaeologist, now in the Department of Pre-history, Brno University; in the middle Dr B. Svoboda, now at the National Museum, Prague

23 Childe displaying a gift from the students at Brno University

24 Childe at the Congress of Prehistoric and Protohistoric Sciences, Zurich 1950: flanking him, from left to right: Kathleen Kenyon, (Childe), R.J.C.Atkinson, Stuart Piggott, Grahame Clark and Christopher Hawkes; by the door, R.J. Braidwood

25 Childe at Tashkent, 1953

26 Childe with Professor F.E.Zeuner

27 Meeting of the Prehistoric Society in Edinburgh, 1954. Left to right: T.G.E. Powell, C.A.Raleigh Radford, Gordon Childe, R.J.C.Atkinson, Stuart Piggott

28 Maes Howe, from the north-east. Childe investigated this tomb on the mainland of Orkney in 1954 and 1955. Excavations by Colin Renfrew in 1973 (in progress here) followed directly on Childe's excavations in the ditch surrounding the monument and produced radio-carbon material

29 Childe relaxing
with a group of
students and staff of
the Institute of
Archaeology

30, 31 Childe on
field trips during his
tenure as Director of
the Institute of
Archaeology

32 At Tara, Ireland, September 1956. Back row, left to right: S.P.O'Riordain, Gabriel MacCarron, Norbert Shannon, Gordon Childe, Howard Kilbride-Jones, John Ryan; front row, left to right: David Liversage, Joan Collins, Mrs H.E.Kilbride-Jones, Rhoda Kavanagh, Joan Burns, Noleen Moran, Rachel Smith, George Eogan

33 Vere Gordon Childe, Director of the Institute of Archaeology, Gordon Square, London 1946–1956. Bronze bust by M. Maitland-Howard

European topic. He later stated that his original interest was in comparative philology. Like Kossinna he began to study European archaeology in the hope of discovering the cradle of the Indo-Europeans and identifying their primitive culture.[4] He sought to trace archaeological links between the Neolithic cultures of Greece and areas north of the Balkans, whence similar connections might lead to Iran and India. In particular he was interested in the painted pottery of the Neolithic and Chalcolithic periods that was being found in Thessaly, and north into Romania, Hungary and the Ukraine. Pottery of this sort had been discovered by C. Tsountas in the stratified mounds of Sesklo and Dimini in Greece at the beginning of the century. These finds, which had been elaborated in 1912 by A. J. Wace and M. S. Thompson in *Prehistoric Thessaly*, were comparable with painted pottery that had been found as early as 1889 by G. C. Butureanu at Cucuteni in Romania, and by F. Laszlo at Erösd in Transylvania. In the course of his research Childe also became familiar with the unpainted pottery of the Danubian culture that M. Vassits had excavated at Jablanica, in the Morava Valley, and soon after at Vinča, near Belgrade.[5]

The abilities of the twenty-three-year-old Childe are displayed in his first published paper, which appeared in the *Journal of the Hellenic Society* for 1915. This study on the date and origin of Minyan ware was based in part on original observations that he had made while visiting Greek museums. His interpretation of the evidence reflected the preoccupation with tracing the origin and diffusion of classes of artefacts that most archaeologists had at this time. More specifically it echoed Evans' concept of an Anatolian-Danubian cultural province. Childe viewed Minyan ware on the Greek mainland and in Asia Minor as being derived from an earlier unitary culture in the northern Aegean and Troad.[6]

Soon after he arrived at Oxford Childe met R. Palme Dutt, then an undergraduate at Balliol, and moved out of college to share lodgings with him. Dutt, who later became a prominent figure in the British Communist Party, recalled that as students he and Childe often debated late into the night about Hegel, Marx and the state of modern society.[7] They joined the Fabian Society at Oxford, which became increasingly unpopular because of its members' stand against the war and conscription. Childe was flatly opposed to the war and in 1916, the year conscription was introduced into Great Britain, he returned to Australia. Jack Lindsay notes that Childe 'had got into some trouble at Oxford – how public I never knew, for he was not a person who unbosomed himself about his private affairs or whom one asked about such things'.[8] Childe joined the Australian Union of Democratic Control, and was active in opposing (and defeating) two successive referenda that proposed conscription for military service outside Australia. He held a number of teaching posts, but in 1919 was appointed private secretary to John Storey, who became premier of New South Wales when a Labour government was elected in that state the next year. When Storey died in 1921 Childe found himself without a job, and was unable to secure a university post, apparently because of his political activities. After a further brief spell of government employment, he again found himself out of work and in London. His thoughts now turned to a career in archaeology.[9]

The final product of what Childe later called his 'sentimental excursion' into Australian politics was his first book, published in 1923, *How Labour Governs: A Study of Workers' Representation in Australia*.[10] This book has been described as the most authoritative published source on the history of the Australian labour movement prior to 1921.[11] He sought to document how, as the labour movement achieved political success within a parliamentary system, its leaders were corrupted by co-optation into a world of clubs, patronage and national traditions, and the party became a machine run for the benefit of individuals. In general, he studied the structure rather than the policies of the labour movement. Yet, in spite of the merits of the book, even F. B. Smith, a sympathetic commentator, finds Childe's interpretation of labour politics narrow and uncharitable.[12] Gathercole construes the work as being 'in the established tradition of Marxist criticism concerning the inevitable way in which leaders of working class movements are corrupted by a bourgeois state machine'.[13] Nevertheless Childe shunned the stereotyped vocabulary of Marxism. A cryptic preface, with which he supplied the book, might be read either as implying that he personally rejected a Marxist interpretation of modern societies, or conversely as an attack on labour parties for not truly seeking to end the exploitation of the working class.[14]

How Labour Governs reflects a distrust and scorn of parliamentary government that was shared by many people at both ends of the political spectrum between the first and second world wars. Childe did not, however, subscribe to authoritarian doctrines. He emphasized the importance of freedom of communication, and pointed out the danger of allowing any one working-class group to control all the newspapers of the labour movement.[15] His sympathy for left-wing political philosophy, his hatred of war and religion, and his liberal commitment to the unrestricted exchange of ideas were themes that were to reappear in his archaeological writings. Yet, in spite of his desire to reveal the shortcomings of the Australian labour movement, *How Labour Governs* was his last political work.[16] He promised, but seemingly never wrote, a sequel dealing with the Storey government. Hereafter Childe remained a Marxist and served on the committees of various left-wing organizations. Yet, as Dutt observed, he was 'fully engaged in his epoch-making archaeological work' and 'did not participate much directly in political activity'.[17]

RETURN TO ARCHAEOLOGY

Childe had run out of prospects in Australia and was clearly disillusioned with Australian politics. Although he corresponded eagerly with the relatives and friends he had left behind, he did not find an opportunity to return there until the end of his career in 1957. F. B. Smith has suggested that Childe turned again to archaeology in order to find evidence that there had existed in the past cohesive, inventive societies in which craftsmen and thinkers were natural leaders; in short, vital, integrated and just societies such as he had failed to see realized in Australia.[18] This suggestion ignores the earlier positive attraction that archaeology had for Childe. It also fails to explain why, for many years after he had come back to England, his archaeological research bore no obvious relationship to any of his Marxist or utopian concerns. In his own words, he sought to distil from archaeological evidence a prehistoric substitute for conventional political history.[19] In 1922, Childe, now thirty years old, concentrated on building a career for himself as an archaeologist. He was staking his talents on the slim chance that a man without considerable financial resources might secure a niche in a profession that as yet had few paying positions.

Although Childe turned again to south-eastern Europe, his main interest was now focused on the Danube Valley. He observed that, while most British archaeologists accepted that cultural diffusion from the Near East was important for explaining the prehistoric development of Europe, one group of them studied the Near East, the Aegean and Italy, while another studied their homeland, and that the two groups tended to work in water-tight compartments.[20] He proposed to bridge this gap, as far as inter-connections could be traced along the Rhine and Danube Valleys. To him it appeared inescapable that these two rivers, which share a common watershed from the Balkans to the North Sea, played a major role in the spread of culture through central and northern Europe. The archaeology of the Danube region was less well known than that of the Rhine; hence he saw there his best chance to do important work. His financial resources were limited, but he took advantage of massive post-war inflation in eastern Europe to travel along the Danube, studying museum collections, visiting sites and interviewing local archaeologists. These travels also gave him an opportunity to observe how the society of landowners, peasants and manual craftsmen in eastern Europe differed from an industrial one, made up of managers, mechanics and farmers.[21] This constituted his closest approximation to ethnographic experience.

John Myres approved of Childe's travels and may have found financial support for them. Childe also earned money translating books from French into English for Kegan Paul's ambitious *History of Civilization* series. These included L. Delaporte's *Mesopotamia*; A. Moret and G. Davy's *From Tribe to Empire*, and L. Homo's *Primitive Italy and the Beginnings of Roman Imperialism*.[22] Childe derived a store of facts and ideas from this work that he made use of in his later writings. *From Tribe to Empire* shaped his view of Egyptian civilization as having developed from a collection of totemic clans, all of whose patron spirits eventually were absorbed into the spirit of a divine king. Davy was a student of the French sociologist Emile Durkheim and, through this book, Childe also became familiar with the broad outlines of Durkheimian sociology. Durkheim had paid particular attention to the effect of technology on the social structures and the latters' role in shaping individual behaviour and religious beliefs. In 1925 Myres obtained a salaried position for Childe in the library of the Royal Anthropological Institute, which he held until 1927.

In 1922 Childe drew upon his earlier work and his more recent observations in central Europe to publish a paper on the eastern European relations of the Dimini culture.[23] Between 1922 and 1925 he published brief notes on various aspects of south-eastern European archaeology, including a report drawing attention to the perilous state of archaeological collections resulting from post-war economic and political chaos.[24] In March 1924 his research was advanced enough for him to read a preliminary synthesis of his findings at a meeting of the Society of Antiquaries in London. Childe defined a sequence of four Danubian periods that was based on Jaroslav Palliardi's stratigraphic analyses of pottery styles for southern Moravia. On the basis of some general similarities, he proposed to synchronize this sequence with Arthur Evans' recently published Minoan chronology. Evans had cross-dated the Minoan chronology with the historical ones of Egypt and the Near East, using trade goods and stylistic parallels in the manner that Montelius had first applied systematically to the study of European prehistory in 1885. Childe concluded his paper by correlating segments of the prehistoric sequences for Britain, Scandinavia, Silesia and the Danube with Evans' periods Early Minoan II to Late Minoan Ia, thus dating them between 2500 and 1500 BC. Although Harold Peake expressed strong reservations about Childe's chronology, the archaeologists who heard this paper praised its discussion of Britain's links to the continent. It was not seen as marking a break with the Montelian chronological approach, with which British archaeologists were familiar.[25]

The Dawn AND The Aryans

His *The Dawn of European Civilization* and *The Aryans* were published in quick succession, both in the *History of Civilization* series.[26] These books sought to trace the 'foundation of European Civilization as a peculiar and individual manifestation of the human spirit'.[27] Nevertheless, they did this in very different ways, and subsequently had very different histories. *The Aryans* reflected Childe's early interest in philology and Indo-European origins. It went through only one printing, and was later ignored by its author who vacillated between viewing the search for an Indo-European homeland as 'naturally fruitless' or as 'legitimate' but unsuccessful.[28] *The Dawn of European Civilization*, which surveyed European prehistory to the end of the Middle Bronze Age, was based almost entirely upon archaeological evidence. It went through six editions, being considerably restructured and revised during its author's lifetime. It is still in print. It also presented a picture of European prehistory that was generally accepted by western European archaeologists until recently, when bristlecone pine calibrations cast serious doubt on the conventional radio-carbon chronology. Yet when Childe wrote these two books, they were meant to complement one another and to treat for Europe, though in far more detail, the same ground that had been covered by Myres' *The Dawn of History*, the title of which was flatteringly echoed by *The Dawn of European Civilization*. While the latter traced the spread of material culture from Egypt and Mesopotamia to Europe, *The Aryans* sought to demonstrate how the benefits of this process had been reaped by Indo-European-speaking peoples, whom Childe, like Myres, believed had come from the grasslands of southern Russia.

Some conservative archaeologists found *The Dawn of European Civilization* overloaded with unfamiliar terminology, and lacking the 'discursions' and 'elements of revelation' that they deemed essential to good archaeological writing.[29] Crawford more perceptively hailed it as the first major synthesis of the whole field of European origins by a specialist who could generalize and apparently was familiar with all European languages.[30] Crawford also recognized that important characteristics of this book were systematic coverage of data on a regional basis, documentation of these data, and the care with which Childe related his interpretations to the evidence.

Interest in the broader European, and even Near Eastern context of British archaeology was not as restricted in England, nor was Childe's work as unique in this respect as Piggott has suggested.[31] Myres' *The Dawn of History* was being reprinted; Volume I of *The Cambridge Ancient History* had appeared in 1923, and the first volumes of Peake and Fleure's *The Corridors of Time* were to be published in 1927. All of these books surveyed the prehistory of Britain, Europe and the Near East. In addition, Peake had just published his *Bronze Age and the Celtic World*, and Fox, in his *Archaeology of the Cambridge Region*, had offered constructive criticism of Montelius' European chronology.[32] It is thus clear that the success of *The Dawn of European Civilization* cannot be attributed solely to its broad survey of the evidence. It must also be due to the original and convincing manner in which Childe analysed and presented his data. It was the combination of these two features that made the book a standard reference work on Neolithic and Bronze Age Europe for over a generation, and a model for prehistoric synthesis in other parts of the world. Luigi Bernabò Brea is quoted as saying that he dedicated his *Sicily Before the Greeks*, published in 1957, to Childe because he felt that he did not begin to understand European prehistory until he had read Childe's early works.[33]

Although Childe had been studying European prehistory intermittently for over a decade, *The Dawn of European Civilization* and *The Aryans* were products of only four years of research, during which time he also had to earn a living. Even with his astonishing ability to assemble and analyse material, it would have been impossible for him to master in detail the vast amount of data on which his two syntheses were based. To a large degree he selected, modified and integrated existing local and regional syntheses to produce a holistic interpretation of European prehistory that was itself original. Clark notes that it was Childe's good fortune to have the talents to do such work at a time when a general synthesis was needed, and was to a fair degree possible for the first time. Over large areas of Europe the gross outlines of local cultural chronologies had been worked out by *c.* 1900, and in some parts the details had been filled in.[34] Along the Danube and its tributaries Childe found considerable material available, but little yet done to draw it together or to interpret it beyond parochial limits.

Implicit in Childe's persuasive synthesis of European prehistory was a fresh combination of ideas relating to the analysis of archaeological data. This package, and his interpretation of European prehistory, were so intertwined in *The Dawn of European Civilization* that the recognition of one encouraged the favourable reception of the other. The rapid acceptance of his synthesis by western European archaeologists reflected the plausibility of the assumptions that he used to structure his data, while the apparent capacity of his propositions to accommodate new data strengthened confidence in Childe's theoretical framework.

Both to determine synchronisms and to define cultural units, Childe used a heterogeneous collection of data, not all of which were as unambiguous or as well understood by him as his confident style of writing often implied. He stressed that only movements of goods, not those of whole peoples, could provide reliable synchronisms.[35] He also stressed that synchronisms based on trade goods occurring bilaterally in two groups were more reliable than ones based on local imitations of exotic goods or on alleged imitations of the products of civilization by less advanced peoples.[36] Yet in his own work he was often unclear about which sort of evidence his synchronisms were based on. In *The Danube in Prehistory*, published in 1929, the metal earrings, pins and daggers appearing in the oldest Bronze Age graves of Bohemia were described as imports from Troy, Cyprus or Syria; elsewhere Childe said they were produced from local ores.[37] Many of his synchronisms were based on vague stylistic resemblances rather than on precisely dated trade goods. He later admitted that he knew of no datable imports north of the Alps prior to 1400 BC and no unambiguous synchronisms for that area before 1200 BC.[38]

Childe's cultural units were defined in terms of miscellaneous sets of traits that varied from one culture to another. As Clark put it, 'He would throw in barrow forms, metal types, ornamental motifs, religious practices, anything in fact that helped to fill out distributional patterns and define territories'.[39] In *The Danube in Prehistory* Childe acknowledged that his European historical synthesis was a 'subjective construction', shaped by his assumption of the historical priority of cultural development in the south-east.[40] One might generalize that Childe's synthesis (and those of other archaeologists) were conditioned more by his assumptions about human behaviour than by the archaeological data that he had at his disposal. It is to Childe's credit that he dared to use the data and concepts available to produce a synthesis that rendered a mass of archaeological data more intelligible. Thus, to understand his interpretations, it is necessary to investigate his assumptions about human behaviour. It is clear that these concepts were eclectic in origin, but derived largely from within archaeology. They were obtained, like his data, by selecting, modifying and integrating ideas of diverse origins to produce a novel, and for western European archaeologists an attractive system.

THE ARCHAEOLOGICAL CULTURE

The most striking innovation of *The Dawn of European Civilization*, as far as British archaeologists were concerned, was Childe's systematic use of the concept of the archaeological culture as the basic unit for the temporal and spatial ordering of archaeological data. In *The Danube in Prehistory* he defined a culture as 'certain types of remains – pots, implements, ornaments, burial rites, house forms – constantly recurring together'.[41] This wording suggests what Lewis R. Binford, founder of the American New Archaeology, has defined as a normative view of culture, which emphasizes the characteristics of human behaviour that are shared by all the members of a particular group.[42] Yet there is much evidence that Childe had already adopted an implicitly functional view of cultural items, even if he did not yet apply this concept to whole cultures. For example he argued that tools and weapons were unreliable as indicators of ethnic identity, since their utilitarian value caused them to spread rapidly from one group to another by means of trade and imitation.[43] On the other hand he believed that ornaments, home-made pottery and burial rites tended to reflect local taste, and not to be traded or imitated; hence their distributions provide valuable clues concerning ethnic differences.[44]

Later Childe was to insist on what would now be called an explicitly polythetic definition of culture. This recognized that within a single culture the same types of artefacts need not occur in both cemeteries and living sites; in winter camps and in summer ones, or in farming hamlets and in urban centres.[45] Another indication of Childe's functional view of culture at this time was his insistence that terms such as 'influence' or 'diffusion' had no meaning, and did not constitute explanations of cultural processes. Instead they must be given a precise meaning in concrete cases, by determining from the archaeological record whether a particular instance of contact involved conquest, federation, friendly visits between neighbouring chiefs, or a particular kind of trade.[46] Childe was especially anxious to provide functional explanations for bronze hoards that would account for the variety and condition of artefacts found in them.[47] Like Kossinna he stressed that all types of artefacts were significant for understanding archaeological

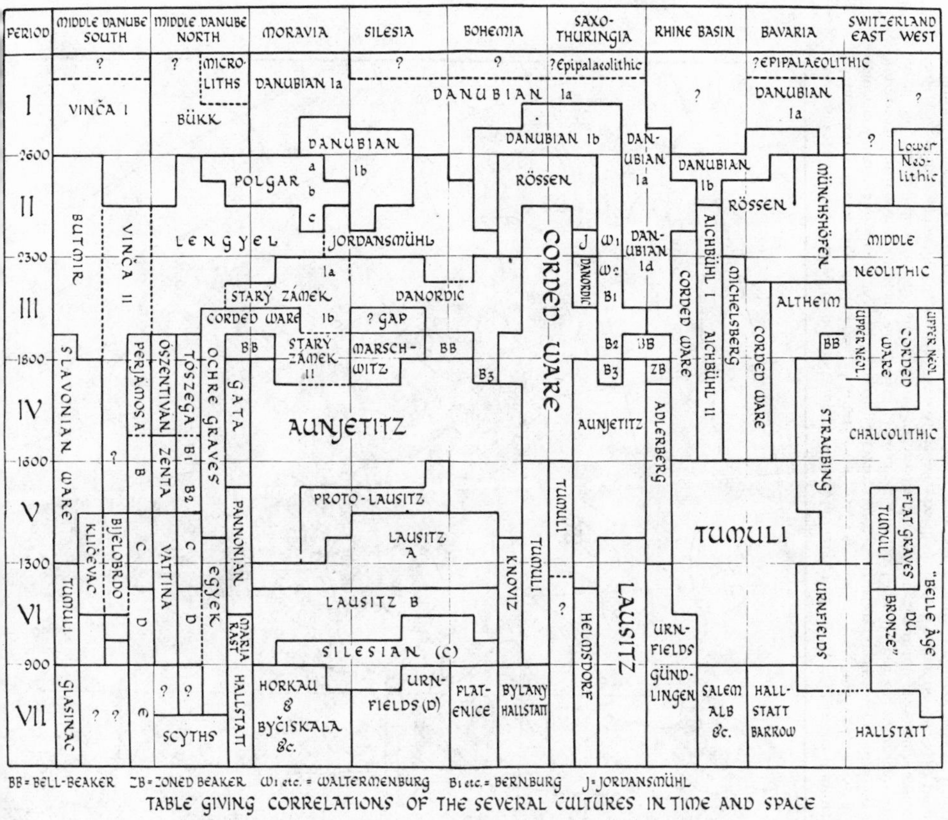
PERIOD
MIDDLE DANUBE SOUTH
MIDDLE DANUBE NORTH
MORAVIA
SILESIA
BOHEMIA
SAXO-THURINGIA
RHINE BASIN
BAVARIA
SWITZERLAND EAST WEST
BB = BELL-BEAKER ZB = ZONED BEAKER W1 etc. = WALTERMENBURG B1 etc. = BERNBURG J = JORDANSMÜHL
TABLE GIVING CORRELATIONS OF THE SEVERAL CULTURES IN TIME AND SPACE

Gordon Childe's first chart correlating archaeological cultures of Central Europe, from *The Danube in Prehistory*, 1929

cultures. While diagnostic artefacts (type-fossils) might serve to define a culture, they could not alone suffice to describe it. For that purpose every artefact type was relevant. Moreover the frequency of a particular type of artefact did not necessarily indicate its social or economic importance to a particular culture.[48]

A detailed chart showing the chronological and geographical distributions of all the archaeological cultures of the Danube Valley was first published in *The Danube in Prehistory*.[49] A more ambitious chart covering all of Europe was prepared by M. C. Burkitt and Childe, and published at the invitation of O. G. S. Crawford in *Antiquity* in 1932.[50] These charts, which Childe had approximated, using sets of maps or tables in *The Dawn of European Civilization*, were the prototypes for ones that archaeologists would use to represent regional cultural chronologies around the world.[51] Childe stressed that the archaeological culture was a formal, not a chronological or

PROVINCES: I The Minoan civilization and empire on the Mainland; III Troy V; IV and non-Minoan cultures of West Greece; V Siculan II civilization; VI Bronze Age of Almeria – El Argar period; VIIa Pyrenaic culture; VIIb Possible survival of cave culture in Liguria; VIII Atlantic megalithic cultures – covered galleries and megalithic cists; IX British bronze age civilization; IXa Intrusive bronze age civilization of North Brittany and Normandy; X Atlantic culture; Xb Hungarian bronze age battle-axe culture; XI ? Survival of Thracian culture; XII Central German bronze age civilization with burials under barrows; XIIa Battle axe cultures still semi-neolithic; XIIIa Scandinavian megalith culture – covered galleries; XIIIa Remnants of North Sea megalithic culture – covered galleries; XIIIb Seine-Oise-Marne culture – covered galleries and artificial grottos; XIVa Swiss lake-dwellings – chalcolithic period; XIVb Bronze age based on the Altheim civilization; XIVc Rhenish bronze age culture – zoned beakers and Adlerburg phase; XV Arctic stone age culture – period of the axes with animals' heads; XVI Italian bronze age civilization. Megalithic areas stippled. NB The Cypriote daggers certainly and the double-axes and eastern amber finds possibly belong to an early period. Amber along the Central and Atlantic routes is not shown. In South Russia the later ochre-graves belong to this period.

PERIOD IV

T Halberds of German type with bronze shaft
U Irish gold lunulae
W Symbolic double-axes of copper
X Cypriote daggers
O Amber finds in the west and east

Cultural distribution in Europe, c. 1600 BC, from *The Dawn of European Civilization* 1925 geographical unit, and that individual cultures had to be defined in terms of constituent artefacts, not by subdividing the ages or epochs of the evolutionary archaeologists.[52] The duration and geographical limits of each culture also had to be established empirically from the archaeological record, and cultures rather than individual artefacts aligned chronologically in relationship to one another by means of stratigraphy, typology and synchronisms.[53] By the time he wrote *The Dawn of European Civilization*, Childe had clearly abandoned the concept of successive ages as the basis for his cultural chronology, and in its place had opted for an inductive, historical approach to the study of prehistory. Yet he did not deny that Thomsen's technological ages were significant features of cultural development. On the contrary, he was to spend much of his life trying to find a useful role for them in relationship to his new analytical scheme.

Childe had been referring to archaeological cultures in his publications since 1922.[54] He did not bother to define the term until he provided a brief sketch of his methodology in his preface to *The Danube in Prehistory* in 1929.[55] He evidently expected the term to be familiar to his readers and, to a large degree, it was. Cyril Fox had organized his study of the Cambridge region in terms of a series of technological and ethnic periods, and he spoke of 'advances in culture', 'new cultures' and 'cultural phases'.[56] In 1922, in *The Bronze Age and the Celtic World*, Peake wrote casually of the Maglemose, Tripolje and other cultures, while Crawford in 1921, in *Man and his Past*, had discussed geographical methods to determine the origins, extent and frontiers of archaeological cultures.[57] In his articles for *The Cambridge Ancient History*, published in 1923, Childe's mentor John Myres defined the concept of culture as follows: 'a culture is ... the total equipment with which each generation of men starts on its career ... to the archaeologist ... it is literally the equipment which the men of each generation were discarding'.[58] Myres discussed specific cultures, such as Hallstatt and Tripolje, but his more frequent references to 'Neolithic culture' and 'regional types of neolithic culture' suggest that he still thought of the concept at least partly in terms of evolutionary stages.[59] Childe did not introduce the idea of the archaeological culture to British archaeologists; what he did was to clarify its significance by showing them for the first time how it could be used to interpret archaeological data in a systematic fashion. It was for doing this that *The Dawn of European Civilization* has rightly been described as 'a new starting-point for prehistoric archaeology'.[60]

In none of his early writings did Childe inform his readers whence he had derived this idea. Even in his 'Retrospect', he merely observed laconically that 'from Continental literature I absorbed the German concept of a culture'.[61] It is clear, however, from the definitions that he offered, that his understanding of the archaeological culture came in particular from Kossinna's *Herkunft der Germanen*.[62] In that work Kossinna had used the concept of the archaeological culture to synthesize the archaeology of much of central Europe, just as Childe was to apply it to the whole continent. Childe followed Kossinna in viewing archaeological cultures as material expressions of particular peoples, who were united by a common social tradition. But the terms 'people' and 'society', which Childe used interchangeably to express this concept, lacked the connotations of blood and soil inherent in the German term *Volk*. Because he regarded archaeological cultures as expressions of particular peoples, he believed them to be observed facts rather than constructs of the archaeologists.[63] Like Kossinna he preferred the expression 'cultural group' (*Kulturgruppe*) to 'culture' because of its ethnic connotations. Yet he decided that it was hopeless to try to persuade English-speakers to adopt the longer form.[64] Towards the end of *The Dawn of European Civilization*, he reverted to using 'culture' and 'civilization' interchangeably to refer to the technologically simpler societies, thus following the inconsistent ethnological usage of the previous century.

But Childe was not prepared to accept many of Kossinna's other ideas. He specifically rejected his equation of peoples and cultures with specific races and Kossinna's efforts to explain the alleged cultural creativity of the Germans in terms of their ethnic purity. Childe noted with evident relish that sound-shifts in the German language seemed to indicate that its speakers were much mixed with foreign blood, and he argued that their true achievement in prehistoric times was to have built a harmonious civilization out of divergent ethnic and cultural elements.[65]

DIFFUSIONISM

Childe's opposition to Kossinna's nationalism reinforced his adherence to diffusionism. We have already noted that this was the preferred explanation of cultural change among British archaeologists of that period. Nevertheless Childe drew his specific conceptualization of diffusion from the work of Montelius, to the extent that Piggott and others have described him as being Montelius' spiritual heir.[66] Like Montelius, Childe was a moderate, empirical diffusionist. He shared with most of his contemporaries the belief that people naturally prefer established ways of doing things and are generally unwilling to modify them.[67] Because of this it seemed reasonable to consider major technological innovations such as the wheeled cart, effective copper smelting and the rotary quern as having been made only once, except where the archaeological record proved otherwise. At this time Childe appears to have thought it unlikely that metallurgy had developed more than once in the eastern hemisphere, or indeed throughout the world.[68] Likewise he thought that changes that had occurred in seemingly arbitrary cultural features (especially stylistic ones) in more or less adjacent areas were unlikely to have done so independently. It seemed improbable, for example, that such a distinctive artefact as the European battle-axe could have been invented twice.[69]

Yet as early as 1922 Childe suggested that high-footed bowls had been invented numerous times in Europe by the fusion of a spheroid bowl with a ring base.[70] In *The Aryans* he argued that all cremations in Europe – let alone in the world – could not be traced back to a single source in central Europe.[71] He frequently cautioned against relying too heavily on isolated and casual resemblances, although he did not always follow his own advice on this score. For all of its uncertainties, his position struck his contemporaries as a sensible middle ground between discredited unilinear evolution and the unacceptable hyperdiffusionism of Elliot Smith and his followers.

Childe also tried to formulate rules for spotting convincing evidence of migration in the archaeological record. He allowed that the infiltration of a new ethnic group might leave no mark, particularly if they were quickly assimilated by a culture that was more evolved and better adapted to the local environment than was their own. On the other hand, he suggested that the replacement of a more developed culture by a more primitive one, or the appearance of less evolved artefacts in a cultural sequence, generally must be interpreted as indicating population movement.[72]

In opposition to Kossinna's Germanophile interpretations of prehistory, Childe maintained that civilizations had first developed in the Near East, and that higher culture had diffused from there to Europe, generally in a piecemeal fashion. The tenets of this position had been spelled out in detail by Montelius in *Orient und Europa*, published in 1899. Childe was aware of Montelius' position prior to 1925, and later carefully reviewed his arguments in a paper called 'The Orient and Europe', first published in 1938.[73] In *The Dawn of European Civilization* he attempted to delineate how Near Eastern influences had penetrated Europe by way of the Mediterranean and the Atlantic seaboard, along the Danube Valley, and north and west across the Caucasus and Russian steppes. Although he dealt with the

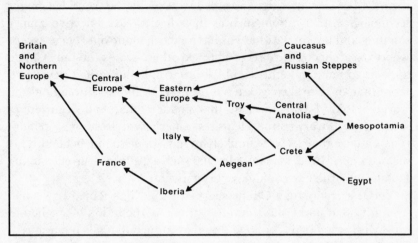

Gordon Childe's concept of the diffusion of culture from the Near East in Prehistoric Europe

Mediterranean route in the opening chapters of the original edition of this book, even at that time he viewed the Danube Valley as the main avenue along which Near Eastern influences had entered Europe. In the third edition, published in 1939, Childe placed the chapters dealing with the Balkans and the Danube immediately after those on the Aegean, to accord better with the importance he attached to this region.[74] Unlike Kossinna, who sought to trace the Indo-Europeans back to the Maglemosian culture, Childe saw little evidence of cultural continuity between the Palaeolithic and Neolithic periods in his early work. A diffusionist position had no vested interest in such cultural continuity, whereas Kossinna's theories required it, at least for the Indo-European homeland.

In recent years Colin Renfrew has stressed that Montelius' claim that cultural development took place more slowly in Europe than in the Near East was not only a conclusion to be drawn from the archaeological record, but also an hypothesis for dating it.[75] Childe was painfully aware of this and regretted that there was no independent means of dating archaeological material. In general he based his synthesis of European prehistory on Montelius' periodization, which he sought to refine in order to incorporate fresh data and adapt it to his more detailed cultural framework. Because no absolute dates were available for most of Europe prior to 1500 BC, he chose to treat the earlier part of his chronology as a bellows that could be expanded or contracted as new evidence indicated. In his published works, and even more so in his letters, he vacillated between a 'long' and a 'short' chronology for this early period.[76] He was not disposed to favour a long chronology for northern Europe because he saw this as supporting Kossinna's arguments concerning the historical priority of German cultural development compared with that of the rest of Europe. Childe also followed John Myres, Harold Peake and Alfred C. Haddon in deriving the Battle-axe cultures, and hence perhaps the Indo-European languages, from southern Russia, rather than having these cultures fan out in the opposite direction from Germany. He realized, however, that the chronology of Europe remained subjective in his own work, as well as in that of Kossinna. Nevertheless he continued to support a Russian origin for the Battle-axe people even when, just prior to the publication of *The Aryans*, the distinguished Finnish archaeologist A. M. Tallgren dated the Kurgan culture, from which the Indo-Europeans might have sprung, so late as to cast doubt on this scheme.[77]

Childe emphasized as well the positive role played by cultural heterogeneity. Like most British historians and geographers, he attributed the pre-eminence in all fields of Britain to the multiplicity of foreign influences to which it had been exposed. By universalizing this concept he sought to refute Kossinna's argument that German greatness resulted from their racial and cultural purity. Childe expatiated on the benefits that accrued from migration, trade and other forms of cultural contact. He maintained that the mingling of peoples with distinct cultures increased the stock of ideas available in a region, and encouraged progress by upsetting established ways of doing things. He also saw the elements of the first states being forged by the clash of cultures and of ethnic groups that had diverse social and economic organizations, whereas isolated cultures lagged in social and economic development, and ultimately became unable to resist conquest. He suggested that the rise of the Prussian Battle-axe culture and the decline of the Fatyanovo culture in Russia may have been correlated with a westward diversion of the commercial routes associated with the amber trade.[78] Though he was basically opposed to warfare and violence, he agreed that military competition and conquest helped to promote cultural development by encouraging flexibility and heterogeneity.

Although Childe relied upon the concept of diffusion to rid his use of Kossinna's concept of the archaeological culture of any Germanic bias, he was not as extreme an Orientalist as was Montelius. Like Myres and Evans, Childe balanced his desire to demonstrate the Near Eastern origins of many items of European culture with a strong emphasis on the creativity of European society. In *The Dawn of European Civilization* he sought to demonstrate how this creativity had allowed Europeans to forge 'the rudiments of arts and crafts' that they had acquired from the Near East into a new organic whole that, by the Late Bronze Age, was developing along original lines, and had already outstripped the achievements of its now moribund oriental teachers.[79]

Childe derived other ideas from the hyperdiffusionists Smith and Perry, and from the speculations they had inspired amongst archaeologists. In particular he adopted the general idea that megalithic culture had been carried to the western Mediterranean and the Atlantic seaboard of Europe by groups from the eastern Mediterranean who were searching for those magical substances, the Givers of Life. Childe was puzzled by the absence of metal objects in the earliest megalithic tombs of Iberia, but believed that the beehive tombs there and in the Aegean region were unlikely to have developed independently of one another. He firmly rejected Hubert Schmidt's dating of the Iberian Chalcolithic as early as 3000 BC, as well as his idea that this was a creative and vital culture that had helped to shape the development of Minoan civilization. Childe believed that cultural influences had moved in the opposite direction. He also saw searchers for magical substances as introducing megaliths and divine kingship to the Russian steppes, and the Beaker-folk as carrying the Iberian Children of the Sun's search for gold, precious stones and copper ore throughout much of central and western Europe.[80]

Childe never passed judgment on the global theories of the hyperdiffusionists, but on at least one occasion he referred without objection to world-wide quests for magical substances.[81] He also did not align himself with a specific formulation of hyperdiffusionism. Although his Iberian colonists hailed from the Aegean and wore 'recognizably the emblems of the Children of the Sun',[82] he was not disposed to be Egyptocentric. In place of Smith's seekers for Givers of Life, Childe accepted as 'in some form . . . the right one' Peake's theory that elements of civilization had been spread by prospectors belonging to a maritime race from the eastern Mediterranean. These were led by Sumerians, whose round-headed descendants Peake bizarrely believed were still dominating European finance in the twentieth century. These prospectors had spread megalithic architecture as far west as Ireland and as far east as India in their search for precious substances.[83]

The hyperdiffusionist theories suggested that a prime factor in the growth of civilization had been the religious aspect implicit in the search for materials with magic qualities of preserving life. While accepting some elements of these theories, Childe sought to reverse their significance by reinterpreting them in much the same manner that Marx had reinterpreted Hegel. He argued that a preoccupation with religion, far from being creative, had sapped the vitality of megalithic cultures, inhibited their technological advance by comparison with their neighbours, and doomed them to eventual conquest and destruction by more progressive groups. In Childe's trenchant phrase 'the legacy left by the "Children of the Sun" was only a dark superstition that retarded progress'.[84] France, as the centre of megalithic culture, had been wholly deprived of progressive development in prehistory. He believed that England and Scandinavia had been saved from the blight of megalithic religion only by having the good fortune to be overrun by more progressive groups, whose cultural development was focused on technology rather than religion.[85]

Glyn Daniel has observed that Childe's view of European prehistory was influenced by the German historical concept of the 'Four Empires', which saw the centre of civilization and world power shifting gradually north-westward from the Near East.[86] This notion, derived from medieval Christian thought, pre-dated the rise of German nationalism, as represented in archaeology by the work of Kossinna. Montelius' views were related to the Four Empires, although a certain mystical quality in Childe's early writings may be derived independently from that idea. In *The Dawn of European Civilization* and *The Aryans* an otherwise unromantic Childe wrote repeatedly of 'civilizing missions'; of the Danube 'pulsing the life blood of progress' through Europe; of the 'spirit of progress' moving northward to Hungary and Germany, and of the ultimate ascendancy of European culture.[87] Equally mystically he spoke of prehistory as still being immanent in the lives of modern Europeans, and of prehistoric peoples being their spiritual ancestors.[88]

ETHNIC STEREOTYPES

Although Childe did not share the widespread predilection of his contemporaries for racial explanations of culture history, he was unable to free himself completely from the trammels of ethnic stereotypes. This was perhaps inevitable, given that the avowed aim of *The Dawn of European Civilization* was to investigate the foundations of European civilization as a peculiar and individual manifestation of the human spirit. Childe followed Evans in discerning a truly occidental feeling for life and nature in Minoan civilization. He also attempted to trace into remote antiquity the qualities of energy, inventiveness and independence that he believed distinguished Western civilization from those of India, Egypt and China.[89] His attitude, far from being unique to him as an Australian, was only a somewhat refined formulation of the belief in the superiority of Europeans that was prevalent in Europe at that time. Despite his disgust with Kossinna's German nationalism, many of Childe's interpretations of prehistory mirrored analogous British prejudices of the 1920s. In *The Dawn of European Civilization* Britain, Germany and Scandinavia were lauded as being progressive in prehistoric times, unlike lands that later were to have Romance-speaking populations.

Something resembling the distinction that the mid-nineteenth century German ethnologist, Gustav Klemm, had drawn between culturally creative and passive races also became embodied in this aspect of Childe's work. He portrayed the peoples of the Aegean, Scandinavia and Britain as having contributed to cultural progress in antiquity, while the peoples of France and the Iberian peninsula had not. In an even more pronounced dichotomy in his thinking, the peoples of the Orient were characterized by stagnation and degeneracy, while true Europeans had a 'peculiar vigour and genius'.[90] The Iberian Los Millares culture was described as perhaps being 'too oriental' to have survived on European soil,[91] while it was only after the islands in the western Mediterranean had become insular and exclusive that they 'fell prey to Orientals'.[92] Although the Danubians were seen as initially having been pioneers of progress, their 'orientalism', and that of the other Neolithic groups in southern Europe, led to their conquest by more truly occidental cultures'.[93] The 'stagnant' megalithic cultures of the west were flatly pronounced to be 'not European'.[94]

Childe suggested that some of these differences might be the result of geographical conditions or specific historic factors. Yet, throughout *The Dawn of European Civilization* and *The Aryans*, these differences tended to be explained in terms of national character. In Germany a 'virile' Stone Age was the prelude to an epoch of original metallurgy. By contrast the Alpine peoples were not seen as a potent civilizing force, but as only progressing under alien inspiration.[95] In his characterization of the Alpines, Childe was influenced by Peake, who saw them as inert and naturally inclined to Communism. Peake had even felt it worthwhile to indicate that Karl Marx had come from a region of Alpine population.[96] Childe ascribed to the Danubians a peasant mentality that he alleged made them (like all peasants) an inert mass that easily fell prey to conquerors. He also suggested that the Virgin

50

cults of twentieth-century Austrian peasants were survivals of the Danubian worship of mother goddesses among a population 'who now as in prehistory served their Indo-European-speaking masters'.[97] Thus, while Childe laudably rejected the more blatant racism of the 1920s, he was by no means immune to the related practice of interpreting particular behavioural patterns as being innate characteristics of specific peoples. In this respect his thinking represented a generally moderate and refined version of contemporary opinion.

Childe's attitude towards language at this period was far from relativistic. In *The Aryans* he argued that a common language implied a common outlook, that intellectual progress may be measured largely by the relative refinements of different languages, and that the advance from 'animalism to civilization' involved the development of more abstract forms of thought that in turn required the evolution of qualitatively superior languages.[98] He maintained that a delicately structured language was a vantage point on the road to progress. He also claimed to find in language a more subtle criterion of individuality than was found in material culture, and suggested that by means of a philological approach archaeologists could learn more about what he ominously called 'racial individuality'. Childe described the latter as approximating the personal initiative that he, like many other anti-deterministic social scientists of that period, saw as playing a major role in cultural development. For him this constituted the apotheosis of national character as an explanation of history.[99] In *The Aryans* he sought to find in the properties of language the answer to questions not too different in principle from those raised by Kossinna: why did the development of Europe outstrip that of Egypt and Mesopotamia, and why did Europe progress when these older civilizations stagnated?

Childe lauded the Indo-European languages as being 'exceptionally delicate and flexible instruments of thought', which conferred special advantages on the peoples who possessed or came to possess them.[100] He pointed out that Buddhism and Zoroastrianism, both of which were founded by Indo-European speakers, appear to have antedated Judaism in extracting divinity from tribal and material trappings. He also drew attention to the then popular idea that the mother of the monotheistic Egyptian pharaoh Akhenaton probably had been an Indo-European.[101] He argued that the first advances towards the formulation of abstract natural sciences were made by the Indo-European Greeks and Hindus rather than by the less theoretically inclined non-Indo-European civilizations in Egypt and Mesopotamia. Additionally he contrasted the 'dignified narrative' of the inscription carved by the Indo-European Persian king Darius at

Behistun with the 'bombastic and blatant self-glorification' of the earlier Semitic rulers of Babylonia and Assyria.[102] While he believed that the Indo-Europeans had learned about agriculture and metallurgy from the ancient civilizations of the Near East, he argued that they were everywhere promoters of true progress, and that they thereby improved the conditions even of those whom they had conquered. He claimed that the expansion of the Indo-Europeans marked the moment when the prehistory of Europe began to diverge from that of Africa and the Pacific.[103]

Childe emphasized that the Indo-Europeans did not achieve success because of their superior culture (which was originally inferior to those of the Near East) or because of their superior natural intelligence. Instead they achieved it because they possessed a superior language and the more competent mentality that accompanied it. In support of this, he pointed out that the Greeks and Romans had only a very diluted Nordic physical type, but that each, having acquired an Indo-European language, realized the high cultural potential that was inherent in these languages. By contrast, in areas such as the Near East where the Indo-European languages were not retained, 'Aryan blood did not come to fruition'.[104] Yet sadly, at the very end of *The Aryans*, Childe bowed to prevailing racist sentiments by suggesting that the 'superior physique' of the Nordic peoples had equipped them to be fitting vehicles of a superior language.[105]

Childe never again championed the idea that languages or ethnic characteristics might constitute independent variables for explaining cultural development. He did not bother to up-date *The Aryans*, nor did he refer to that book in the 'Retrospect' written at the end of his life. Yet there is no reason to doubt that early in his career he had believed what he wrote in *The Aryans*. Its thought was in accord with the ideas of the time. The sharp separation of the themes covered in that book and *The Dawn of European Civilization* may simply reflect the tidiness of his thinking. Yet, if this is so, it is curious that the latter is so wholly devoid of even the slightest reference to his linguistic speculations, especially since we know that his philological interests, as embodied in *The Aryans*, antedated his archaeological studies. It is possible that when he was preparing his first two books for publication, Childe was aware of the relative originality and probable durability of the ideas contained in each of them. Publishing these two studies separately may have been an attempt, either consciously or unconsciously, to separate the solid accomplishments of *The Dawn of European Civilization* from the more vulnerable speculations of *The Aryans*. If so, *The Aryans* may have been more anachronistic, and the future course of his intellectual development more narrowly defined by 1925 than the published record of these early years indicates.

In a review published in *Nature* in 1925, Childe drew attention to what he considered to be the most important developments in archaeology during the previous decade, and tacitly evaluated his own work in relationship to these trends. He argued that scientific progress had left archaeology no alternative but to adopt the concrete methods of history. As a result the Neolithic was no longer defined simply as a stage of cultural development, but as a mosaic of sharply delineated cultural groups. The principal aim of prehistoric archaeology was now to isolate individual peoples or cultural groups, and to trace their differentiations, wanderings and interactions. He noted with satisfaction that the clarity with which the migrations of nameless prehistoric peoples had stood out in the archaeological record when it was thus analysed was a revelation to British archaeologists.[106]

Childe later observed that in the nineteenth century archaeologists had become interested in artefacts rather than in their makers. They had sought to construct evolutionary sequences, but these sequences left the artefacts as dead fossils, rather than as expressions of living societies. Only when archaeologists such as John Abercromby began to use archaeological data to trace the movements of peoples in prehistoric times, did they really become interested in prehistory.[107] In his 'Retrospect' Childe mentioned that when he wrote *The Dawn of European Civilization* he had sought, by tracing the movements of peoples in the archaeological record, to provide a prehistoric substitute for the politico-military chronicles of professional historians.[108]

Both *The Dawn of European Civilization* and *The Aryans* were structured, using concepts that Childe had derived from the fashionable archaeological writings of the period. He did not accept the ideas of any one system *in toto*, but selected, modified and integrated different aspects of their thinking to produce a synthesis of European prehistory that was both novel and widely acceptable. *The Dawn of European Civilization* provided other archaeologists with a model of how they might deal with archaeological data elsewhere, or within a more limited geographical or chronological framework. Childe's basic concepts, which included processes such as innovation, diffusion and migration, and analytical devices such as synchronisms and artefact types, were all relatively straightforward and, with one exception, wholly familiar to British archaeologists. The exception was the archaeological culture, which, although known to British archaeologists by name, had not previously been well defined nor systematically applied to the archaeological record, except for central Europe. His ideas did not provide a mechanical device for the cultural classification of archaeological data, as the Midwestern Taxonomic Method was later to do in America.[109] The latter system sought on a typological basis to assign sites to a hierarchical classification in which they were repeatedly merged on the basis of less specific cultural criteria to form broader groupings. The resulting dendritic pattern implied that cultures, like biological species, developed by differentiation only. Instead Childe's work was based on conceptions of human behaviour, which, right or wrong, infused his interpretations with historical, rather than just chronological, significance.

These ideas embodied a set of beliefs that were shared by the contemporary humanities and social sciences, as well as by the educated public, and represented a full-scale retreat from the propositions of the Enlightenment. Human beings were viewed as being naturally conservative and uninventive, and cultures as being to some degree expressions of qualities that were inherent in specific human groups. He espoused prevailing non-deterministic, and generally idealistic views about the nature of cultural change. He argued that archaeologists can identify the material forces that have shaped certain types of cultures, and the processes of trade and migration that have helped them to grow. He also maintained, however, that the individuality of groups 'eludes explanation in abstract material terms', and that 'personal initiative' lurks behind material factors.[110]

Yet Childe's views retained more of the ideals of the Enlightenment and of evolutionary archaeology than did those of most of his significant contemporaries. He continued to believe that across-the-board cultural progress was natural, rather than thinking of it as being accidental as the hyperdiffusionists did, or maintaining that material advances were paralleled by moral retrogression. His 'conservatism' in this respect may reflect his commitment to Marxism, since Marxism had selectively accepted and preserved many concepts of the Enlightenment, while non-Marxist thinkers had abandoned most of them. If so, this is one of the few manifestations of Marxism that can be detected in Childe's archaeological theorizing at this time. Another archaeologically less relevant manifestation was his contempt for nationalism.[111] This contempt was later to play an important role in undermining his respect for the culture historical approach that he had pioneered in *The Dawn of European Civilization*.

54

The most important element in Childe's success at this time was his avoidance of extremes. He adopted a moderate diffusionist approach and used it to strike a balance between the conflicting doctrines of *le mirage oriental* and *ex oriente lux*. He also adopted Kossinna's view of the archaeological culture but, by associating it with Montelius' notions of diffusion rather than Kossinna's of migration, he purged the concept of its Germanic connotations. The general outline of Childe's compromise was in line with the position that had been adopted by Evans and Myres, and had already won considerable support among British archaeologists.

In other aspects of his thinking, Childe was less willing to compromise. While his work was not wholly devoid of biological explanations of cultural differences, he rejected racial considerations more than did most of his colleagues. In his later publications, the last vestiges of racial explanations were to disappear. The most idiosyncratic characteristic of his archaeological interpretations was his loathing of religion. In *The Dawn of European Civilization* he explicitly identified an over-emphasis on religion as an important cause of cultural stagnation. Yet, because his comments applied to areas considered by many English readers in the 1920s to be backward in modern times owing to their adherence to Roman Catholicism, his views probably did not appear as outrageous then as they do now. To many readers, Childe, in spite of himself, probably appeared more Protestant than anti-religious.

CHAPTER IV

Prehistoric Economics

IN HIS FIRST TWO archaeological books Childe had ceased to use the technological model of successive ages of Stone, Bronze and Iron as a chronological framework. Instead he constructed the chronology of Europe as a mosaic of cultures individually positioned in time and space. Yet, not long after he had published *The Aryans*, he began to doubt whether much could be learned about ethnicity from archaeological data alone, and hence whether ethnicity was a concept that could give significant meaning to the study of prehistory.[1] He also began to doubt whether it was profitable to go on trying to produce a substitute for conventional political history in which, as he put it, cultures replaced statesmen and migrations replaced battles.[2] He turned again to the technological model in his search for a way to read more meaning into the study of prehistory.

Childe had realized that Thomsen's Three Ages were not simply chronological divisions, and also that each sub-stage in their evolution did not produce the same sort of societies in every part of the world. Nevertheless he continued to regard the development of stone, bronze and iron-cutting tools as a significant aspect of human progress. To circumvent the limitations inherent in the narrowly technological concept of the Three Ages, he began to examine prehistory in terms of broader economic trends. The results of these investigations were individually formulated and then drawn together as an integrated system in four books that Childe published between 1928 and 1934: *The Most Ancient East*, *The Danube in Prehistory*, *The Bronze Age* and *New Light on the Most Ancient East*.[3] These books will be examined in the order in which they were written.

The Danube

Childe continued to work for the Royal Anthropological Institute throughout 1926, while writing *The Danube in Prehistory*. This was to be the longest and most detailed work of historical synthesis that he produced. It documented a part of Europe for the most part unknown to British archaeologists, but which he had argued in *The Dawn of*

European Civilization was crucial for understanding the origins of European civilization. It was also to establish beyond question his credentials as a prehistorian. In the summer of 1926 Childe and C. Daryll Forde travelled together for six weeks in Yugoslavia, Romania and Hungary, gathering fresh data and checking personally the stratigraphy at important sites such as Vinča. Taking advantage of the inflated currencies of the region, they were able to move about in a large American car driven by an emigré Russian general.[4] In the autumn of that year, Childe was invited to deliver some lectures on prehistory and early man at the London School of Economics, which were well received.[5] The following year saw a second edition of *The Dawn of European Civilization* (in effect a reprint of the first edition with a brief addendum), and by September *The Danube in Prehistory* was finished, although it was not in print until 1929.

Many of the key themes of *The Danube in Prehistory* had already been outlined in *The Dawn of European Civilization*. Childe viewed the River Danube as the most extensive natural highway across the European continent, and therefore probably the principal route along which civilization had diffused from the Near East. He sought to document the role that it had played in the development of European culture to the end of the Bronze Age.[6]

Childe continued to regard the main elements that had promoted European cultural development during the Neolithic period and Bronze Age as being of Near Eastern origin. Yet, despite his earlier tendency to emphasize the alleged hiatus between the Palaeolithic and Neolithic cultures of Europe, he now saw the survival of certain elements of Palaeolithic culture as helping to explain the distinctive character of later cultures in the Danube region.[7] In his new book he also stressed that the Danube Valley was not only easy to penetrate from the south-east, but in addition possessed the natural resources that in early times would have attracted traders and settlers from that direction. As he had done in *The Dawn of European Civilization*, Childe argued that by the Late Bronze Age the peoples of central Europe had developed a sufficiently advanced technology to enable them to invade the already civilized Aegean region, while southern influences were not again to pass up the Danube until the Macedonian era.[8]

Most of *The Danube in Prehistory* was taken up by detailed descriptions of the archaeological cultures of the Balkans and the rationalization of a cultural chronology that was synchronized with the civilizations of the Aegean and the Near East. While *The Dawn of European Civilization* was the first study written in English to be organized in terms of archaeological cultures, its vast scope had precluded a detailed demonstration of how this idea could be applied to the analysis of archaeological data. Because of its narrow focus *The Danube in Prehistory* provided a better demonstration of the strengths and weaknesses of Childe's use of this concept.

Childe described each archaeological culture in terms of a more or less inclusive list of traits, from which a shorter list of distinctive traits was abstracted to facilitate its easy recognition. As in *The Dawn of European Civilization*, he attempted no systematic ordering of traits, nor did he seek to achieve comparable coverage for each culture. Cultures often were characterized very impressionistically. Like Kossinna Childe conceived of them as ideally having sharply defined boundaries that indicated tribal frontiers. He observed, however, that in reality local ceramic groups often melted imperceptibly into one another.[9] The origins of cultures were frequently expounded as certainties, even though the evidence he cited showed them to be obscure.[10] The culture at the end of a proposed migration route often was quite unlike that found in its alleged homeland.

The basis of Childe's chronology was his synchronism of Vinča I and Troy II, which would have dated Vinča as early as 2700 BC. Despite his strictures against relying on 'abstract common traits', his synchronisms for the Danube Valley were based mostly on general resemblances, such as red-slipped ware, anthropomorphic lids, female figurines, signs scratched on clay and metallurgy.[11] Vinča I is now radio-carbon dated much earlier than Troy II, between 5300 and 4000 BC.[12]

In 'Retrospect' Childe claimed that he had introduced the idea of post-glacial climatic changes and ecological re-adaptation to English readers in *The Dawn of European Civilization*.[13] Yet ideas of ecological adaptation and change first played a significant role in his work in *The Danube in Prehistory*, and had already been considered by other British archaeologists, such as O. G. S. Crawford, prior to 1925.[14] In this book the restriction of Neolithic settlement in Europe to loess soils and lake shores was ascribed by Childe to the inability of early farmers to clear dense forests. He also stressed the role of climatic alteration in bringing about cultural changes during the Bronze Age.[15] In 1930, a year after the publication of *The Danube in Prehistory*, Childe noted with approval Cyril Fox's dichotomy between highland and lowland Britain.[16] Fox argued that the highland areas in the north and west were characterized by cultural continuity and the selective acceptance of foreign traits, while the lowland areas in the south-east had been exposed to repeated invasions, and their history was characterized by radical replacements of one culture by another. Childe was clearly interested in employing ecological explanations when they permitted a better understanding of cultural change in Europe. On the whole, however, he was content to make use of other people's explanations. He did not contribute significantly to the formulation or refinement of these ideas.

The most important innovation in *The Danube in Prehistory* was Childe's economic interpretations of the evidence. This was something that was barely hinted at in *The Dawn of European Civilization*, where economies were alluded to only in passing references to commercial links and the use of local resources.[17] In *The Danube in Prehistory* he began to formulate concepts that were to remain part of his intellectual equipment for the rest of his life. He noted the presence of *Spondylus* shells from the Mediterranean in sites along the Danube already in Vinča I times, and interpreted this as evidence of trade during the early Neolithic period, possibly in return for cinnabar ore.[18] On the basis of much flimsier evidence, Childe proposed that after 2600 BC traders, prospectors and metallurgists had come into the Danube Valley from Anatolia to mine gold, copper and tin for export to the Near East.[19] Yet the only metal products that he could suggest they had supplied to the local market were some pins, earrings and daggers with Anatolian affinities. The best evidence he could produce for their hypothesized expeditions and trading posts was pottery bearing certain general resemblances to that found in the Near East.[20]

Childe argued that the destruction of Troy II, which he dated about 1800 BC, had disrupted trade between the Danube and the Near East. This compelled immigrant metal-workers in the Danube Valley to produce for local consumption rather than for export to their homelands. The result was the development of the bronze industry associated with the Aunjetitz culture.[21] Childe described the cultures of the Early Bronze Age, perhaps too enthusiastically, as the first European societies in which manufacturing and trade played a role on a par with agriculture. He did not, however, see any sign of differential social status associated with this industrial specialization.[22] He argued that the production of bronze presupposed contact between tin-producing areas such as Britain and Bohemia, and copper-producing areas such as Slovakia, Transylvania, Austria and Yugoslavia. This suggested the existence of a 'continental economic system'.[23] He was later to describe this 'system' as two loosely connected trade zones, one centred on Britain and the other on Hungary, each of which was a commercial network integrated by travelling tinkers.[24] He interpreted the wide distribution of new artefact types at this time as evidence of extensive trade and exchange. This was what made it possible to use typology to interrelate the development of culture on a continental scale. He noted that the typological method could only be used to construct chronologies covering areas where different cultures had been in constant and regular contact.[25]

Childe specifically denied that *The Danube in Prehistory* was a treatise on prehistoric nationalities; instead, it sought to clarify the role of the Danube in the development of European culture.[26] His historical interpretations did not lack tribal movements or even Aryan invasions, but he did not treat such events as primary explanations of historical processes. Though his economic formulations were as yet developed only in a rudimentary fashion, they were playing an increasing role in his explanation of archaeological data.

THE ABERCROMBY PROFESSORSHIP

He went to Edinburgh University in 1927 to take up his appointment to the Abercromby Chair of Prehistoric Archaeology, which had been established by the will of John, Fifth Baron of Aboukir and Tullibody, who had died three years earlier. Born in 1841, John Abercromby had served in the army from 1858 to 1870, and had then devoted himself, among other things, to studying the archaeology of northern Europe. His principal work, *The Bronze Age Pottery of Great Britain and Ireland*, was published in 1912. As early as 1905 Abercromby had expressed his dissatisfaction with the archaeological methods that were sanctioned by the Society of Antiquaries of Scotland. His quarrel with the Society, and his desire to improve Scottish archaeology, led him to propose the setting up of a department of archaeology at the university.

Childe thus joined the small band of prehistoric archaeologists who occupied professional posts in Great Britain. Reginald Smith, Christopher Hawkes and T.D. Kendrick worked at the British Museum; M.C. Burkitt was Disney Professor at Cambridge University, where Dorothy Garrod was also; R.E. Mortimer Wheeler and Cyril Fox were employed at the National Museum of Wales, in Cardiff, and O.G.S. Crawford worked for the Ordnance Survey. In addition H.J. Fleure taught in the Geography Department at Aberystwyth. Harold Peake had private means, Gertrude Caton-Thompson was excavating in Egypt and the young Grahame Clark was a research student at Cambridge. R.G. Collingwood, whose studies of Roman Britain were to exert some influence on prehistoric archaeology, taught philosophy at Oxford University. These archaeologists had been trained in subjects ranging from classics to chemistry. While several of them were interested in ecological problems, they can hardly be said to have shared a common theoretical orientation. There was at this time no clearly defined British school or schools of prehistoric archaeology into which Childe and his work might or might not fit.

In Abercromby's will, which Glyn Daniel has described as an example of 'remarkable testamentary writing', it was laid down that the holder of the new chair should be familiar with the prehistoric archaeology of Europe and the Near East; proficient in the French and German languages, and to some degree in Italian; able to impart his knowledge to the general public, and actively engaged in research on some archaeological problems. To ensure the success of the project, Abercromby also stipulated that the first incumbent should be a 'vigorous man in the prime of life'.[27] Stuart Piggott, Childe's successor at Edinburgh, has observed that these clauses were 'designed to exclude rather than to accommodate certain potential applicants – but they might have been framed for the benefit of Gordon Childe'.[28] For as long as he held the chair, Childe showed great scrupulousness in living up to both the spirit and the letter of Abercromby's will; hence in many ways these clauses were also instrumental in shaping the direction of his research.

In his inaugural lecture Childe reconsidered Abercromby's account of the arrival of the Beaker-folk and the beginnings of metallurgy in Britain in the light of recent research. Hereafter he often cited Abercromby's work on the Beaker-folk as marking the beginning of modern prehistoric research in Britain.[29] He also drew up a programme for a Bachelor of Science degree in archaeology at Edinburgh – the choice of degree clearly indicating that he regarded archaeology as a scientific discipline. But, while his influence on the students who attended his lectures was considerable, only one candidate read Honours Archaeology during Childe's tenure.[30]

The Most Ancient East

In 1928 Childe published *The Most Ancient East*, which was based on a course of lectures he had given during his first year at the University of Edinburgh. It was intended mainly to provide students with the oriental background that he believed was necessary to understand European prehistory. He sought to detail the origins of major innovations that had later spread to Europe, and to illustrate artefact types from the Near East that seemed important for cross-dating European material. In accordance with the terms of his academic appointment, Childe also tried to provide the general public with the context necessary to understand the many spectacular archaeological discoveries that were being made in the Near East. Widespread interest in archaeology had been aroused by the excavation of the intact tomb of the Egyptian pharaoh Tutankhamen, which had been found in 1922. Childe wished to survey other important discoveries that were shedding light on the development of civilization such as the Early Dynastic royal tombs at Ur, the Badarian culture in Egypt and the entire Indus Valley civilization. These were so far known only from brief reports in archaeological journals and notices in the *Illustrated London News*.

The Most Ancient East was criticized by reviewers for showing obvious signs of having been written too quickly.[31] Yet they also recognized that it filled a real need. More importantly it marked the beginning of some significant trends in Childe's thinking about prehistoric economies. As in *The Dawn of European Civilization*, Childe drew many of the main ideas for his work from the writings of contemporary archaeologists. Unlike his use of ecological concepts, these ideas became the basis for sustained and original thought.

Childe later noted that as early as 1915 Elliot Smith had characterized the development of food-production as being one of the most crucial stages in human history and an indispensable pre-condition for human progress.[32] Harold Peake and H.J. Fleure, among others, helped to promote this idea, which gradually made food-production appear to be a far more important criterion of the Neolithic than were pottery or polished stone tools.[33] Childe saw this view as endowing a technological stage with new economic meaning and eagerly espoused it. He described the development of agriculture and stock-raising as a 'revolution whereby man ceased to be purely parasitic and . . . became a creator emancipated from the whims of his environment'.[34] He was later to adopt the view that Neolithic societies had learned how to co-operate with nature in order to increase their food supply.[35] This is similar to the more recent eco-systemic approach which is concerned with the reciprocal interactions between human beings and their environment. He also suggested that the inhabitants of parts of the Near East may have been primarily collectors rather than big-game hunters, and that the versatility of such an economy would have made it easier for them to effect the transition to food-production.[36] Like many other archaeologists, he regarded the Upper Palaeolithic cultures of Europe as over-specialized dead-ends of cultural development.

To explain the origins of agriculture, Childe adopted Pumpelly's 'oasis hypothesis', which had been transmitted to a wider audience not long before in Peake and Fleure's *The Corridors of Time*, published in 1927.[37] Childe accepted that post-Pleistocene desiccation in the Near East had forced men and animals to gather around surviving pools and wadis, as their former range was transformed into desert. This propinquity encouraged symbiotic relations between human beings and animals that eventually led to the domestication of some animal species, as well as of wild cereals, in an effort to increase productivity.[38] In 1924 W.J. Perry had popularized T. Cherry's claim that agriculture had begun in Egypt when someone thought of increasing the amount of barley that grew spontaneously along the flanks of the Nile Valley by irrigating dry land adjacent to wild stands and planting barley seed in the wet mud left behind by the retreat of the annual inundation.[39] Childe viewed this as one variant of the oasis hypothesis, but he did not agree with Perry that food-production had necessarily begun in Egypt.[40] In 1928, however, the priority that is currently accorded to the development of food-production in south-western Asia, as a result of Robert Braidwood's excavations at Jarmo between 1948 and 1955, had not yet won support. Childe continued to emphasize the more familiar sequence of development in Egypt, while according second place to Mesopotamia.

Childe did not claim that the development of food-production was an inevitable response to increasing desiccation. He suggested that a hunting and gathering group confronted by such a challenge might move farther north or south, following the prey to which they were accustomed, and thereby maintaining their traditional way of life. Alternatively they might remain where they were, eking out a miserable existence on such game as remained, or they might liberate themselves from dependence on the whims of their environment by becoming agriculturalists.[41] This view had little in common with unilinear evolution. Instead it was akin to the possibilism which at that time was in vogue in human geography. In keeping with this non-deterministic view, Childe treated migration and diffusion as having played an important role in the establishment of a food-producing economy throughout the Near East and Europe.

Only three 'oases' in the Near East were generally thought large enough to have supported the development of major early civilizations: the Nile, Tigris-Euphrates and Indus valleys. In each of these areas, Childe saw the growth of wealth, the concentration of political power and the rise of city life reflected in the progress of the industrial arts.[42] He also saw societies becoming increasingly hierarchical and falling under the control of princes, priests and officials, while their security was guarded by well-trained and well-equipped armies.[43]

Yet, while Childe believed that these civilizations had developed from an interrelated, largely common neolithic base and had continued to maintain contact with one another, each civilization was seen as developing along separate lines, and as having a 'ripe and distinct individuality by 3000 BC'.[44] Far from treating them as examples of parallel development, he carefully delineated their differences. This was especially so with Egypt and Mesopotamia. Mesopotamian civilization was described as a series of city states, each focused on a major temple complex, while the whole of Egypt constituted a single state, ruled by a divine monarch. His view of Egyptian kingship was deeply influenced by James Frazer's concept of the divine 'corn king' and by Emile Durkheim's theory of the totemic origins of monarchical authority.[45] Childe also contrasted Mesopotamia, as an ethnically diverse culture area, with Egypt, which was an ethnically homogeneous one. Mesopotamia was portrayed as threatened by foreign enemies and rent by destructive internecine wars, while Egypt was seen as having quickly achieved and largely maintained internal peace and order. He suggested that because of this Egyptian civilization had prospered and was able to pull ahead of Mesopotamian civilization during the third millennium.[46]

Childe's ideas about the contrast between Egyptian and Mesopotamian civilization did not change in later years. He has, however, erroneously been interpreted as treating these two civilizations as examples of parallel evolution, while Henri Frankfort's *Birth of Civilization in the Near East*, published in 1951, has equally erroneously been seen as redressing this position. In fact Frankfort and Childe offered very similar accounts of the differences between Egyptian and Mesopotamian civilization. Where Frankfort's interpretation differed from that of Childe was by insisting that every culture has a unique pattern, or cosmological view, remaining constant throughout its history, that can never be fundamentally altered. Frankfort regarded such a pattern as the mainspring of a civilization's life and creativity.[47]

Childe viewed the development of civilization as resulting from major inventions that had been made during the Neolithic period. He noted, with respect to Mesopotamia, that the spectacular progress achieved at the dawn of history was 'expressed not so much in revolutionary industrial inventions as in the stabilization of institutions, increased amenities of life and a widened horizon opened up by the extension and regularization of foreign trade'.[48]

The large cities of Mesopotamia were seen as having been produced by synoecism (or the coming together) of smaller towns; an inference that seems to be borne out by recent archaeological evidence.[49] Childe believed that the growing demand for specialized tools and luxury goods associated with urban life had stimulated a market for exotic raw materials. Efforts to obtain these goods encouraged colonization and foreign trade, while refugees, fleeing from dynastic wars within the early civilizations, also carried know-how to peripheral regions. He saw trade as the principal factor promoting the diffusion of knowledge. It also helped to bind the Near East together and to maintain some degree of cultural unity in opposition to strong tendencies towards regional divergence.[50]

All of these processes promoted the development of a 'higher barbarism' on the fringes of Near Eastern civilization. In return for raw materials, the rulers of less developed, outlying societies received manufactured goods from the earliest civilizations, and eventually grew wealthy enough to employ surplus artisans who would have remained unemployed in their civilized homelands.[51] As Childe later put it, the Mediterranean peoples could draw upon the social surplus of oriental states, and use it as capital to develop a rudimentary commercial and industrial civilization of their own.[52] The closer geographically this capital was, the sooner a secondary Bronze Age civilization emerged.

Childe argued that it was necessary to give the term 'trade' a precise connotation whenever it was used, by defining the particular sociological, economic and environmental conditions that favoured and shaped such activity in a particular area.[53] He drew upon what seems to have been a rather superficial knowledge of industry and trade in modern industrialized societies in order to accomplish this. He produced some fairly simple models illustrating internal development, and relations between centres and peripheries, which he believed helped to explain the archaeological record. Childe saw specific political events like wars or migrations as factors contributing to the realization of the possibilities inherent in the economic situations he had thus defined.[54]

In *The Most Ancient East* Childe embraced the doctrine of *ex oriente lux* more completely than he had done in his earlier works. This change might be interpreted as simply reflecting the geographical orientation of the book, except that it continued into later works having little to do with the Near East. He argued that the accuracy of the diffusionist postulate was 'guaranteed by the fundamental continuity that characterized the Oriental world no less than its antiquity'.[55] He also asserted that 'the same threads that held together the various centres of Oriental civilization can be shown to bind thereto the European barbarisms of prehistory'.[56] Armed with this assurance, Childe ascribed all early inventions of any significance to the Near East. European prehistory, until its latest stages, remained a story of the imitation, or at best the adaptation, of Near Eastern achievements.[57] To understand how or why these achievements came about, one must study the archaeological record of the Near East.

We have already mentioned that Childe shared the mistrust of unilinear evolution felt by most social scientists of his generation. He postulated a variety of alternative responses to regional desiccation and, while noting that the early civilizations shared certain common features, laid greater emphasis on their differences. More explicitly, he affirmed that 'archaeology's revelations ... disclose no abstract evolution but the interaction of multiple concrete groups and the blending of contributions from far-sundered regions'.[58] In keeping with his mistrust, he felt ambivalent about the value of broad ethnographic analogies for interpreting archaeological evidence. He considered that societies at approximately the same level of development as those of Bronze Age Europe could be found in modern Borneo or Africa, and that the apparel worn in all of these societies must have had an equally barbarous appearance.[59] Yet Childe did not attempt to draw any specific parallels between these societies.

Like most others who rejected unilinear evolution, Childe was more hopeful about comparing societies that seemed to be historically related. He believed that the practices of the ancient Near Eastern civilizations, as revealed by written texts, might shed light on the coeval Bronze and Iron Age societies of Europe.[60] He also described the modern Dinka and Shilluk peoples of the Sudan as a 'living museum', whose arrested social organizations illustrated early stages in the development of the ancient Egyptian civilization. He stressed, however, that this analogy was valid because these tribes were related to the ancient Egyptians in 'appearance, stature, cranial proportions, language and dress'; in short, they were historically related.[61] When Childe later observed that these same groups constituted the closest modern analogues to the Neolithic and Bronze Age cultures of the British Isles, he also had an historical relationship in mind, since he believed that the Neolithic cultures of Britain were ultimately derived by migration from Neolithic Egyptian cultures, such as those found at Merimde or in the Fayum.[62]

The Most Ancient East contains specific interpretations that now appear wildly speculative. Most of these reflect the anti-evolutionary and diffusionist views of the period. The microliths and conventionalized art associated with the Mesolithic period in Europe were treated as signs of degeneration among groups that were unable to cope with a worsening environment.[63] Southern Arabia was proposed as perhaps being the ancestral homeland of the Beaker-folk.[64] Childe dismissed as hardly even a legitimate inference the suggestion that the Mesopotamian and Egyptian civilizations were derived from a southern steppe culture, where adherents of a Lower Palaeolithic tradition had first learned to plant grain and tame animals. Nevertheless he accepted the possibility that many similarities between these two civilizations could be explained by postulating a third, still earlier centre from which influences had radiated simultaneously to both regions.[65] His conclusion that the debate about whether similarities between Egypt and Mesopotamia resulted from trade or invasion was not a profitable one seems more in line with current opinion.[66]

When he wrote *The Most Ancient East*, Childe felt that not enough archaeological evidence was available to construct a coherent and detailed explanation of the development of civilization in the Near East.[67] Yet he saw, particularly in the increasing variety of tools, the material expression of greater control over nature and the general enrichment of life.[68] He therefore sought to use archaeological data to endow prehistory with economic significance. He later maintained that one of the benefits he derived from writing *The Most Ancient East* was that it familiarized him with how archaeological data can be 'illumined' from associated written texts; although, not reading any of the ancient languages of the Near East, he had to use this material at second hand.[69] More importantly, however, at least in the short term, writing this book brought him to grips with the problems of the origin and significance of food-production. His interest in the consequences that flowed from this process constituted the theme that was to be elaborated in his next book on the Bronze Age.

The Bronze Age

The Bronze Age was published in 1930 not, Childe claimed, as a sequel to M. C. Burkitt's *Our Early Ancestors* (1926), but rather to take up the story of 'prehistoric industrial development' where that textbook left off.[70] Childe defined the Bronze Age as a stage of development characterized by the regular use of copper or bronze, as distinguished from the occasional manufacturing of artefacts from nuggets of native copper. In his book, he tried to determine the economic and social significance of bronze-working, and thus to rehabilitate the Bronze Age as a major stage of economic, as well as technological development.[71]

Childe considered the possibility that metallurgy might have been invented independently in Egypt, the Near East, Hungary and Spain, but dismissed this idea as highly unlikely.[72] He regarded bronze-working as being such a complex process, and the discoveries leading to it so abstruse, that it was likely to have been invented only once in human history. He also interpreted specific similarities in the processes used to work bronze in Europe and the Near East as proof of a single origin.[73] He asserted that the design of the earliest metal goods in Europe could be traced back to Mesopotamian and Egyptian prototypes. Finally widespread evidence of trading connections in Neolithic and Chalcolithic times militated against completely independent development in areas that were so close to one another. Childe was uncertain whether copper-working was more likely to have been invented in Egypt or in Mesopotamia. Evidently the rapidity of cultural development in these two areas made them seem more promising points of origin than other areas closer to major sources of ore.[74]

Childe assumed without question that bronze-working was impossible without various types of full-time, often itinerant craftsmen. He believed that smiths were probably the first full-time specialists in human history, and saw miners, prospectors and smeltermen as requiring even more abstruse knowledge.[75] He later equated the development of metallurgy with the beginning of Engels' separation of handicrafts from agriculture, and thus viewed it as marking a major social, as well as technological transition.[76] He assumed that miners and smiths were the first human beings who functioned independently of tribal bonds.[77] He does not appear to have seriously tried to check any of these assumptions against the ethnographic record. He noted vaguely that in parts of Africa smiths travelled from one tribal group to another to serve their clientele, and wrongly concluded that this was a universal practice. Childe derived this conclusion mainly from a passage of Homer, which states that in ancient Greece a soothsayer, doctor, singer or craftsman was sure of a welcome anywhere.[78] He continued to stress the importance of this passage throughout his life.

Childe also believed that in early times knowledge of metal-working had been guarded as a professional secret by masters who practised the craft. These masters would instruct only non-kinsmen who could offer them something of special value in return, especially access to additional sources of raw materials.[79] He suggested that knowledge of metal-working had been slowly diffused by smiths looking for sources of metal ores, and by the younger sons of smiths seeking new areas where they might work.[80] Because of this, craftsmen often belonged to different ethnic groups from the people for whom they worked. This model did not contradict Sidney Smith's assertion that foreign craftsmen were frequently attracted to major urban centres as the latter evolved and offered new sources of employment.[81]

Childe was interested in the effects on individual communities that bronze-working had. Although he viewed metal tools as being desirable, he believed the spread of metallurgy to have been slow and far from inevitable, and attempted to delineate the social and economic conditions that might have accelerated or retarded this process. In Childe's own wording, it required a double loss of Neolithic self-sufficiency for most communities to begin using bronze tools on a regular basis. First, it required every family in the community to become dependent on craftsmen who were often unrelated to them. Second, because copper and tin occur only in a few places, it required most communities to become dependent on trade. The regular use of copper thus necessitated the development of extensive trade routes that were not interrupted by periodic outbreaks of tribal warfare.[82]

The cost of securing copper and tin was seen as a major factor limiting its routine use in most areas. At first it was employed extensively only in regions such as Mesopotamia, where the lack of naturally occurring stone tended to offset the high cost of metal.[83] Childe observed that bronze tended to be used for weapons and specialized tools before it was employed for farm implements. He argued, however, that even such limited use could produce the irreversible dependence on it that characterized the Bronze Age. He believed that specialized carpentry, such as the manufacture of cart and potter's wheels, was impossible without metal tools.[84]

Childe also considered the role that the employment of copper and bronze had played in the development of scientific lore. Copper ore, unlike flint, occurs in hard rock and had to be mined by specialists. The reduction of copper ore produced more dramatic changes in its chemical properties than did the firing of pottery. Hence, in his opinion, the elaboration of this process marked the beginnings of chemistry as a practical science.[85]

Childe was no more a unilinear evolutionist in *The Bronze Age* than he had been in *The Most Ancient East*. He maintained that bronze-working had played an important role in the development of more complex societies, but that its effects had been quite different in Europe than in the Near East, where it had been invented and where the Bronze Age lasted twice as long as in Europe. In the Near East, bronze-working had been an important prerequisite for the rise of civilization, which Childe defined as being characterized by cities, animal traction, writing, consciously ordered government, the beginnings of science, specialization of the industrial arts, and international trade and commerce.[86] He also noted that, after a precocious start, Near Eastern civilization had stagnated. In Iraq no new types of metal tools were invented after the collapse of the Akkadian Dynasty, about 2230 BC.[87]

By contrast Childe believed that bronze-working had been introduced into Europe by miners and artificers from the Near East, who were looking for copper and tin for their home markets. When commercial contacts between Spain and the Danube and these traditional markets were interrupted, at the end of the Copper Age (*c.* 1900 BC), these craftsmen began to produce goods for a European clientele.[88] The Middle Bronze Age saw the development and spread of new 'schools' of metallurgy, especially in those parts of Europe that were again engaged in direct or indirect trade with the eastern Mediterranean. These metal-workers made original contributions to a common European stock of metal types.[89] By the Late Bronze Age (*c.* 1600 BC), an increasing population, combined with altered climatic conditions that favoured the spread of forests, was producing a greater need for agricultural land, and hence more warfare and an increased demand for metal weapons. This led to the growth of the scrap metal trade, more intensive mining and more competition to control mines.[90] This aspect of Childe's work was influenced by the publications of Cyril Fox, who saw the founder's hoard and the reorganization of the metal industry as important characteristics of the Late Bronze Age.[91]

Childe continued to stress inter-tribal contact and competition as major forces promoting growth. That it was a meeting place for several currents of influence from the eastern Mediterranean was accepted as explaining the 'intense vigour and originality' of Bronze Age Britain,[92] while the 'clash of African and Asiatic traditions' in Gerzean Egypt accounted for a general spurt in progress and growing specialization in all the arts.[93] Childe now insisted on the principle of *ex oriente lux* even more strongly than he had done in *The Most Ancient East*. He argued that it was 'not possible to point to a single vital contribution to material culture originating in Europe outside the Aegean area'.[94] Western civilization as a whole was seen increasingly as simply the culmination of a tradition of inventions and discoveries that was rooted in the Near East.[95] He argued that post-war discoveries in the Near East had emphasized the 'debt' that Europe owed to that region.

In 1934 Childe produced a synthesis and further elaboration of the economic ideas he had formulated in *The Most Ancient East* and *The Bronze Age* in a wholly rewritten version of the former book, to which he gave the title *New Light on the Most Ancient East*. Whereas the original had been based solely upon published source material, he prepared to write this one by visiting Iraq and the recently excavated sites of the Indus Civilization. In Iraq he inspected the excavations of the Oriental Institute of the University of Chicago, under the direction of Henri Frankfort, in the Diyala region east of Baghdad, the German Expedition at Uruk, and Leonard Woolley's Joint British and University of Pennsylvania Expedition at Ur. In the course of his journey, Childe noted 'how the beginnings of literacy in the ... great river valleys coincided with the erection of the first monumental tombs and temples and the aggregation of population in regular cities'.[96] He fancied a parallel between the expansion of rustic settlements in the ancient Near East into cities, such as Ur and Lagash, and the recent growth of English villages into manufacturing towns. This transformed his habit of casually interpreting economic developments in ancient times in terms of what he knew about the Industrial Revolution of the eighteenth–nineteenth centuries into a formulation that was to dominate much of his subsequent work.

Childe had hitherto referred to cultural revolutions in an informal manner. In *New Light on the Most Ancient East* he drew upon previous work to define and label as such two economic revolutions that had preceded the Industrial Revolution, and which he claimed were similar in historical importance to it. The first was the change-over from food-gathering to food-production. The second was the transition from self-sufficient food-producing economies to urban civilizations, which he believed were based on industry and commerce. He also believed that, like the Industrial Revolution, both prehistoric revolutions were followed by a large increase in population. Among hunters and gatherers having many children was regarded as a liability for a family, whereas in food-producing societies children could be put to work at a young age, and thus constituted an economic asset for a family.[97]

Childe based the delineation of his two prehistoric revolutions mainly on conclusions he had arrived at in *The Most Ancient East* and *The Bronze Age*. Food-production was seen as resulting from desiccation, which compelled large numbers of people to subsist off a small area of land. Hitherto he had suggested that growing scarcity of resources and increasing population densities in the surviving oases were major factors promoting innovation and change. In *New Light on the Most Ancient East*, he accorded less importance to this ecological explanation, and reformulated his account of the development of food-production in terms of increasing diffusion and culture contact. Childe suggested that the 'first revolution' came about in the Near East as worsening desiccation compelled hunting groups to travel greater distances in search of food, and thus brought increasing numbers of people, who often possessed diverse knowledge, into contact with each other.[98] Migration and diffusion were both assigned an important role in spreading a food-producing economy throughout the Near East and Europe.[99] This process created a realm of villages that itself became increasingly a theatre of diffusion. Childe noted evidence of considerable trade among these villages, but he believed that prior to the Bronze Age this trade had not negated their essentially self-sufficient status, since it was invariably in non-essential items. The contact associated with this trade nevertheless helped to disseminate technical knowledge. He believed that specialized trading groups might already have existed at an early food-producing stage, since 'specialized traders are found on a lowly economic plane in modern Africa'. These traders might have been either pastoralists or hunters living outside the settled communities.[100]

Childe believed that the food-producing cultures of the Near East shared a common origin, or at least that their origins were historically inter-connected. Nevertheless within this region he distinguished 'two irreducible cultural provinces'. The African-Anatolian province was distinguished by its monochrome black, and later red pottery, straight-handled sickles, hollow-based arrows and disc-shaped mace heads. The Asian province was characterized by pale pottery – often painted, pear-shaped mace heads and crooked sickles. Although Egypt was overrun by an expansion of the Asian province at the beginning of the Gerzean period, cultures of African–Anatolian type reached Europe by way of north Africa and Spain, Crete and central Europe. On the other hand, the painted-ware cultures of Thessaly, Bulgaria, Transylvania and the Ukraine were seen as derived from the Asian province, with which they also shared more advanced features, such as stamp-seals, copper-working and probably brick architecture.[101] The concept of two cultural provinces continued for a long time to play an important role in Childe's writings about British prehistory, and was only gradually abandoned by him.

Childe's 'second revolution', from barbarism to civilization, was characterized by an increase in the total wealth of society and by the accumulation of surplus wealth by kings and temples, primarily in the form of foodstuffs. Part of this surplus was used to pay for productive works such as systems of drainage, irrigation and flood control, and for the importation of primary materials that were now essential for the operation of the economy.[102] Much of it was used, however, to sustain craftsmen, merchants, artists and soldiers, many of whom were no longer engaged in any sort of agricultural production.[103] Though Childe admitted that the growth of militarism was justified in order to defend the wealth of civilizations against raids by neighbouring barbarians, he believed that much wealth and manpower were destroyed in futile conflicts between city states. He now interpreted the synoecism of early Mesopotamian towns as being the forcible consequence of warfare.[104] Yet, while he deplored the wasteful behaviour of the early civilizations, he argued in a teleological fashion that the emergence of such societies was essential in order to integrate human effort on a vaster scale than had been achieved hitherto.

Childe vastly under-estimated the degree to which most of the inhabitants of the early Mesopotamian city states were engaged in agriculture. He saw industry, trade and commerce as the basis of the pre-industrial as well as the prehistoric city. He also argued that, as with the Industrial Revolution, a new means of livelihood had resulted in the multiplication of the proletariat, who gradually outstripped in numbers the demand for their labour, and some of whom were thus forced to emigrate. These, together with groups defeated in war, carried civilization, or elements thereof, into neighbouring, less developed regions.[105]

At the same time growing industry and an increasing market for luxury goods created a demand for more raw materials. The rulers of the early civilizations traded surplus food for these materials with their less advanced neighbours. They also conquered neighbouring regions in order to secure control of needed supplies of raw materials. Both activities encouraged the development of new civilizations. The urban centres that grew up, or were deliberately founded in these peripheral regions created new proletariats. These, combined with the efforts of tribal peoples to resist the aggression of their civilized neighbours, produced independent states, which in turn, as soon as their own economies ceased to be self-sufficient, began to encourage the growth of tertiary centres still farther removed from the primary areas in which civilization had first developed.[106] The more remote developments were usually not as complex as the original ones had been. Childe also attributed the spread of food-producing cultures in Europe to the rise of secondary civilizations in Anatolia and the Aegean, which were themselves products of his second revolution in the Near East.[107]

Childe enunciated two principles that he believed governed relationships between primary and secondary centres. The first was that of the archaism of provincial regions. He postulated that while secondary civilizations can borrow ideas from primary centres they are unable to improve these borrowings as quickly as can their originators.[108] Hence old-fashioned or archaic forms in a secondary civilization may be contemporary with more developed forms of the same item in a neighbouring primary civilization. His second principle was that the political and military institutions of Near Eastern civilizations ultimately wasted more resources than they produced, thereby causing the development of these civilizations to grind to a halt. The growth of secondary civilizations also undermined the prosperity of primary regions, as the former gained control of trade routes and their own needs reduced the amount of raw materials that reached the primary civilizations.[109] He believed that the last two points explained why the civilizations of the Near East ultimately were outstripped and came to be dominated by those of Europe.

EVALUATION

Christopher Hawkes has defined four levels of increasing difficulty in interpreting archaeological evidence. He argues that technological inferences can be made fairly easily, while economic ones are harder, social and political ones harder still, and ideological ones the hardest of all.[110] Childe's effort to read more significance into archaeological data had led him to seek to master the second level in this hierarchy. His interest in the economies of prehistoric societies may to some degree have reflected his Marxist political views. Yet archaeologists who were not Marxists, such as Harold Peake, were also interested in economic problems, and Childe had made use of their ideas to construct his own more detailed and comprehensive model of economic growth, which was meant to explain the development of the Near East and Europe to the end of the Bronze Age.

Childe had modelled his 'pageant of economic development' on the assumption that in some respects his first two revolutions were analogous to the Industrial Revolution. His view that all three revolutions had been followed by spectacular rises in population was admittedly an assumption for the first two, not a relationship that he could demonstrate from the archaeological evidence. He also overlooked the fact that in England a significant growth in the population had preceded as well as followed the Industrial

Revolution, and that the whole increase had been due mainly to improved medical technology and growth in agrarian productivity.[111] Hence the expansion of the eighteenth century was unlikely to apply to earlier periods, especially when many urban populations were not self-reproducing. Childe's assumption that Sumerian cities were 'regular industrial and commercial' centres inhabited by an 'industrial proletariat' was also a naive parallel, even in terms of the limited information that was then available.[112]

Childe's efforts to offer functional interpretations of archaeological data were clearly limited by his lack of awareness of alternative patterns of behaviour, that he might have been familiar with had he had better knowledge of the ethnographic record. He knew of Hobhouse, Wheeler and Ginsberg's *The Material Culture and Social Institutions of Simpler Peoples*, an ethnographic comparison of 640 societies that aimed to discover to what degree variations in the method of food-production were correlated with the evolution of other aspects of culture. Their economic classification established three types of hunting societies, three grades of agriculturalists and two grades of pastoralists,[113] but most of his references to ethnographic data were vague in the extreme. Although he cited the occurrence in Africa of wandering smiths who were not associated with any particular tribal group as support for his interpretation of the prehistoric economy of Europe, he did not attempt to find out how commonly this occurred, or what alternative arrangements existed in other cases.[114] This omission was serious, since virtually no archaeological evidence relating to the activities of smiths was available for northern or central Europe prior to the Iron Age, when there was some evidence of community-based bronze-workers. Childe squared this evidence with his speculations about earlier times by postulating the 're-tribalization' of bronze-workers in an Iron Age economy.[115] Because of his unfamiliarity with ethnology, even the basic distinction between part-time and full-time specialists was unknown to him until much later.[116] He remained suspicious of the relevance of ethnographic analogy as an interpretative device, and was unwilling to use it systematically to expand his awareness of alternative explanations for this data. He also made little effort to substantiate key elements of his explanations of prehistory, such as locating actual graves or houses belonging to his postulated Anatolian prospectors in Europe.

Childe's use of ethnographic data was typical of the period. Most archaeologists continued to follow the nineteenth-century evolutionists' practice of selecting from ethnographic data around the world random examples that supported the point they wished to make, while ignoring contrary cases. The new social anthropology was so preoccupied with describing individual societies that it offered no alternative to this practice, and systematic cross-cultural studies were not to become common in anthropology until after World War II. Though some archaeologists, such as O. G. S. Crawford, stressed the value of ethnographic analogy for interpreting archaeological data,[117] most social scientists were so mistrustful of cross-cultural regularities that they regarded them as being of little explanatory value.

The developmental sequences outlined in *New Light on the Most Ancient East* were still more linear and inevitable than they had been in *The Most Ancient East*. Yet Childe continued to argue that cultures did not develop in the same way in different areas. He sought to correlate his economic stages with the traditional Palaeolithic, Neolithic and Bronze Ages, but at the same time stressed that the effects of the new technologies had been different in the Near East and in Europe. He also believed that the spread of a food-producing, and later of a bronze-working technology in Europe had largely been a consequence of the second revolution in the Near East.[118]

There was already the making of a multilinear evolutionary approach in Childe's contrast between cultural development in Europe and the Near East. Yet he was not primarily concerned with evolution at this time. All archaeologists and anthropologists admitted that technological progress had occurred, in the sense that more complex technologies had appeared later than simpler ones. What they disagreed about was the significance of this phenomenon. Cultural evolution had formerly been viewed as a universal manifestation of human reason unfolding in the course of time. By the 1920s, however, many social scientists had ceased to believe that man was naturally inventive or disposed to change his way of life. This led many archaeologists, including Childe, to rely more heavily on diffusion and migration as explanations of the cultural changes observed in the archaeological record. Hence it does not come as a surprise (except anachronistically) to be told at the end of *New Light on the Most Ancient East* that the main aim of the book was to justify the 'general doctrine of cultural diffusion'.[119] Childe had not managed to harmonize his conventional concern with diffusion with his more original and creative interest in economic development. As a result, diffusionary explanations (however reasonable) would continue to inhibit his studies of social development.

CHAPTER V

Scottish Archaeology

CHILDE'S INSISTENCE that his main contribution was to the development of archaeological theory has lent credibility to the claim that he was not much of an excavator or 'field man'.[1] Soon after he had arrived in Scotland in 1927, Childe wrote to a friend that he loathed digging sites as much as he loathed having to spend the summer in the chilly climate of Scotland.[2] Yet Piggott later had the impression that Childe 'in some curious way' enjoyed excavating.[3] Whatever were his personal feelings, between 1928 and 1946 Childe did as much field work as most other professional archaeologists; he recorded his excavations in detail, and he was scrupulous about publishing archaeological reports. Contrary to what is sometimes alleged, his field work did not terminate after he became Director of the Institute of Archaeology in 1946. He continued to excavate in Scotland during four summers in the 1950s.[4]

Piggott has asserted that Childe was a bad excavator. He claims that Childe was unable to appreciate the nature of archaeological evidence in the field, and the processes involved in its recognition, recovery and interpretation. Piggott also claims that this failing blinded Childe to potential inequalities in the data produced by other archaeologists, and hence to the reliability of the data he used in his works of synthesis.[5] No one has bothered to review these charges.

During his tenure of the Abercromby Chair, Childe devoted considerable time to research on Scottish prehistory, which he judged on his arrival in Scotland to be in a very backward condition.[6] He appears to have begun to do this largely from a sense of duty, and as part of the responsibility of his post. Nevertheless the volume and quality of his work shows that he did not take the task lightly. He not only excavated sites, but also sought to familiarize himself with what had been written about Scottish archaeology, did original research on museum collections, and produced *The Prehistory of Scotland*, which was the first comprehensive treatment of prehistoric Scotland since Joseph Anderson had published *Scotland in Pagan Times* in 1886.[7] Childe evidently viewed Scotland as an entity worthy of serious study.[8] His investigations of its prehistory provide us with an excellent

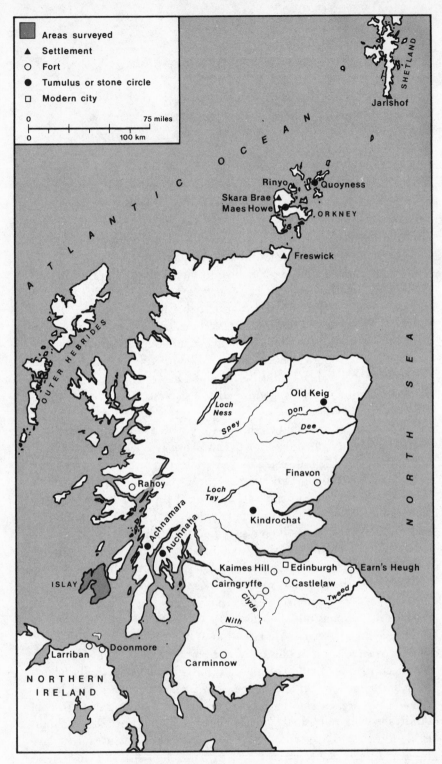

ATLANTIC OCEAN

SHETLAND

Jarlshof

Rinyo   Quoyness

Skara Brae

Maes Howe   ORKNEY

▲ Freswick

OUTER HEBRIDES

Loch Ness

Spey

Don

Old Keig ●

Dee

Finavon ○

Loch Tay

● Kindrochat

Rahoy ○

Achnamara

Auchnaha

ISLAY

Kaimes Hill ○   □ Edinburgh   Earn's Heugh ○

Cairngryffe ○   ○ Castlelaw

Clyde   Tweed

Nith

Doonmore ○

Larriban

Carminnow ○

NORTHERN IRELAND

NORTH SEA

Location of the major archaeological sites investigated by Gordon Childe in Scotland and Ireland opportunity to examine the relationship between his field work and his culture-historical syntheses. Because *The Prehistory of Scotland* is Childe's most narrowly focused synthesis, it reveals in even more detail than does *The Danube in Prehistory* the strengths and weaknesses of his approach.

Childe lauded Joseph Anderson, J. Geikie, R. Monro, John Abercromby and T. H. Bryce as former students of Scottish prehistory who, like himself, had overcome British insularity and approached their subject with an international outlook. He claimed that because of this they had done work of international importance.[9] Yet, in spite of his research, there is no indication that, prior to his return to England in 1946, Childe was aware of the work of Daniel Wilson, even though Wilson had written the first major synthesis of Scottish prehistory. The fact that Anderson did not emphasize the work of his distinguished predecessor may in part explain this lapse. It also demonstrates that Childe's knowledge of the early archaeological literature remained incomplete, even for Scotland.

Childe recorded little about his study of museum collections; however, in 1945 he wrote to Robert Braidwood that he was spending more time serving temporarily as director of the National Museum of Antiquities than in teaching at the university.[10] As a product of this work, he assembled systematic lists and distribution maps of chambered tombs, stone circles, pottery types, Iron Age forts and grave offerings, all classified in detail. Childe enjoyed travelling about Scotland in his motorcar and on foot, visiting known sites and searching for new ones. He undertook many excavations in response to requests from the owners of sites and government agencies, and during the war worked for the Royal Commission on Ancient Monuments, carrying out emergency surveys of sites and monuments threatened by bombing and construction projects.

SKARA BRAE

Childe's first excavation in Scotland was at Skara Brae, on the Bay of Skail in the Orkneys. There, along the bleak, windswept west coast, an unusually well preserved complex of inter-connected stone huts dating from prehistoric times was partly buried under a sand dune eight to nine feet deep. Inside the houses was equally well preserved stone furniture. Skara Brae had been discovered and partly plundered by antiquaries in the nineteenth century, and had been plundered again in 1913. In 1924 another house belonging to the complex was damaged by a severe storm. In 1928 the Chief Inspector of Ancient Monuments invited Childe to supervise the clearance of the structures at the site and their consolidation as a national monument. Childe was aware of the paucity of prehistoric habitation sites that had been studied north of the Alps, and worked at Skara Brae for three summers from 1928 to 1930. He published the results of this work in a series of preliminary reports, and in a detailed monograph that set a new standard for the publication of prehistoric sites for the British Isles.[11]

Childe concluded that while the same culture had occupied Skara Brae throughout its history, four building periods could be distinguished stratigraphically, and had been followed by the light reuse of the site after period IV. In his final report he recorded in detail the changing architecture and stone furniture of Skara Brae, noting the relationship of artefacts to these features. He also drew parallels between the Skara Brae huts and rural houses inhabited in the Scottish Highlands and the Hebrides during the nineteenth century.[12] Although he noted no traces of grain cultivation, the bones of domesticated sheep and cattle were common, as well as the remains of shellfish. He described the artefacts from the site under the twin headings of material culture and spiritual culture. The former embraced items of practical use; the latter burials and objects that he associated with religious practices, ornamentation, art and games.

D. J. Mulvaney has rather uncharitably attributed the success of Childe's excavations at Skara Brae more to the solid construction of the huts and the looseness of their sand fill than to the skill of the excavator.[13] Yet, by the standards of the time, Childe had done an excellent job of unravelling the stratigraphy and reconstructing the way of life of Skara Brae. The complaint of a contemporary reviewer, that he was confused by Childe's structural and occupational periods, reflected his unfamiliarity with the kind of detailed analysis that Childe was presenting.[14] Skara Brae had given Childe an exceptional opportunity to study the ethnography as well as the history of occupation of a prehistoric community. This challenge was in accord with his interest in prehistoric economies. His main failure to respond was that he did not learn anything about the use of plants at Skara Brae. Even the pottery was not scrutinized for grain impressions, although this technique ought to have been known to Childe by this time. In spite of this Skara Brae stands as a thoroughly competent and innovative study of prehistoric social life. Since this was Childe's first significant archaeological excavation, and he had few good models to follow, it augured well for his future as a field archaeologist.

The glaring shortcoming of *Skara Brae*, published in 1931, was Childe's dating of this site. He noted some traits that were then considered characteristic of the Bronze Age and would now be considered late Neolithic. Nevertheless he concluded that it was a much later Pictish or proto-Pictish village because a distinctive type of carved stone ball that occurred there had the same geographical distribution as did known Pictish monuments.[15] On the basis of this single piece of evidence, he decided that the early traits at Skara Brae did not prove that it dated from the Bronze Age; the difference between Skara Brae and the Broch culture, which was more certainly associated with the Picts, instead might reflect the humbler status of Skara Brae's inhabitants. They had perhaps preserved a more primitive culture, much as peasants in eastern Galicia continued to live in an almost medieval style near the nineteenth-century mansions of their Polish lords.[16] In 1936 Piggott discovered that grooved ware, similar to that found in the lower levels at Skara Brae, occurred in what was then considered to be a Bronze Age context in south-eastern England.[17] This was a striking demonstration of the weakness of the methods that Childe used to establish synchronisms. They did not measure up to the high standards that he had repeatedly advocated in his publications.

OTHER EXCAVATIONS

Childe continued to excavate Neolithic and Bronze Age village sites. In 1937 he supervised the excavations carried out by the Office of Works at Jarlshof in southern Shetland.[18] In 1938, and again in 1946, he excavated with W. G. Grant the site of Rinyo at Rousay in Orkney. The plans of the houses, furniture and pottery at this site were like those at Skara Brae.[19] In 1937 Grant found a beaker vessel in the upper level of this site, thus confirming the contemporaneity of the Skara Brae culture with the English Bronze Age, as it was then defined.[20] Childe's experience excavating such village sites enabled him to record some Viking Age houses at Freswick prior to their destruction in 1941.[21]

For ten years Childe excavated hillforts in an effort to clarify the pre-Roman Iron Age chronology of Scotland. Some of this work was done in association with the League of Prehistorians (initially the Edinburgh League of Prehistorians), a society that Childe had started with the intention that it should become a more popular alternative to the Society of Antiquaries of Scotland. Although there were no qualifications for membership, and Childe hoped to rake in hundreds of subscriptions, the society did not flourish. Its membership rose to no more than forty and then declined.[22] He did not refer to it after 1935.

The forts that Childe excavated were mostly south of Edinburgh. They included Castlelaw Fort, on the south-eastern slopes of the Pentlands, dug by the League in 1931–32; two multi-vallated forts at Earn's Heugh, near Coldingham in Berwick, dug with Daryll Forde in 1932; Carminnow in Kirkcudbright, examined as a work of rescue archaeology in connection with the completion of the Kendoon Reservoir in 1935; Cairngryffe, near Lanark, another site threatened with destruction by quarrying, in 1939–40, and Kaimes Hillfort, in Midlothian, also an endangered site, in 1940.[23] In 1934 Childe surveyed sixteen of the twenty-seven known forts on the island of Islay, noting that most of them were of castle rather than of town size.[24]

During this period Childe also excavated two vitrified forts farther north in Scotland. He worked at Finavon in Angus for three seasons between 1933 and 1935, and at Rahoy in Argyll with W. Thorneycroft in 1936 and 1937.[25] Prior to this time it had been uncertain if the fusing of stone in this sort of fort had been a deliberate feature of their construction or an accidental one resulting from fierce conflagration at the time of their destruction. In 1937 Childe and Thorneycroft carried out two experiments to see if the vitrified walls were related to the timber-reinforced *murus gallicus* construction employed at other Iron Age forts. In March a section of wall of fire-clay and timber was constructed at Plean colliery, and then burned. In June another wall was constructed at Rahoy, using stone from the fort, and it too was burned. These experiments proved that Gallic and vitrified forts were one and the same.[26] Although Childe carried out no more archaeological experiments on this scale, he remained interested in technical subjects, such as factors affecting the colour of pottery and the relative weight of different kinds of bronze axes.[27]

Childe excavated two fortified sites for the Prehistoric Research Council of Northern Ireland. One, at Larriban on the Antrim coast, was determined to date from the Christian era, while the other, near Fair Head, turned out to be a Norman castle.[28]

He also investigated megalithic remains. He dug a cairn at Kindrochat, near Comrie, in 1929 and 1930; at the Old Keig stone circle in Aberdeenshire in 1932 and 1933; and a round cairn near Achnamara, in Argyll, in 1936. In addition he studied two cairns near Kilfinan in 1932.[29] After World War II he excavated chambered tombs in the Orkneys. In 1951 and 1952 he superintended excavations by the Ministry of Works at Augmond's Howe, a corbelled cairn at Quoyness, on the island of Sanday. Over twenty years before Childe had persuaded the owner of this monument to put it under the guardianship of the Ministry. In 1954 and 1955 he investigated the great tomb of Maes Howe on the mainland of Orkney. Alone among the Orkney cairns, it had a surrounding ditch and a tumulus of earth rather than of stones.[30]

In 1941 Childe surveyed all of the megalithic tombs on Rousay which was a poor, self-contained and little disturbed island, where few if any such tombs appeared to have been destroyed. He noted that clusters of these tombs occurred adjacent to large tracts of fertile soil that in recent times had supported small farming settlements, while individual tombs occurred near isolated crofts. He assumed that in Neolithic times the island had been inhabited by fewer than the 770 people who had lived there in A D 1800. On these grounds he concluded that each tomb belonged, not to a chief, but to one extended family that had owned a well defined tract of arable land on the island.[31]

Childe clearly devoted much time and energy to Scottish archaeology. His most innovative work related to the study of settlements, and is best represented by *Skara Brae* and his survey of Rousay. In both projects he sought to elucidate the social dimensions of prehistoric cultures. The work at Skara Brae was done at a time when archaeological research in northern Europe was focused mainly on forts and tombs; hence his study was innovative in terms of its subject matter. The experiments that finally settled the status of vitrified forts were also major pioneering efforts, applying the experimental method to archaeology. His sustained attempts to unravel the Iron Age chronology of Scotland indicate that much of his other field work was designed to serve broadly conceived objectives. Nevertheless his Iron Age chronology remained shaky, and the specific inferences that he drew from most of the data he collected were not outstanding. His field work compares favourably with that of most archaeologists of the 1930s. Yet he failed to wrest novel kinds of information from the archaeological record. In this respect even his work at Skara Brae fell short of what Grahame Clark later accomplished at Star Carr. Because of this Childe's interpretations of prehistory had to be based on conventional categories of archaeological data. His insights into the past were never broadened by techniques of observation or analysis that were of his own invention. Childe's contemporaries thus were correct when they judged him not to be an innovative or even an exceptionally perceptive excavator.[32]

BRITISH PREHISTORY

The Prehistory of Scotland appeared in 1935. The stated aim of this book was to stimulate interest in Scottish archaeology among the general public, and to reveal its significance to students of prehistory abroad.[33] Childe also sought to demonstrate to Scottish academics that he stood squarely in the tradition of the great Scottish archaeologists of the past (including Abercromby), who had approached the study of their country's prehistory with an international outlook. In 1940 he published *Prehistoric Communities of the British Isles*, a broader survey of British prehistory that was intended to articulate it to a 'world view' of what had happened in ancient times.[34] Although both books were written after *New Light on the Most Ancient East*, their general organization and outlook were little influenced by Childe's new economic approach. Instead they tried to do for the United Kingdom what *The Dawn of European Civilization* had done for Europe as a whole. Because they are similar in organization and execution, they can be discussed together.

Like Childe's other works, these books were based on the assumption that all major innovations in prehistoric times had originated in the vicinity of the eastern Mediterranean and spread westward across Europe. Childe saw this same pattern applying within Britain. New influences were believed to have reached it, either across the English Channel or up the Irish Sea. He conceived of British prehistory in terms of sloping developmental horizons, with new cultures and traits generally appearing first in the south and spreading slowly north. In some cases they did not reach the far north, where the cultural sequence was abbreviated.[35]

These books also reflected the increasing influence of the geographical and ecological approaches in British archaeology. Childe frequently alluded to Fox's characterization of the differences between highland and lowland Britain, and he used these differences to assure Scottish readers that their country's prehistory was distinct from that of England.[36] Chapter I of *The Prehistory of Scotland* was entitled 'The Personality of Scotland', in imitation of Fox's recently published *The Personality of Britain* (1932). Childe agreed with other British archaeologists that the chalk downs were areas of easy settlement suitable for primitive farming, while clay soils were more difficult to work, but ultimately more productive. He also followed these archaeologists in dating the beginning of the cultivation of clay soils to the Belgic rather than to the much later Anglo-Saxon period, as had formerly been done.[37]

Childe stressed the role that climatic change had played in the development of prehistoric cultures, as he had already done in *The Danube in Prehistory*. In *Prehistoric Communities of the British Isles* he stated that the main theme of prehistory was 'Man's conquest of Nature', an over-enthusiastic cliché that he quickly modified by asserting that the interactions of peoples are no less part of the 'drama of prehistory' than are their reactions to the external environment.[38] Yet, while he appreciated the work done by ecologically-orientated archaeologists, he continued to regard it as merely providing a background for the detailed study of prehistory, rather than as being its principal focus.

The organizational principles followed in *The Prehistory of Scotland* and *Prehistoric Communities of the British Isles* were only a slightly modified version of those Childe had utilized in *The Dawn of European Civilization*. He divided Scotland and Britain into a fixed set of geographical regions, and his time-scale into numbered periods representing intervals of time that were applicable to the whole territory under discussion. Each period was defined for a particular region by one or more archaeological cultures that were characterized primarily by pottery types. Childe was able for the most part to interpret all of the cultures occurring in a particular region at one period as representing a single pattern or stage of cultural development. Because of diffusion the same pattern might be found in several regions at the same time, or in different regions at different times. For example, the pattern he labelled Cinerary Urns occurred in southern England in Period V, but not before Period VI in the Scottish Highlands.[39]

In *The Prehistory of Scotland* Childe delineated six successive stages of Neolithic and post-Neolithic cultural development, not all of which occurred in the Highlands. In *Prehistoric Communities of the British Isles* he defined nine stages for southern England, but as few as five each for the Scottish Highlands and Ireland. Many of the cultures that characterized particular stages were interpreted as having been introduced into Britain by migrations. Childe thought that the Windmill Hill culture, which was believed to have been the first food-producing culture to reach Britain, was ultimately of African origin; that the Beaker cultures had arrived in waves from the continent, and that further putative migrations accounted for the Deverel-Rimbury, Hallstatt, La Tène and Belgic cultures. In order to explain why many of these cultures did not precisely resemble their alleged continental prototypes, he, no doubt with his homeland in mind, proposed that a loss of traits normally accompanied transmarine migrations, so long as water transport remained inefficient.[40]

Childe interpreted some arrivals of new peoples as having wiped out older cultures. In other cases newly arrived cultures and their bearers mingled with existing ones.[41] He continued to vacillate in his assessment of the Mesolithic. In *The Prehistory of Scotland* he argued that the Mesolithic period was unimportant for understanding subsequent developments. In *Prehistoric Communities of the British Isles* he accepted the idea that knowledge, especially concerning how to cope with the natural environment acquired in England during the Mesolithic stage of development, had been transmitted to later times, especially in the Peterborough culture.[42] This did not represent a change in his thinking, since similar vacillations concerning continuities from pre-Neolithic times had occurred earlier.[43] By 1944 Childe was prepared to acknowledge that the concept of a major hiatus between the Mesolithic and Neolithic periods was erroneous, even though this admission did not greatly affect his treatment of the Mesolithic thereafter.[44] In general his insistence that the cultural history of Britain represented a fusion of traditions, rather than a succession of novel, independent adjustments to the British environment, was in line with the importance that he had always ascribed to cultural diffusion as a source of progress, and with his insistence that cultural diversity was especially characteristic of prehistoric Britain.

Childe allowed for the local development of some cultures. He suggested that the Food Vessel and Wessex cultures might have evolved as a result of the concentration of wealth and power in a local setting. In his interpretation of the Wessex culture, he disagreed with Piggott, who sought to derive it from Brittany.[45] He also disagreed with the suggestions of Crawford, Fox and Peake that the traits that were characteristic of the Late Bronze Age had been introduced into Britain by an invasion from central Europe. He argued that these traits could not be correlated with any one culture, nor was their development marked by any significant change in pottery or burial rites. Childe concluded that the Late Bronze Age was the result, not of ethnic change, but of a change in the economy of detribalized smiths, who had already been producing for the international market in the Middle Bronze Age.[46]

Nevertheless Childe postulated mobility on the basis of limited evidence. He accepted a single antler axe as proof that fishermen had crossed the North Sea from Denmark or Germany to Scotland in Mesolithic times, and the outline of what appears to be an elk's head in a cave at Wemyss as probably attesting a similar visit by Scandinavian fishermen during the Bronze Age.[47] Although he considered the possibility that the English fossed circles of the Early Bronze Age had developed locally, he argued that extraneous influences were needed to explain the causewayed fosse and its similarity to monuments in Ireland and Anglesey.[48]

Childe regarded similarities between the megalithic tombs of

Scotland and those of Iberia as being too close and too numerous to be accidental. He agreed with Perry that only actual settlements of people trained in the techniques of building such tombs could have reproduced in Scotland monuments that he was convinced had originated in the Mediterranean region.[49] He assumed that the Scottish tombs that reproduced the most widely distributed plans were the oldest.[50] They were also located at convenient landing places along the coast, while apparently later more divergent types appeared to spread out from these areas of initial settlement.[51] He suggested that in some areas these monuments grew more elaborate through time; for example, the vast dimensions of Midhowe and the Holm of Papa Westray seemed to him to be 'the final outcome of long brooding in isolation'.[52] Recent radio-carbon dates suggest that his relative dating of these tombs in relationship to neighbouring ones was correct.[53] On the other hand, in the Clava cemetery he saw a 'complete degeneration series', marking the breakdown of the practice of collective burial.[54]

Like many other archaeologists during the 1930s, Childe interpreted megalithic tombs as evidence of a religious cult that had spread from the western Mediterranean northward along the Atlantic seaboard. This religion was not associated with a particular culture, but, like Christianity and Islam, was believed to have spread among many different cultures. Childe playfully elaborated the parallels between this putative megalithic religion and the international religions of historic times by hypothesizing 'passage grave' and 'gallery grave' sects and 'cremation heresies', and proposing to explain variations in tomb construction in terms of these concepts.[55] He suggested that megalithic tombs might have been introduced into Scotland by Iberian or Pyrenean traders, who travelled by sea with crews they had recruited among the Windmill Hill people of southern England. He proposed that at this period the north-east coast of Scotland had functioned as a sort of Cape Colony in the sea trade between Iberia and Denmark.[56]

CHILDE AND HYPERDIFFUSION

Childe's thinking about the megalithic tombs of western Europe remained coloured by the ideas of Elliot Smith and Perry, even though he rejected their specific historical speculations and the idealist view of human behaviour on which these speculations were based. In *The Prehistory of Scotland* Childe toyed with the idea that the Iberian traders were chiefs endowed with the magical attributes that James Frazer had seen as universal characteristics of divine kingship.[57] The prestige of these chiefs secured for them and their families, even in remote regions like Scotland, the funerary honours that were their right in their homeland. Childe also drew attention to the theory held by Smith and Perry that their voyages were part of the search for ores, precious stones and other materials that were valued for their supposed magical qualities as Givers of Life.[58] The influence of such ideas was more attenuated in *Prehistoric Communities of the British Isles*, but even there he speculated that 'on a quest for Isles of the Blest or Givers of Life fanatics might brave the perils of voyages across the Bay of Biscay to the Bristol Channel or the Firth of Clyde. Once wafted to the shores of the British Isles, such adventurers might be accepted as wizards by the local Windmill Hill peasants and installed as chiefs'.[59]

Childe was never a disciple of Elliot Smith. On the contrary *The Dawn of European Civilization* was a defence of moderate diffusionism and a clear rejection of Smith's model. Yet as late as 1940 Childe saw some merit in Smith's and Perry's conceptualization of megalithic religion, even though he regarded this cult as an evolutionary dead-end. In his 1935 presidential address to the Prehistoric Society on 'Changing Methods and Aims in Prehistory', Childe had argued that, while Smith and Perry generally relied on superficial resemblances, they had contributed to the development of archaeology by insisting that archaeologists study the concrete implications of diffusion, and also by stressing the value of evidence concerning spiritual culture as a means of supplementing material arguments for diffusion.[60] In *Man Makes Himself* Childe had agreed that the Neolithic inhabitants of the Near East had valued precious stones for their presumed magical properties. He also stated that, even though Perry exaggerated, he had correctly pointed out that this search had resulted in the exploration of uninviting regions and the invention of metallurgy.[61]

Childe gave up these ideas only slowly. In the third edition of *The Dawn of European Civilization* he argued that in western Europe the cost of erecting giant tombs and importing magical substances had precluded the use of accumulated wealth to buy ores or support smiths.[62] As late as 1954 he wrote that the megalithic religion had been spread by missionaries, who were perhaps also prospectors seeking ores or the magical substances needed for funerary rituals. Yet he noted again that no metal was associated with their tombs.[63] He did not formally abandon the Children of the Sun until he brought out the final edition of *The Dawn of European Civilization* in 1957. There he argued that the absence of metal in association with the construction of European megalithic tombs was fatal for the theory, since one would expect it to be present if trade had been the main stimulus for the development of megalithic culture.[64]

Childe's study of the archaeology of the British Isles contributed only to a very limited degree to the elaboration of his economic models. He interpreted the abundant supplies of copper and tin that were available in Britain as delaying the acceptance of iron-working there.[65] He also viewed the introduction of iron-working as forcing hitherto independent coppersmiths to become dependent once more on tribal society. By breaking down international networks of merchant-artificers, it also led to the multiplication of local styles of metal implements.[66] Childe came to regard the agricultural revolution, which was brought about by the introduction of the plough and iron tools into Europe during the Early Iron Age, as being historically more important than the abortive 'industrial revolution' of the Late Bronze Age.[67] Iron-working, unlike bronze-working, provided every farmer with cheap and durable tools, and weapons. [68]

CONCLUSIONS

Childe's excavations, while not innovative in terms of techniques and methods of analysis, represented useful contributions. His work at Skara Brae and Rinyo helped to redirect Neolithic and Bronze Age archaeology from the almost exclusive study of tombs and stone circles to the study of habitation sites. These excavations and his survey of Rousay foreshadowed Childe's later interest in social organization.

The Prehistory of Scotland and *Prehistoric Communities of the British Isles* are the most historical of Childe's books in content, and represent the most detailed application of the methods he had developed in *The Dawn of European Civilization.* Childe drew upon the ecological studies of other British archaeologists, but neither their interests nor his own concern with economic problems became the focus of these two works. The main burden of his explanations was placed on diffusion and migration. His approach to British prehistory and his specific interpretations of data did not differ greatly from those of other British archaeologists, whose work was influenced by Childe's *Dawn of European Civilization,* and whose writings were now reinforcing Childe's own views.[69] The principal exception was Grahame Clark, whose popular synthesis, *Prehistoric England,* was arranged topically rather than chronologically in order better to reflect its author's socio-economic interest.[70]

Childe continued to view a mosaic of cultures as constituting the reality studied by the archaeologist.[71] In 1933 he had noted that prehistoric archaeologists mainly sought to identify cultures and peoples, and to trace their diffusions, wanderings and interactions.[72] This was clearly the approach that he applied in his two books on the prehistory of the British Isles. Yet, as explained in the last chapter, Childe had begun to have misgivings about the value of this approach as early as the late 1920s. He had stressed the tenuous nature of the culture-historical interpretations that were produced within such a framework, noting that its preconceptions tended to produce circular arguments. He even noted that if a longer chronology were accepted 'The whole "megalithic religion" threatens to vanish in smoke.'[73] In reaction to what he perceived as the boring, trivial and largely inconclusive task of tracing the development of particular peoples in prehistory, Childe began to explore how knowledge had been shared on a world-wide basis in prehistoric times, and how this sharing had contributed to the progress of mankind as a whole.[74] While writing *The Prehistory of Scotland* and *Prehistoric Communities of the British Isles*, he had elsewhere been seeking ways of using archaeological data to investigate more significant aspects of cultural development. Yet he did not apply the results of this search to his work on the British Isles, which remained conceptually arrested by comparison with his coeval writings about the Near East. The latter will be examined in the following chapter.

CHAPTER VI

Human Progress and Decline

WHEN ADOLF HITLER became dictator of Germany in the spring of 1933, the event made Childe painfully aware of how dangerously archaeology and politics were becoming intertwined. Gustaf Kossinna's ideas about the biological and cultural superiority of the Germans had arisen out of the same cultural tradition as had the doctrines of National Socialism, and his version of European prehistory enjoyed the public approval of leading Nazi officials. The fact that Childe had borrowed his concept of the archaeological culture from Kossinna seems to have made him particularly anxious to reveal to the general public the errors of Kossinna's racist views. Yet Childe had no cause to apologize for the use he had made of Kossinna's work. The emphasis that he and other British archaeologists had placed on the concept of diffusion was wholly alien to Kossinna's teaching that among allegedly superior peoples racial purity leads to cultural progress.

In the autumn of 1933 Childe published in the semi-popular journal *History* a persuasive attack on racial explanations of archaeological evidence. He demonstrated that in general archaeological cultures could not be equated with specific racial types, and that racial differences never explained the relative cultural status of different peoples.[1] That autumn he also began a course of lectures in prehistoric archaeology at the University of Edinburgh by proposing that archaeology demonstrated the very opposite of fascist doctrines. Crawford recognized the importance of this address and was quick to publish it in his journal *Antiquity*.[2]

In this paper Childe denounced both the notion of racial superiority and the great man theory of history, which also explained behaviour in terms of biological differences. He denied that his own concept of 'peoples', assumed to be the ethnic equivalent of individual cultures, had any racial implications. He maintained that for the most part archaeologists should speak of peoples rather than races in connection with prehistory. He also argued that to regard only what belongs to a single people as being good or valuable was unscientific and unhistorical, and that for the believer it was also a form of spiritual suicide. The achievements of scholars, such as Newton and Einstein, depended not on their racial affiliations, but on 5,000 years of collective human effort. Cultural progress had resulted from breaking down the isolation of human groups and pooling their ideas on an ever-increasing scale. Because of this, tracing the histories of specific peoples could be only one part of archaeology. A more important task was for archaeologists to examine the development of mankind's common cultural heritage, even though Childe still thought of this heritage primarily in terms of Europe and the Near East. He had long employed diffusion as an antidote to the nationalistic theories of Kossinna and other German archaeologists, and had now recruited it to play an important role in the struggle against fascism.

SOVIET ARCHAEOLOGY

In 1935 Childe briefly visited the Soviet Union, spending time in Moscow and Leningrad. He later spoke about what he had observed there sympathetically but not uncritically and in America in 1936 he did not hesitate to describe Russia as a 'totalitarian state'.[3] One of his aims in visiting Russia seems to have been to collect information about the current state of prehistoric research in the Soviet Union, and to try to establish relations with Soviet colleagues that would allow him to keep abreast of future developments in Soviet archaeology. Data concerning the Soviet Union were vital both for up-dating his synthesis of European prehistory and for trying to locate the homeland of the Indo-Europeans. The latter activity remained an important part of his crusade against Kossinna and German nationalism.

While in Russia Childe obtained some recent publications by Soviet archaeologists. These included A. P. Kruglov and G. V. Podgayetskiy's study of the clan societies of the steppes of Eastern Europe, as well as books by Y. Y. Krichevskiy, who studied the Battle-axe cultures of central Europe and later the Tripolje culture, and P. N. Tretiakov, who specialized in Russian and Slavic archaeology. There is no evidence that Childe was influenced by the specific contents of these studies prior to the 1940s, when he 're-read' them and applied some of their more interesting interpretations to his own work. Nevertheless he did not exaggerate when he claimed that he had learned from this visit how Soviet archaeologists were explaining 'without appeal to undocumented external factors the development of certain prehistoric cultures'.[4]

Childe had visited the Soviet Union when its archaeology had just passed through a five-year period of directed change designed to bring it more closely into line with Communist party policy. In 1929 many archaeologists, who had been allowed to conduct their research relatively freely during the period of the New Economic Policy, were accused of being reactionaries who sought to avoid building socialism by retiring into the past and studying artefacts in isolation from the societies that had produced them. The latter charges were directed in particular against archaeologists who followed the typological approach of Oscar Montelius and Joseph Déchelette. To remedy this, the designation archaeology was prohibited, and archaeological activities were subsumed under the study of the History of Material Culture, and later the History of Pre-Capitalist Societies. Within the State (formerly the Russian) Academy for the History of Material Culture (GAIMK), archaeology came under the control of Nicholai Marr who maintained that all linguistic change reflected social rather than ethnic history. Until they were denounced by Stalin in 1950, Marr's ideas were to continue to dominate Soviet social science.[5]

The primary task set for Russian archaeologists was to investigate the archaeological record in terms of the societies that had produced it. Archaeologists were required to abandon the belief that material culture develops by virtue of some internal logic, and therefore independently of society. Instead it was assumed that technologies develop because of internal contradictions within societies. This required that in any explanation of cultural change the principal emphasis had to be on the development of society. The standard series of technological ages was replaced by a unilinear sequence of social stages, each of which was characterized by distinctive productive forces, relations of production and ideology. These stages were labelled pre-clan society, clan or gentile society (itself divided into formative, matrilinear, patrilinear, and dissolutionary sub-stages), and class society (also with divisions). Migration was ruled out as a mode of explaining changes in the archaeological record, and strong emphasis was placed on independent parallel development. In this the ideas of Marr played an important role. By denying that close similarities between languages necessarily indicated an historical relationship between their speakers, it could be argued, for example, that the Crimean Goths had not been Germans, but a group resulting from a blending of local tribes that merely resembled Germans. Given its commitment to parallel evolution, it is not surprising that Soviet archaeology laid heavy emphasis on the use of ethnographic analogy. In excavations increased attention was paid to camp-sites and workshops, which it was claimed illustrated the life of ordinary people better than did the rich tombs that hitherto had been the major concern of archaeologists. Nevertheless, between 1930 and 1935, more emphasis was placed on the production of theoretical and programmatic works than on excavation.[6]

In 1935 the Finnish archaeologist A. M. Tallgren had also visited the Soviet Union. He had long been interested in Russian archaeology, and the journal he edited, *Eurasia Septentrionalis Antiqua*, was a major forum for the dissemination of information about Russian archaeology and for the publication of articles by Russian scholars. Tallgren was thus far better equipped than was Childe to understand what was going on in Soviet archaeology. When he returned to Finland, Tallgren published a detailed report in his journal describing the political purge of Soviet archaeologists that had taken place between 1930 and 1935.[7] In retaliation for this report, he was never again allowed to visit the Soviet Union.

Tallgren's report was discussed in various English publications. In 1936 Grahame Clark summarized it in the *Proceedings of the Prehistoric Society* and in 1940 an editorial based on it appeared in *Nature*.[8] In a reply to *Nature*, Childe deplored the fanaticism that Tallgren had complained about, but drew attention to some hopeful trends that had appeared in Soviet archaeology since Tallgren's visit. In particular he noted a new emphasis on excavation, the founding of a respectable new journal (*Sovetskaya Arkheologiya*), and a more tolerant attitude towards the interpretation of data, including a cautious rehabilitation of the concept of migration. Childe admitted that Soviet archaeology had its faults, but argued that these should not be used as an excuse for Western archaeologists to break off contacts with their Soviet counterparts.[9] His position reflected his desire to exchange information with Russian archaeologists, and his consistent opposition to barriers against scholarly communication anywhere or on any subject.

Moreover Childe was correct in believing that a change had taken place in Soviet archaeology. In 1935 the polemical literature of the preceding five-year period was declared obsolete and a new emphasis was placed on technical expertise. 'Soviet Archaeology' emerged anew as a discipline. The concept of stages of social development continued to play a pre-eminent role in Soviet archaeology, but archaeologists were allowed once more to write about the sequence of technological ages and, to some degree, discuss diffusion and migration.[10] On the other hand, during the international crisis of the late 1930s, Soviet archaeology developed a strong commitment to problems of Slavic prehistory, which led to employing some of the analytical procedures of German archaeology, while adapting them for Soviet use. It is not surprising that Childe later regarded the Soviet archaeology of the period 1930 to 1935 as constituting on the whole a more stimulating inspiration for his Marxist interpretations of prehistoric society than anything the Russians were to produce later.

In his 'Retrospect' Childe stated that his first visit to Russia led him to adopt the 'Marxist terms' 'Savagery', 'Barbarism' and 'Civilization', and to apply them to the archaeological ages or stages that were separated by his two revolutions.[11] Yet Childe had used these terms informally in the past, and he did not employ them systematically in the manner described above until he published *What Happened in History* in 1942.[12] It was also not until then that he designated his two revolutions as 'Neolithic' and 'Urban'.

Engels had borrowed the terms Savagery, Barbarism and Civilization from the nineteenth-century American ethnologist Lewis Henry Morgan. The terms ante-date Morgan, having been used in approximately their modern sense by William Robertson and other Scottish writers in the eighteenth century. During the nineteenth century these terms acquired common currency in anthropology. Childe had learned about Morgan as a result of reading Engels, but in a letter to Braidwood he confessed that at first he had considered the writings of both men to be horribly old-fashioned. Only when he saw how the Russians 'applied the general theory', did he find their work 'helpful in many points'. Engels differed from Morgan by emphasizing the distinction between Savagery and Barbarism as being primarily an economic one: food-gathering as opposed to food-production. Childe accepted this clarification, which was in line with his own thinking. He also regarded Engels' original contributions as being generally better than the material he had 'cribbed' from Morgan, 'because Engels really knew something of German history and archaeology'.[13]

About the same time that Childe visited the Soviet Union, he had been asked to write the prehistoric and early oriental chapter for a projected Marxist history of science. This led him to read a number of works on early science, especially by Otto Neugebauer who was noted for his studies of the exact sciences in antiquity. Childe later maintained that these studies had helped him to move further away from an ethnic-political view of prehistory and to adopt a more explicitly materialist approach to his analysis of archaeological data. He came to view tools as embodiments of scientific knowledge as well as expressions of social traditions and a means of coping with nature. He also began to insist that craft lore had contributed as much to the development of modern science as had the speculations of astrologers or alchemists.[14] Childe's thinking about such matters ran along lines similar to that of his fellow Marxist, Benjamin Farrington.[15]

Childe was especially intrigued by the efforts of Soviet archaeologists to explain the development of prehistoric cultures in terms of internal social changes, and without appeal to external factors such as diffusion and migration. His desire to understand the implications of this approach was to shape much of his later work. In 1935 he outlined his new theoretical orientation in his presidential address to the reorganized Prehistoric Society (formerly the Prehistoric Society of East Anglia). This address expounded for the first time in archaeology an explicitly functional view of whole cultures.[16] Childe argued that individual cultures must not be regarded as collections of shreds and tatters, as the diffusionists tended to view them. Instead archaeologists must study cultures as if they were composed of functionally interrelated parts. They must also seek to discover how innovations or diffused items have fitted into pre-existing contexts.[17] Childe's employment of an organic analogy indicates that his functional concepts owned much not only to Marx, but also to Durkheim and to contemporary social anthropologists, such as Bronislaw Malinowski.[18]

Childe did not view archaeological data as fossilizing whole cultural systems. He saw them as directly informative mainly about subsistence, the division of labour and what he called economic knowledge. In spite of this he maintained that all archaeological data must be analysed as parts of functioning cultural systems. He pointed out that if the materialist position were correct, detailed knowledge of the economy ought to allow an archaeologist to infer much that is significant about the social organization and belief systems of archaeological cultures.[19] If ideas are largely products of human adaptation to their environment, the fact that archaeologists cannot study either ideas or behaviour directly, but only the concrete products of behaviour, was a less serious liability than if ideas played a major independent role in determining that adaptation.[20] Childe accepted the ecological and economic approaches that interested many British archaeologists in the 1930s as materialist orientations that, like his own, were leading to a functionalist analysis of archaeological data.

Childe's functionalism showed the clearest evidence of Marxist influence in his treatment of causality. His views, like Marx's own, were not entirely free from ambiguities and seeming contradictions. Although he sometimes suggested that material culture could be viewed primarily as a response to the environment, he rejected as pseudo-Marxist the idea that cultures could be explained as adjustments determined by the environment.[21] He cited with approval

Marx's dicta that ultimately it is the mode of production that determines social organization, beliefs, aesthetics and legal systems, and that change comes about as a result of the evolving forces of production contradicting the existing relations of production and ownership.[22] Childe occasionally interpreted this to mean that in the long run technology or material culture determined the rest of the cultural system, or even more narrowly that cutting tools decided the course of history.[23] Sometimes he pushed his materialist view of prehistory to the point where he argued that early man had acted rather than thought. Like some anthropologists, beginning with William Robertson Smith, Childe conceived of rites evolving as concrete and passionate acts, long before the development of the myths that served to explain them.[24] He also recommended this position as one enhancing the value of archaeological data.

Elsewhere, however, Childe explicitly rejected Leslie White's technological determinism and argued the need for a broader view of causality.[25] Like Marx Childe assumed that technology could function only in a concrete economic and social setting, which inevitably contained many elements that antedated and conditioned any particular technological innovation.[26] The production and distribution of goods were determined not only by technology, but also by social and political relations. The latter influenced the assembling of materials, assured co-operation among specialists, and provided society with its central direction.[27] Relations of production, ownership of property, and the application of objective scientific knowledge were vital factors that, in addition to the means of production and the environment, influenced historical change.[28]

Childe further cautioned that to a Marxist 'determines' does not signify 'causes' in the sense of any linear cause-effect relationship. While the economic factors embodied in the relations of production might be the key ones producing change, he did not underestimate the role played by social values and religious beliefs in shaping the history of any particular society.[29] He maintained that no complex set of beliefs could be inferred in detail from the economic system with which they were associated. While certain beliefs might facilitate the operation of a particular type of economy, their concrete expression enjoyed great latitude, and was shaped by various historical and environmental factors. He argued that the precise forms of the English constitution or of Protestantism in the nineteenth century could not be deduced from the capitalist system alone.[30]

Childe's espousal of a functionalist approach compelled him to refine some of his ideas about religion. He now viewed religion as being determined largely by the 'internal environment' and social needs of individual groups.[31] Like the ethnologist A. M. Hocart, he stressed that the fundamental aim of all early religions was to promote good harvests, health and long life rather than morality.[32] This was compatible with his long-standing political commitment to materialism. He also assigned religion and art a role in promoting social solidarity and the efficient operation of society.[33] Later he even suggested that in Egypt and the eastern Mediterranean, the production of goods for funerary purposes might have encouraged the development of specialized crafts, and the consolidation of more complex social and political units.[34] In these examples Childe ascribed to religious beliefs a 'progressive' role in social development. Generally, however, he analysed religion more neutrally as a means of lubricating the relations of production with sentiment. He maintained that in order to provide motives for action, such relations had to be transformed in the minds of individuals into ideals, which thereby acquired a certain degree of independent historical reality.[35] By holding a society together and promoting the development of technology, which is itself a social product, a healthy ideology helped to encourage cultural survival and development.[36]

This did not mean that Childe had abandoned his earlier negative attitude towards religion. Instead he refined his thesis that religion often impeded innovation.[37] He argued that, in order to control the natural environment, human beings required specialized tools, scientific knowledge and economic skills. To manage their spiritual environment, they needed psychic tools, in the form of religious beliefs, superstitions, loyalties and artistic ideals. He viewed adequate material and spiritual tools as both being necessary for human beings to cope effectively with their total environment. Religious tools differed from scientific ones, however, by consistently ignoring failure. Thus, while religious beliefs in the short run might play a positive role, by encouraging technological and social development, magic and religion must ultimately prove illusory as a means of controlling nature. Because of this, religious and magical beliefs, if sustained unchanged over long periods, inevitably must shackle social development.[38]

Childe believed that religion, ideologies and artistic ideals can only survive in the long run if they encourage the growth of the economy: 'if "every word that proceedeth out of the mouth of God" does not directly or indirectly promote the growth, the biological and economic prosperity of the society that sanctifies them, that society and its god will vanish ultimately'.[39] Childe argued that natural selection operates on ideology as on any other aspect of human adaptation, thus ensuring that in the long run the ideals of society are 'just translations and inversions in men's minds of the material'.[40] Yet he allowed that an entrenched political system may obstruct changes in its economy for a long time before both break down.[41] He also argued that ideology can hamper change longer than most Marxists would care to admit.[42] While Marx had foreseen that a revolution might be necessary to allow further technological progress, Childe considered that such revolutions were by no means inevitable. Instead social progress might be halted indefinitely.[43] In spite of this, or perhaps because of it, he stressed the need for archaeologists to study the economies of prehistoric societies, since in this sphere of behaviour alone can be found the clues that will explain their progressive development. Yet he saw all too much of the archaeological record reflecting 'magical ends, as distorted in an ideological medium'.[44] He interpreted the pre-eminence of temples and 'sepulchral shrines' in the early civilizations as evidence of 'ideological devices appropriate to the mechanical solidarity of barbarism'.[45]

Despite his Marxist orientation, Childe remained sympathetic towards the possibilist views that were current in human geography and ethnology. This led him to stress that every society can be thought of as a co-operative organization that not only satisfies existing needs, but also creates new ones. Changes in culture could be initiated, controlled or delayed by social choices. Progress was not automatic, but consisted of the specific responses of societies to particular situations. Social traditions circumscribed human behaviour within certain bounds, but left choice as to what line further developments might follow. Because human beings in the long run collectively shape their traditions, Childe felt it appropriate to maintain that Man Makes Himself.[46] In these pronouncements, he was echoing, perhaps unwittingly, formulations that others had articulated within a strongly anti-deterministic framework.

The anti-evolutionary, and even some of the anti-functionalist, biases that had influenced Childe's work in the 1920s continued to do so in various ways in the 1930s. These are evident in his still negative opinions concerning ethnographic analogy. Childe now cautioned that no one could be certain that the social rules, ceremonies and beliefs of modern hunting and gathering peoples closely resembled those of ancient times. Like many ethnologists, he was unprepared to believe that the cultures of groups such as the Australian Aborigines had ceased to evolve, simply because their stone tool technology did not seem to have altered significantly in the archaeological record over a long period of time. In his view, Aborigine culture, instead of developing technologically, had evolved along 'blind-alleys of superstition'. Hence the 'painful' rites and 'puzzling', 'incoherent' beliefs about totems found among such groups might be recent developments reflecting technological stagnation, rather than characteristics of the early hunting and gathering societies from which our own and other civilizations had developed. He also believed that surviving hunting and gathering groups had lost many of their more progressive characteristics as a result of being pushed into poorer environments by expanding complex societies.

Childe likewise saw no reason to believe that the political or religious systems of modern food-producing societies at the tribal level were as stagnant, and therefore as archaic, as were their economies.[47] He believed that most such groups had been strongly influenced by political and religious concepts that had evolved in the early civilizations, and then diffused among their less developed neighbours. Because of these developments, the thoughts and beliefs of prehistoric man could not be regarded as analogous to those of modern technologically less advanced societies. The beliefs of ancient times had perished irretrievably, except insofar as they had resulted in actions that had shaped the archaeological record. Modern less complex societies could not be used as a 'gloss' of how ancient peoples had lived.[48]

By the time he wrote *What Happened in History*, Childe's growing understanding of the significance of functionalism made him more optimistic that surviving hunting and gathering societies could indicate at least the general nature of the social organization and beliefs that were associated with similar economies in antiquity.[49] Still later, he proposed, as Binford was to do subsequently, that ethnographic parallels only provided clues as to the direction in which explanations might be sought in the archaeological record itself. The chief value of ethnographic analogies was that they indicated a broader range of possible explanations than archaeologists might be able to think of on the more limited basis of their personal experience.[50] Childe's strongest endorsement of world-wide ethnographic analogies appeared in his 'Archaeology and Anthropology', published in an American anthropological journal. There he allowed that ethnographic data might supplement archaeological findings, so long as they were treated with due reserve and not used to determine how particular odd artefacts had been used.[51]

Yet, throughout his life, Childe's use of ethnographic generalizations continued to be selective and imprecise. It was generally confined to undocumented *ex cathedra* pronouncements, such as that ethnology shows professional potters in most societies to be male.[52] In situations where there was historical continuity, Childe saw ethnographic parallels as having more weight. He regarded the studies of European folklore by Cecil Curwen and Grahame Clark as being especially valuable for the interpretation of European prehistory.[53]

Childe also continued to believe that human beings are inherently conservative and not inclined to change their accustomed ways.[54] He frequently expressed doubt that isolated societies could be progressive and, at times, he was prepared to argue that all progress resulted from the stimulus of cultural contact and cross-fertilization.[55] In an even more negative vein, he maintained that, however well innovations might correspond with the changed needs of a society, their acceptance was usually a response to 'shocks' from the outside. Migrations and the resulting clash of cultures were credited with breaking down the rigidity of established societies and promoting the acceptance of new ideas.[56] Even invasions, although destructive, brought about changes that were 'logically necessary but that might have been indefinitely postponed'.[57] This was what Childe meant when he asserted that the most important element in man's environment was his fellow man.[58]

Childe maintained, like many anthropologists of that time, that groups that were poor, or that had simple technologies, and therefore lacked surplus resources, dared not risk experimenting with innovations. Yet he also maintained that a particularly successful adaptation, whether achieved by advanced hunters, Neolithic cultivators, or civilized peoples, likewise encouraged resistance to change, which was justified by magico-religious beliefs and fears. He thought that such fears had been shown to be a powerful factor inhibiting change among surviving simpler societies.[59] Thus, for one reason or another, primitive communities rarely invented new processes or adopted innovations from their close neighbours, even if the superior utility of these devices was apparent to them.[60] Childe considered that food-production had developed as a result of a change in attitude of a few communities, whose inhabitants somehow conceived of controlling nature by co-operating with her.[61] This interpretation implied that to some degree the development of food-production might have been an historical accident. Childe at first described women as being especially suspicious of radical innovations; however, he soon reversed his position and suggested that women had invented many things, including potting and weaving, which were the most complex processes found in the early Neolithic cultures.[62]

Childe also thought that the mental process of innovation had to be understood in relationship to the social context in which it occurred.[63] Each invention was the result of a symbolic operation that involved the re-combination, rearrangement and modification of familiar elements to create new wholes.[64] Because each new invention was built upon preceding ones, he believed that they had to occur in a specific order; however, because of the complexity of technology, the details of this order could not be predicted or deduced from any general principles.[65] Childe also stressed that what he had come to call 'revolutions' were not sudden events. Instead they were the climaxes of slowly occurring processes that appeared as a single event because archaeologists could recognize only their consequences.[66]

DIFFUSION AND MIGRATION

Unlike Soviet archaeologists and most western European social anthropologists, Childe did not think that an interest in migration and diffusion was antithetical to a functional view of individual cultures. He found the two points of view to be complementary, and argued that all archaeologists should be both evolutionists and diffusionists.[67] As a functionalist he maintained that it was necessary to understand the social background of inventions and the conditions under which new ideas were accepted and integrated into specific societies. He also assumed that the successful introduction of any new element into a culture brought about changes in the relationship among the rest of the elements of that culture.[68] Accounting for such changes was a vital part of any discussion of cultural diffusion.

For the rest of his life, Childe continued to argue that contact between different societies had played an important role in cultural development.[69] Because of denser populations and improved methods of transportation, inter-societal contact became a more important source of innovation as societies grew more complex. Childe saw both the Neolithic and the Urban revolutions as being brought about by the application of a series of interlocking discoveries of varied origins that were brought together as a result of widespread networks of contact.[70] He also regarded diffusion, rather than parallel development, as the key process justifying the holistic study of world-wide processes of evolution, in addition to studying the growth of individual societies and cultures.

Childe maintained that, as a result of progress, individual cultures were tending to merge into a single world culture. He regarded the civilizations that had first developed in Egypt and Mesopotamia, and had later flowered in Europe, as being the mainstream of cultural development. In the course of human history, this mainstream had captured or was in the process of capturing all parallel streams, such as those that had produced the civilizations of India, China and the New World. He believed that ultimately all cultures would flow together in a single, essentially European stream. As part of this process of assimilation, life had been enriched by the world-wide spread of various items of culture; in particular, he cited the great economic importance of cultigens, such as maize, potatoes and bananas.[71]

Childe was greatly troubled by Soviet archaeology's denigration of migration and diffusion as factors promoting cultural change. He could understand the Soviet rejection of migration as a reaction to the importance that German nationalists had accorded to this process as a means of claiming German priority in the cultural development of eastern Europe, yet he believed that their rejection of the process went too far.[72] He particularly resented Soviet scepticism about diffusion, since he had already made that concept the cornerstone of his intellectual opposition to fascism.

Childe agreed that Western archaeologists were too prone to explain their data in terms of migrations and conquests. He also admitted that the Soviet approach obliged prehistorians to undertake a more detailed study of the internal aspects of cultures which, in turn, resulted in a better understanding of cultures as functioning units.[73] He urged that archaeologists should try, as far as possible, to explain changes in the archaeological record in terms of internal developments or alterations in the natural environment.[74] Yet, for the benefit of Marxists, he also pointed out that neither Marx nor Engels had ruled out migration in prehistoric times.[75]

Childe was delighted when an article in the second issue of *Sovetskaya Arkheologiya* urged a more tolerant view of migration.[76] Yet the anticipated liberalization of Soviet attitudes did not come to fruition. In 1951 Childe noted glumly that while Soviet archaeologists had rejected migration almost entirely as a factor producing changes in prehistoric societies, even they had to attribute some importance to diffusion.[77] In his latest works he was once again protesting that the Russians did not pay enough attention to diffusion. While he found merit in their efforts to explain the Battle-axe cultures as products of parallel or convergent evolution, he also believed that some diffusion of ideas was required to account for the development of at least the common stylistic aspects of these cultures. He was hesitant to view them even as products of a series of shared revolutions provoked by related technological advances and commercial reorganizations.[78]

When he visited Russia in 1945, he was delighted to find an anatomical researcher who told him that she believed the population from a Fatyanovo cemetery was not descended from the hunters and gatherers who had lived in the region previously. Childe observed that 'ten years ago this suggestion might have been penalized as fascist so, although now not illegal, the evidence must be very convincing'.[79]

Man Makes Himself

In spite of Childe's now overt materialism and his long-standing interest in cultural development, his thinking remained strongly influenced by the pessimism about human creativity and the particularism that had characterized European social science during the previous half century. If anything this pessimism was reinforced by the growing power of fascism, which made him and others fear that European civilization was about to relapse into a new age of barbarism.[80] Yet Childe's desire to find out if there was any hope for the future also led him to explore theories of cultural evolution, which had remained important in Marxist thinking, but in which he had so far taken only a marginal interest. These two streams of thought, the evolutionary and the pessimistic, were brought together in his two best known books, *Man Makes Himself* and *What Happened in History*. Although meant for the general reader, neither was a popularization. They were significant discussions of the relevance of archaeology for understanding broader problems of human history. Their stated purpose was to encourage renewed faith in cultural progress among readers who had largely abandoned such a belief in favour of biological, and even supernatural explanations of history and human behaviour. Childe saw himself as battling with the extreme diffusionists, who had revived the Biblical concept of the fall of man, and with the even more benighted fascists, who had equated cultural progress with biological evolution.[81] Yet his faith in the likelihood of progress in any one situation was weak enough that he felt involved in an uncertain and up-hill struggle.

These two books covered largely the same archaeological and historical material as had *New Light on the Most Ancient East*. Childe's presentation of this evidence in all three was essentially the same. The principal characteristic of his later books, rather ironically in view of his expressed aim in writing them, was their detailed examination of factors that he believed could impede or halt cultural development. This analysis added a powerful social and ideological dimension to the economic analysis of his earlier works.

A novel feature of *Man Makes Himself* was Childe's effort to establish a quantitative index of cultural development. In 1935 he had stressed numerical increase as an objective measurement of the success with which groups of human beings coped with their environment.[82] In this book he sought to use population increase to measure cultural development. Successful cultures were those with expanding populations, while over-specialized ones were characterized by static or declining numbers, which might eventually lead to their extinction. Childe admitted that it was difficult for an archaeologist to determine either absolute population sizes or relative changes in population. Yet he argued that there seemed to be more people in Europe during the Iron Age than there had been in the Bronze Age. As before Childe made little effort to determine whether population increases had preceded or followed his two prehistoric revolutions. He assumed that they followed them and were a result of technological innovations.[83]

In *Man Makes Himself* and *What Happened in History* Childe re-analysed his two prehistoric revolutions in terms of these new concepts. A comparison of his new interpretations with those offered in *New Light on the Most Ancient East* is highly instructive. Childe now admitted, at least in principle, that it was wrong to underrate the economic potential of hunting and gathering as a way of life. He traced the roots of biology and chemistry back to knowledge won during the Palaeolithic period.[84] He also recognized groups, such as the Kwakiutl of British Columbia and the Upper Palaeolithic hunters of western Europe (the higher hunters of Hobhouse's classification), as constituting examples of prosperous food-gathering cultures. Yet he saw these groups as using their food surpluses only to support specialists devoted to the cultivation of magical arts – shamans. This produced a brilliant spiritual culture, but did nothing to increase food production, so the population remained low. As a result the more prosperous hunters developed highly specialized and conservative ways of life that represented dead ends of evolutionary development. The inflexibility of such cultures doomed them to stagnation and in the long run to extinction. Childe interpreted this as evidence of the defects of food-gathering as an economy and therefore as an impasse or contradiction that had to be surmounted.[85]

Childe believed that in most parts of the world the more prosperous hunting cultures had been destroyed by climatic changes (and their own inflexibility) at the end of the last ice age. At the same time some of the less specialized hunters in the Near East accomplished the transition to a food-producing economy.[86] The new economy, while transcending the limitations of savagery, required new forms of co-operation that were consolidated and reinforced by magico-religious sanctions, which he saw as constituting a Neolithic ideology.[87] Because the early food-producing cultures lacked a wide variety of crops and were unable to import large amounts of food from adjacent regions, they remained heavily dependent on nature, and relied on magic and ritual to influence it. This provided individuals with opportunities to acquire wealth and power by alleging that they were able to control nature. Such superstitions impeded the growth of scientific knowledge and the establishment of an international economy. Where they became entrenched, they developed into passionately held beliefs that were able to block social change and scientific advancement.[88]

Childe saw his second (or urban) revolution beginning in areas where the first revolution had sapped faith in 'hunter's magic', but where no rigid ideologies or firmly rooted institutions had yet been elaborated that would impede the material progress of food-producing societies. At the time civilization developed in the Near East, the superstitious forces that were opposed to progress in that area were still weak enough for cultural development to occur relatively easily. The emergence of complex societies created yet another ideology that embraced a belief in astrology, divine kings and the worship of ancestral spirits. Childe interpreted such worship and a belief in divine rulers as two aspects of a widespread fertility cult. He also believed that when ideas of this sort 'irradiated' neighbouring cultures still at a simple food-producing stage, they produced specialized developments, such as megalithic tombs, which he thought were unlikely to be associated with pristine Neolithic cultures.[89]

Childe viewed his second revolution in a broader cultural framework than he had done formerly. He saw more than the desire for bronze tools and ornaments as necessary to explain what motivated certain peoples to produce the surpluses required to sustain complex societies.[90] The second revolution involved a vast increase in scientific knowledge, which developed more quickly in the Near East in the fourth millennium than it was to do anywhere else in the world prior to the time of Galileo. This period saw the harnessing of the power of oxen and of the wind; the invention of the plough, wheeled cart, sailing boat and copper-smelting, and the development of the solar calendar, various scripts, and systems of measurement and calculation.[91] Although irrigation agriculture was believed to have begun in small oases like Sialk and Anau, where the pressure on land was the greatest, it soon provided the rulers of Egypt and Mesopotamia, assumed by Childe to control these public works, with potent physical sanctions to supplement the moral force on which their authority formerly had rested.[92] He also noted the growing interdependence and declining self-sufficiency that was brought about by increasing economic complexity at this time.[93] Warfare, which was waged by the upper classes both to protect society and to increase the wealth at their disposal, encouraged the elaboration of metallurgy and an increase in the number of slaves. Royal power emerged in the course of this transitional period as a result of economic success, military victories and magico-religious prestige.[94] At the same time, the state developed as a means for controlling class conflict.

Childe continued to interpret different civilizations as developing in different ways, each as evolving its own distinctive pattern. Egyptian civilization was presumed to have been dominated by a ruling class that set an extravagant value on the preservation of royal corpses and the acquisition of exotic materials for magical purposes; Mesopotamia was seen as a collection of temple-dominated city states.[95] This divergence was regarded as normal, even though the civilizations of the Near East had developed from a common Neolithic base. He assumed that geographical separation would inevitably lead to cultural divergence. This divergence was somewhat offset by cultural diffusion, which he believed accompanied contact among these societies at all periods of their history.[96]

Childe argued that the early civilizations, like the more prosperous Neolithic and hunting and gathering societies, tended to enshrine their success in increasingly rigid and conservative social systems, which in turn were rationalized by magico-religious beliefs and fears.[97] With the assistance of written records, he analysed this process in detail. He attributed the growing conservatism of complex societies to the development of a differentiation between high status occupations, which did not involve manual labour, and lower status crafts, which did. History, mathematics, medicine, astrology and alchemy were recorded in written form, after these domains of knowledge were appropriated by literate people of high status. As a consequence of this appropriation, these studies became divorced from practical life and were prevented from developing into true sciences. They became subjects of idle philosophical speculation that were gradually incorporated into systems of magico-religious practices. Childe maintained that whenever a craft or high art was co-opted to the service of religion it was purged of scientific value.[98] He agreed with Egyptologists that the general absence of magical practices in the Edwin Smith medical papyrus suggested that it had been composed at an early stage in the development of Egyptian civilization.[99] Yet he did not go so far as to deny Neugebauer's thesis that the data assembled by Babylonian astrologers had made possible the development of Greek astronomy.[100]

On the other hand, the technical knowledge possessed by farmers, carpenters, metallurgists and other manual labourers was scorned by the upper classes, and went unrecorded by them. Childe believed that because these crafts remained illiterate, and were transmitted only by example from father to son, they were denied the opportunity for systematic elaboration that was possible for the arts of the scribal class. He also considered that in the ancient civilizations craftsmen were supplied with raw materials and had their tasks assigned to them by scribes, who had little if any knowledge of craft lore, and sought only to have the workmen in their charge turn out required amounts of familiar items.[101] Because of this, craftsmen were turned into industrial serfs and denied the right to control their own processes of production. This further deprived them of the freedom to innovate. As a result the technologies of the ancient civilizations ceased to improve. The social development of the early civilizations had arrested the technological progress that had produced them.

Childe pointed out that few significant technological innovations were made between 2600 and 600 BC. Those that were, such as decimal notation, coined money, iron-working, the alphabet and aqueducts, occurred in areas peripheral to the Near East, where conservative forces were relatively weak. The potential for social and economic development inherent in iron-working was realized most fully in maritime areas, such as Greece, where the legacy of the Bronze Age civilizations was diffuse.[102]

Childe did not explain the stagnation of Bronze Age civilization only in terms of the subordination of craftsmen to the scribal class. He also saw it resulting from what, using Marxist terminology, he called internal contradictions. In general, he argued that the concentration of wealth by the ruling class resulted in the economic impoverishment and social degradation of the mass of the population. This in turn restricted the latter's purchasing power and ultimately halted economic expansion. He often supposed, though on the basis of no sound archaeological evidence, that most of the wealth produced by the development of early civilizations quickly fell into the hands of the upper classes, and that the majority of people probably were poorer than they had been as Neolithic peasants. Only occasionally did he allow that the development of civilization had resulted in a better standard of living for all.[103] Childe also assumed, as he had done previously, that the internal development of Bronze Age civilizations was halted by an 'external contradiction', which involved their failure to obtain raw materials, such as copper and tin, in sufficient quantities to supply their needs. In an effort to obtain essential supplies, these societies resorted to military force, which ultimately destroyed more wealth than it produced. Such activities encouraged the political and military development of neighbouring barbarian societies, thus laying the basis for barbarian invasions that 'put back the clock of progress'.[104]

Thus Childe posited that the development of a ruling class was the principal factor halting technological progress in the early civilizations. Except when pressured by economic and military competition with neighbouring societies, the ruling class sought to minimize technological change in order to forestall associated social changes that might threaten their control of society. Prior to the second revolution, progress had been made by craftsmen innovating in the face of superstitions that opposed all progress. In the early civilizations the ruling classes sought to preserve their power by patronizing the reactionary forces of religion and superstition, and by rejecting rational science. Because they controlled unlimited amounts of human labour, the rich did not have to look for labour-saving devices. The scribal class shared this attitude, and devoted themselves to esoteric learning and the cultivation of superstition. Craftsmen were relegated to the lower classes, and their creativity was impeded by the bureaucratic control of their production.[105]

Childe viewed magical and religious beliefs as a scaffolding that during the rise of civilization was required to support growing complexity in social organization and the accumulation of technical knowledge. Yet the rulers of the early civilizations rejected the pursuit of scientific knowledge and enthroned magic and superstition in their place, thus effectively cutting off the growth of science.[106] In this manner, Childe, like Farrington, identified superstition as being (among other things) a technique of social control in the hands of the upper classes. He regarded this as a specific application of his theory that all societies successfully adapted to their environment tend to be conservative, and are likely to change only as a result of immigration or conquest, when the clash of cultures spreads new ideas and breaks down their rigidity.[107] Although Childe once more denounced warfare as unproductive, he also saw it as promoting cultural contact and hence progressive cultural change.

In 'Retrospect' Childe recalled *Man Makes Himself* as interpreting the archaeological record as 'a directional process wherein men by applications of science steadily increased their control over non-human nature so that their species might multiply and incidentally secrete laws and political institutions, religions and art'.[108] Yet the most characteristic feature of this book was his concern with ideology as a factor impeding societal development. If he thought of technological change as the only source of healthy social progress, he assigned great importance to political and religious factors as forces that can arrest social development for long periods of time. Thus religion and politics took their place alongside technology, as major although negative forces shaping human history.

What Happened in History

What Happened in History, which was conceived as early as 1938,[109] was written with the conviction that the growing power of Hitler's Germany was driving European civilization, Capitalist and Communist alike, irrevocably towards a Dark Age. Childe stated that its purpose was to convince himself and his readers that this Dark Age was not a 'bottomless cleft' from which civilization would never re-emerge. In keeping with his professionalism, it was also written for the more optimistic purpose of demonstrating to the general public that no 'chasm' divides prehistory from history, and that history can be extracted from archaeological as well as from archival data.[110]

This book recapitulated the main points of *Man Makes Himself*, but extended Childe's account of the development of civilization in Europe and the Near East until the collapse of the Roman Empire. He made extensive use of F. M. Heichelheim's recently published *Wirtschaftsgeschichte des Altertums* for understanding the economy of Classical antiquity, about which he pronounced himself to be 'lamentably ignorant'. He had originally intended that this book should cover the Byzantine and Islamic periods, but had reluctantly abandoned these periods when he found no source that could provide the same kind of information as had the *Wirtschaftsgeschichte*.[111]

Childe may have been correct when he maintained that the conceptual framework of *What Happened in History* and its explanations of human history were scarcely more advanced than those he had offered in *Man Makes Himself*.[112] Nevertheless in the former he placed greater emphasis on the role of social organization, and hence relied more heavily on an explicitly Marxist view of historical processes. He viewed the application of scientific knowledge in relationship not only to competing systems of belief, but also to an institutional framework made up of more than economic factors. He now attempted to explain many of the most significant differences that he had hitherto noted between Egyptian and Mesopotamian social organization in terms of different techniques for controlling the surpluses that had developed in the course of their transition from clan to class societies. He viewed the social and economic organization of Egypt as centralized and totalitarian, an arrangement reflecting the homogeneity of an isolated land that was watered by a single river. He was uncertain whether the Sumerian temple priesthoods had begun as secret societies or whether temple estates had grown out of tribal or clan territories.[113]

Childe elaborated his view of contradictions as part of his growing interest in social organization. He identified the main contradictions in Neolithic society as being the growth of population beyond what its subsistence technology could support and local self-sufficiency, which left each community vulnerable to climatic fluctuations and other natural disasters.[114] These contradictions were first transcended in the Near East, when the surpluses inherent in an intensive Neolithic economy practised in a highly productive riverine environment were used to support specialists who did not produce their own food. Childe believed that 'industrialism', which he still imagined had been as characteristic of urban life in the Bronze Age civilizations of the Near East as it was of modern Europe, was the ultimate solution for providing employment for a surplus population. He argued that, while Bronze Age Europe had possessed the technological skills needed to achieve a similar solution to its problems, everywhere except in Greece the social surpluses had been too small and too widely scattered to provide the capital necessary to support urban life. Because of this, civilization did not develop and warfare became more common as the struggle for arable land grew more intense.[115]

Childe now stressed the social rather than the technological character of the Urban Revolution. The governments of the early civilizations of the Near East were viewed as providing massive storage systems for their agricultural surpluses, abolishing internal feuds, reducing the frequency of war, increasing production, and hence making it possible to support much larger populations.[116] Yet building these civilizations had mainly been accomplished employing tools that were already in use during the Neolithic period. Childe argued that the cart, plough and potter's wheel could not have been manufactured without metal carpenter's tools. In the Near East all of these items were being made prior to the rise of urban society. Copper and bronze came to be used in Mesopotamia to manufacture not only weapons and luxury goods, but also to some degree knives, hoes, sickles and other agricultural implements. Yet raw materials were too scarce for these metals to be employed on a vast scale. Hence copper and bronze did not extend man's control over nature as much as the revolutionary possibilities inherent in them as items of technology suggest they might have done.[117]

Childe believed that kings controlled much of the surplus produce of the early civilizations and dominated their foreign trade. Their power, in turn, was enhanced by, and perhaps based on their control of imported metal.[118] Although the development of social classes correlated with the breakdown of clan-based societies, he considered that the full implications of this transformation had only begun to be realized by the Early Dynastic periods in Egypt and Mesopotamia.[119] The fact that only the rich had enough wealth to purchase the specialized products of the early civilizations meant that the demand for such goods was small and the capacity of crafts to employ a surplus population remained limited. Hence there continued to be people who either had to migrate elsewhere or be killed off in warfare.[120]

A limited external expansion of the economy was possible. Luxury goods were sold to the ruling classes of less advanced neighbouring states in return for raw materials. The conquest of adjacent regions increased the internal wealth and purchasing power of victorious states, and spread wealth among a new class of professional soldiers.[121] Nevertheless, as the external market reached the limits of its expansion, the expenditures required to maintain the state, together with an unacceptable concentration of wealth, worked to undermine the economy. These factors promoted renewed self-sufficiency, which foreshadowed the collapse of the system.[122]

According to Childe these terminal periods also saw greater reliance on superstition to control the masses, whose economic and social conditions were rapidly deteriorating. He cited the promotion of Christianity as a state religion by the Emperor Constantine as a classic illustration of this process.[123] Childe was now in a better position to answer the question he had posed (but dismissed as childish) in *Man Makes Himself*: why did human beings not progress straight from the squalor of pre-class society to the glories of a classless paradise? Formerly he had suggested that the conflicts and contradictions of early civilizations had constituted the dialectics of progress.[124] He had now spelled out in much greater detail the probable nature of these dialectics.

Viewed in a broad perspective, the decline of individual early civilizations was not an unmitigated catastrophe. Disorder returned hoarded wealth to general circulation, ideas (or what Childe called cultural capital) survived, and freedom from the superstitions and political control of entrenched social systems facilitated technological innovations and their practical application. Because of this rejuvenated or secondary civilizations tended to be more productive, and to share wealth among more of their citizens than their predecessors had done. They also had more merchants and skilled artisans who were free of the control of temples, palaces, or other great households, and were politically more pluralistic.[125] In the Iron Age civilizations of the Mediterranean region, kingship withered and money replaced land as a source of power and influence. The last great epoch of expansion in antiquity was during the Hellenistic period. This was an era of many competing states, when scholars and craftsmen were mobile and were welcomed by rulers who were anxious to develop the resources and enhance the prestige of their domains. Cosmopolitanism also freed men from the coercion of state religions and local mythologies. Yet after 200 BC economic expansion ceased and purchasing power shrank as wealth fell increasingly into the hands of kings and a small ruling class.[126] After a brief period of recovery under the Roman Empire, the external market began to contract. Rome tried unsuccessfully to save the economy by means of state control, which became to an even greater degree and counter-productively totalitarian and theocratic. Rural estates evolved into self-sufficient economic units, urban life disappeared, and ultimately the empire vanished.

Childe concluded that the most significant achievements of the past could survive even such a major catastrophe as the fall of the Roman Empire. Many intellectual refinements were permanently lost, but these had been enjoyed only by a small upper class. Craft skills and other 'real' achievements had survived in manors, monasteries and the shells of cities, where they acquired a solid basis of popular support. The medieval European town stood at a higher level of development than the Sumerian cities, since it knew itself to be part of a far larger world than had been known to the Sumerians. He thought that, even if progress were discontinuous, it was real. He conceived of progress as an upward curve consisting of a series of crests and troughs. No trough ever declined to the level of its predecessors, and each successive crest out-topped the one immediately before.[127] In this way, he was able to reconcile the concept of temporal continuity in the development of culture with clear historical evidence of social and political discontinuities. This view was chronologically analogous to Childe's concept of diffusion, which postulated the spatial continuity of major aspects of culture in spite of important social discontinuities.

In *What Happened in History* Childe attempted to formulate an explanation of the forces promoting and inhibiting cultural development that was focused on social, political and economic institutions. This was complementary to the explanation that he had offered in *Man Makes Himself* of these same processes in terms of systems of knowledge and belief. In his new book Childe tried to account for the subordination of craftsmen in Bronze Age civilizations in terms of the behaviour of a self-perpetuating upper class, rather than in terms of superstitious beliefs that were part of a false consciousness emanating from a static social order. In *What Happened in History* he also came closer to realizing the Marxist ideal of demonstrating how science is applied and production carried out within a framework that is not wholly economic. Nevertheless he later felt that the explanatory mechanisms of this book fell short of his ideals, and that discredited fictions, like the idea of 'Economic Man', still haunted its pages.[128] In spite of his Marxist orientation and his detailed study of the hierarchical social institutions of early civilizations, he did not attempt to examine closely the classic Marxist problem of class conflict in these societies. To some degree he may have believed that this was not a concept susceptible to archaeological study. Yet he was later to refer to the interests of classes in the early civilizations as being only seemingly opposed.[129] In this instance the concern of Durkheimian social anthropology with functional integration, and perhaps the Fabian orientation of much socialist thought in Britain, seem to have been influencing Childe as much as was orthodox Marxism.

Progress and Archaeology

In 1944 Childe published *Progress and Archaeology*. In contrast to his two previous books, this one expressed an ebullient view of progress; no doubt reflecting his satisfaction with the alliance between the Soviet Union and the West, and the approaching defeat of fascism. *Progress and Archaeology* offered a topical review of the archaeological evidence concerning progress that complemented the historical view that he had adopted in *Man Makes Himself* and *What Happened in History*. It sought to delineate clearly defined, uni-directional, cumulative and progressive trends in human history. The perspective of the book was a universal one; knowledge being viewed as the common heritage of mankind rather than as the possession of individual societies.[130] Childe now maintained with more self-assurance than ever before that archaeological evidence concerning cultural evolution was more important than any speculative reconstruction of particular folk migrations, religious reforms or social cataclysms. Yet he did not reject history. On the contrary, he asserted that archaeology was helping to revolutionize the study of history by emphasizing the practical things that have affected the lives of human beings more than have any battles.[131]

Childe found it relatively easy to document a general trend towards increasing control over nature in respect of food-production, tools, machines and materials, and clothing and shelter. He believed that these changes could be shown to have helped peoples adapt more successfully to their environments, in terms of better health, greater longevity and higher densities of population.[132] He continued to insist that, although these advances were cumulative, they were not necessarily continuous. Yet even in any one area regression was likely to have been only temporary. He also stressed that economies of any one type, such as food-gathering or simple food-producing ones, developed divergently in different environments.[133] He was not convinced that every technological advance would be of long-term economic value. While he noted that the mode of farming devised in Iron Age Europe had survived for several millennia, he interpreted the American Dust Bowl as evidence that large-scale mechanized farming might not prove to be a viable mode of subsistence.[134] What survives, rather than what is technologically more complex, was a true measure of success.

Childe later cautioned that the relative efficiency of specific types of artefacts could not be predicted by archaeologists, because efficiency was too complex to be calculated mathematically.[135] For this reason, there are seeming anomalies in the development of material culture. Childe cited the replacement, during the course of the European Bronze Age, of shaft-hole axes by technologically more primitive socketed ones. This happened because the socketed type required only half as much metal, and its employment therefore permitted an increase in the production of needed metal axes. With the introduction of ironmongering, scarcity of metal no longer impeded production and shaft-hole axes again replaced socketed ones, because they were easier to forge and more efficient to use.[136]

Childe acknowledged that the results of technological progress were not shared equally within societies. He argued that rural housing had seen no radical improvement since the Stone Age. The Hebridean black house or croft of AD 1900 was no brighter, warmer or more sanitary than the houses he had excavated at Skara Brae had been 4,000 years before.[137] On the other hand, in *What Happened in History* Childe had suggested that the quarters the Romans had provided for their slaves were better than the tribal hovels many of these slaves would have lived in as free people.[138] As usual he was ambiguous about warfare. Weapons had clearly improved over time, but so had defenses. Because of this it was hard to tell for any particular period if weapons had become more effective or wars more destructive. It was also hard to tell if wars had become more or less frequent. He abandoned the effort to find clear regularities in this sphere.[139]

Like many archaeologists before and since, Childe found trade to be an activity that was especially amenable to archaeological study.[140] He believed that dependence on imported materials probably explained the precocious rise of civilization in the Near East, and that it had stimulated cultural contact and development everywhere. While trade networks could be reconstructed by examining distributions of exotic goods, the evolution of trade had to be understood in terms of the development of physical means of transport. These had become increasingly efficient through time, and had moved items ever more inexpensively over long distances. Childe proposed, as an empirical generalization, that in Upper Palaeolithic times cultures normally had received imported items from a distance of no more than 500 miles, while by 2000 BC trade goods might be carried up to 5,000 miles.[141] In fact trade goods have been documented as passing from band to band over several thousand miles among hunting and gathering peoples.[142]

Childe also sought to demonstrate progressive change in terms of social institutions, beliefs and values. This reflected a renewed interest in the approach of Soviet archaeologists. The most detailed and successful of these studies was of interments.[143] He noted a general tendency for extended burials to replace contracted ones, although both positions are attested as early as the Upper Palaeolithic. He explained extended burials as correlating with more efficient digging tools, and as reflecting a new sleeping posture related to increasing wealth, a rising standard of living and warmer bedding. The contracted burial position persisted longest in marginal areas, such as Scotland where it was still practised as late as AD 200. In addition he noted the gradual development of a tendency to separate graves from dwelling areas, the transitional stage being marked by poorer burials being made inside the village, while richer ones were located in special cemeteries outside it. He interpreted this trend as reflecting an increasing awareness of the value of sanitation, which became especially important as communities increased in size.

Childe also proposed that in stable and progressive cultures less real wealth was buried with the dead as the total wealth of the society increased. He followed Kruglov and Podgayetskiy in attributing this to the greediness of heirs who, as private property became a growing source of wealth, prestige and status, begrudged burying valuable items with dead relatives and sought to appropriate them for themselves.[144] An exception to this rule occurred when a barbarian society underwent rapid social and political change (including the breakdown of its kinship organization) as a result of internal factors or the opening up of trade and other forms of contact with a developed civilization. For a time this produced royal burials on an extravagant scale, often accompanied by human sacrifices. He cited examples of this practice for the early phases of most ancient civilizations and for more ephemeral barbarian states elsewhere. Eventually, as the material culture of these societies progressed, less energy was expended on tombs, and more wealth was appropriated by the living. Again he argued that the percentage of a society's wealth that was expended on temples and sacrifices declined as technology developed. People relied more on natural, and less on supernatural means of controlling the environment. He concluded that progress had occurred in respect of human beliefs and values, inasmuch as most civilized societies were gradually abandoning the attempt to secure material ends by spiritual means and spiritual ends by material means.[145]

Childe claimed that he was not competent to detect unilinear trends in costumes or graphic art, and that no one saw them in language or music.[146] His thinking about costumes may have been influenced by A. L. Kroeber's studies of cyclical patterns in women's dress.[147] Childe's observation about music overlooked, the extraordinary advances in instruments, notation and composition that have characterized European music since the Middle Ages. This is strange since, while he is alleged to have been insensitive to the aesthetic qualities of visual art, he was fond of music.

Childe concluded that the archaeological record demonstrates that progress has occurred in many areas of human endeavour. As a result people have become healthier, live longer and the overall population has increased. The increasing internal heterogeneity of cultures has provided individual human beings with new interests, needs and pleasures, and more choices in their lifestyle. Yet, as the individual has grown less dependent upon his immediate natural environment, he has grown more dependent on his social environment. As a result of greater inter-dependence, individuals and societies have been increasingly affected by political and natural events that occur far off, through their impact on trade and communication.[148]

Childe used this conclusion to refine his earlier proposal that the only objective criterion of progress is the order in which things actually happened in history.[149] He suggested that progress may be objectively defined as what is cumulative in the archaeological record. He sought to refute the idea that prehistory, like history, is primarily concerned with the evil, strife and intrigue of the ages. He argued that, on the contrary, for the archaeologist evil is what is not cumulative. In his opinion archaeology demonstrated that in the long run the destruction and misery wrought by strife and ignorance were outweighed by progress.[150] To arrive at this conclusion, however, he had to equate progress with scientific knowledge, while he rather casually expanded evil, which he identified with the Marxist concept of false consciousness, to embrace the social institutions, and most of the religious and moral beliefs of mankind.

Childe's growing enthusiasm for progress led him to write several papers opposing the notion of degeneration as a pervasive motif of human history. In one paper he argued against the idea expounded by the extreme diffusionists, and by the Austrian school of ethnologists, that war is a perversion of human nature resulting from the development of civilization. He pointed out that, while it is difficult to detect evidence of warfare in the archaeological record for simpler societies, modern hunters and gatherers wage war. He rather uncharacteristically interpreted this as suggesting that, although the motives for warfare may change as societies become more complex, conflict has characterized all phases of human history.[151] In his Frazer lecture, in Liverpool, November 1949, Childe argued against the idea that magic was a recent development that occurs when knowledge fails human beings and hence is associated with societies that are degenerating. He maintained that magic is as old as practical science, and cited possible evidence of its existence back into Lower Palaeolithic times.[152] While his opposition to ideas of degeneration echoed the earlier arguments of John Lubbock, it was directed not against fundamental religious opposition to evolutionism, but against anti-evolutionary thought that had dominated the social sciences in the first half of the twentieth century and influenced Childe's thinking.

RETREAT FROM OPTIMISM

While the challenge of fascism had led Childe to become increasingly interested in problems of cultural evolution, it had a rather different effect on his culture-historical work. This is evident in the third edition of *The Dawn of European Civilization*, which was published in 1939. In the preface to that book, he noted that his conclusions of 1925 generally held true, but that new archaeological discoveries had raised his original abstractions of prehistory nearer to the complexity of real history.[153] In deference to his more systematically functionalist views, he endeavoured to describe each archaeological culture in a standard, though loosely applied format that embraced subsistence, secondary industries and trade, and thereafter social and religious institutions, as far as these could be inferred. Childe also emphasized the social factors underlying cultural change. These included the various ways in which social surpluses were concentrated and the role of the economy as an integrating force in society.[154]

The third edition of *The Dawn of European Civilization* was also characterized by a far stronger emphasis on the role that diffusion from the Near East had played in the cultural development of Europe in prehistoric times. Childe wrote unblushingly of rays of oriental culture penetrating the darkness of Europe and of 'the neolithic economy', as if it were a unitary entity that had arrived from the Near East.[155] In *Man Makes Himself* he had stressed that there was no such thing as a Neolithic civilization, but that the Neolithic was a stage made up of many different cultures at a similar level of development.[156]

Childe was fully aware of how and why this change in his thinking had come about. In 'Retrospect', he noted that 'embittered hostility to and fear of the archaeological buttresses of Hitlerism enhanced my reluctance to recognize the positive aspects of all European barbarisms'.[157] Diffusion, which he had already used to argue against fascism insofar as it stressed the inter-connectedness of all human development, was here being used in a different way, which tended to negate the emphasis that he elsewhere had placed upon the creativity of all peoples. He remained fully aware that the hypothesis of *ex oriente lux* was based on assumptions that were undemonstrable until an independent chronology had been established.[158] He noted that there were arguments in favour of a long as well as a short chronology for Europe, and that there was as yet no way to decide which was more nearly correct. Yet, because the long chronology favoured the interpretations of Kossinna, Childe was still motivated to support a short chronology.[159] In 1935 he had argued that cultural parallels between Europe and the Near East that had been found in the last ten years had rehabilitated the idea of *ex oriente lux* and won support for the short chronology.[160] He now felt less certain. He admitted that he knew of no objects of eastern Mediterranean manufacture in Chalcolithic Spain and, while he disagreed with it, drew attention to Bosch-Gimpera's theory of the indigenous development of megalithic culture in northern Portugal.[161]

Nevertheless Childe believed that the zoning that seemed apparent in the archaeological record offered strong support for the idea that cultural diffusion had played an important role in the prehistoric development of European culture, especially the elaboration of bronze-working with all of its economic implications. In *Man Makes Himself* he had alluded briefly to the development of concentric zones of culture around the primary centres of civilization in the Near East. Each of these zones was characterized by a different grade of culture that varied in its approximation to the standards set by the primary centres.[162] In 1939 he stated that about 3000 BC these zones had been as follows: urban civilizations in Egypt and Mesopotamia; smaller cities in Syria; Copper Age townships in Anatolia and Greece; permanent Neolithic villages in south-eastern Europe; shifting hamlets along the Danube and the Rhine, and primordial hunters and gatherers on the northern European plain. In 1500 BC there were metropolitan civilizations in Egypt and Mesopotamia; literate provincial civilizations in Syria, Turkey and the Aegean; literate and illiterate Bronze Age towns in western Turkey and Greece; stable villages with some knowledge of metallurgy in Macedonia, the Balkans and along the Middle Danube; less permanent settlements in Czechoslovakia and southern Germany; herdsmen and small hamlets in northern Germany, Denmark and southern Sweden, and hunters in the extreme north. In this system the Danubian I culture was four stages down the scale of cultural development from the civilizations of Egypt and Mesopotamia, just as it was four zones away from them geographically.[163]

Childe accounted for this zoning in terms of diffusion. He also saw it involving the degradation of culture as it was transmitted outward from the primary centres of innovation. In his opinion secondary centres diverged increasingly from the pattern of the eastern Mediterranean primary civilizations until, among the rude tribesmen who built the megalithic tombs of western Europe, the material and technical elements derived from the east had been swamped by the extravagant elaboration of oriental funerary ritual.[164] In this instance, he abandoned (or refused to adopt) a functional view of society. Instead he reasserted his ill-explained principle of the archaism of the periphery, even though this view did not accord with the strong emphasis that he now placed on the static, fossilized nature of the mature Near Eastern civilizations, or with his claim that the development of European technology and society soon outstripped that of the Near East. For Childe this theory had the attraction of uniting his long-standing views about the degenerate nature of megalithic religion with his belief in the importance of the diffusion of culture from the Near East. As he had done in other contexts, he argued that Britain represented an exception to his notion of zoning as a result of the attraction of its metallic ores, and its location at the termini of various lines of trade and communication that led across continental Europe from the Near East.[165]

Childe's optimism about progress did not long outlive the end of World War II. In *History*, which in other respects as well marked an important turning point in his thinking, he returned to his preoccupation with factors impeding human progress. Once again he argued that if history and archaeology disclose the continuous development of humanity as a whole, they also reveal the stagnation, decadence and extinction of many of the societies into which mankind is divided. Progress was characterized as being neither automatic nor inevitable; some historical sequences led to dead ends, others to annihilation. Childe, now confronted by the spectre of the Atomic bomb, believed that there was no certainty that Western civilization would evolve in a rational manner, rather than vanishing like that of the Maya, or fossilizing like that of the Chinese. He cautioned that social change is not a mechanical process, as some of Marx's and Engels' writings suggest.[166]

Nevertheless Childe offered a Marxist explanation for this: that the adjustment of ideology to economic changes is not automatic. On the contrary, ideas have an independent reality. If a system of beliefs is hostile to change it may be able to postpone technological and economic transformations indefinitely.[167] However, such a situation can do a society little good. Childe argued that the index of a society's fitness to survive was the harmony that existed between its means of production, its social institutions and its dominant system of beliefs. A society can flourish only insofar as its relations of production favour rather than oppose an expansion of productive forces.[168] Where ideology is able to block change, a society will decay and with it will perish the ideas that it cherished. It is only in the absence of external competition that its final collapse will be delayed for a long period. The idea that ideologies, creeds and national loyalties are potent forces impeding social change is in line with the Marxist argument that political activism is essential for bringing about political change. This, it is believed, justifies Communism as a political movement. It also suggests that successful political action (or an understanding of change as it has taken place in the past) requires the ability to distinguish 'old' ideas serving moribund institutions from 'advanced' ones that further material and social progress.[169]

Although Childe had succeeded in harmonizing his pessimism about progress with Marxist philosophy, the pessimism itself was an older element of his thought and of non-Marxist origin. It had grown out of the rejection of the ideals of the Enlightenment, which also had led social scientists to glorify the inductive approach, emphasize the conservatism of human beings and regard diffusion and migration as the main factors producing social change. Childe retained these ideas, but by 1946 had managed to purge them of their idealistic basis and to align them with Marxist materialism.

CONCLUSIONS

The menace of National Socialism had challenged Childe to rethink the nature of society and history. He was aided in doing this by the functionalist views of Durkheim and Malinowski. Durkheim's ideas had been familiar to him, at least in a general way, since he had translated *From Tribe to Empire*. Childe was also aided by the materialist views of Marx and Engels, which he did not misunderstand as a crude technological determinism. Because Childe believed that the relationship between ideology and the productive forces of society might be rather remote, and that archaic concepts might survive into more advanced stages of social development, he continued to maintain that living societies constituted poor models for understanding any particular prehistoric culture. What archaeologists may know in detail about the social organization and beliefs of a specific culture, just like what they may learn about its economy, is limited to what can be inferred directly from the archaeological evidence. Childe did not consider that there was a close or direct enough relationship between the economy and the superstructure of any particular culture for the latter to be inferred on the basis of archaeological knowledge of the economy alone. For this reason he quietly resisted Soviet efforts to define prehistoric stages of development primarily in societal terms. He maintained that because mankind acts on and alters its environment mainly with tools, tools are a reliable index of any group's control of nature. Thus archaeologists should retain techniques of tool manufacture as the basis of their overall cultural classification.[170] Childe also saw the loose relationship between the economy and superstructure combining with ecological diversity to produce an overall pattern of multilinear, rather than unilinear, evolution. He still viewed diffusion as a uniquely human process, and as an aspect of cultural evolution rather than as its antithesis. While Marxism was not the only influence on Childe's thought, it is clear that his understanding of Marxism was not the 'naive and optimistic' variety that Ravetz has attributed to him for this period.[171]

Man Makes Himself and What Happened in History have generally been viewed as important for their advocacy of cultural evolution. Yet, in the context of Childe's life work, their main value seems to be that in them he began to use archaeological evidence to transcend a narrowly conceived economic approach to prehistory. In *Man Makes Himself* he was concerned with tracing the development of various types of knowledge and in *What Happened in History* the development of social organization. In trying to cope with these areas of increasingly difficult archaeological analysis, lay the future direction of his labours.

CHAPTER VII

Archaeology and Scientific History

CHILDE'S APPOINTMENT AS Professor of European Archaeology and Director of the Institute of Archaeology at the University of London in 1946, where he remained until his retirement in 1956, provided him with his first opportunity to influence the rising generation of professional archaeologists through his teaching. There, in the Institute's old quarters on the Inner Circle of Regent's Park, Childe won the respect and devotion of students reading for the Post-Graduate Diploma in Archaeology.

While he continued to up-date his two major culture-historical works, *The Dawn of European Civilization* and *New Light on the Most Ancient East*, his new publications were largely theoretical in orientation. Some of them, such as *Piecing Together the Past*, were attempts to sum up principles that had guided his earlier work; others sought fresh solutions for problems that his earlier work had raised. For Childe this was a period of lonely innovation, much of which was too easily dismissed by contemporary British archaeologists as more examples of 'Gordon's naughtiness'. It was also a period when major shifts occurred in his thinking, which produced real or seeming contradictions in his writings. Even today this theoretical work remains ignored or badly understood. This is unfortunate, since it represents an important creative phase in his thinking that significantly altered and developed his earlier contributions.

SOVIET AND AMERICAN INFLUENCES

After Russia was drawn into World War II, Childe renewed his contacts with archaeologists in the Soviet Union, an activity that he observed was now commended by 'public opinion and the State', although it was later to make him *persona non grata* with the American State Department.[1] He was a member of the Society for Cultural Relations with the USSR in the 1940s, and in June 1945 he was one of the scholars who represented Britain at the celebration of the 220th anniversary of the Academy of Sciences in Moscow. In August and September 1953 he toured Moscow, Tashkent, Stalinabad

(Dushanbe) and Leningrad. On both trips he had an opportunity to visit museums and laboratories and to meet many archaeologists, including S. I. Rudenko and S. A. Semenov. This allowed him again to collect first hand information about an archaeological province that, in his own words, 'was crucial for my own special interests'.[2] Personal meetings were especially important to him because of the difficulty he experienced in obtaining books and up-to-date information from the Soviet Union.[3]

Apart from their political symbolism, Childe seems to have valued these post-war contacts with Soviet archaeologists more for the data he obtained than for the theoretical stimulation that current Soviet scholarship was providing him. Intellectually pan-Slavic patriotism cannot have appealed to him as a motive for archaeological research any more than German nationalism had done.[4] He gradually became less reticent about revealing what he saw as shortcomings in Soviet archaeology; in particular their prehistoric chronology, which he regarded as a series of hopelessly vague guesses that did 'not even attract, still less convince him'.[5] In 1957 he refused to write a book on prehistoric Russia for Glyn Daniel's *Ancient Peoples and Places* series, giving as his reason that the evidence was so weak that any book based on it would be premature and misleading.[6]

In spite of this Soviet archaeology continued to influence Childe's later thinking. This resulted from his re-reading and apparently studying in detail for the first time in the early 1940s, the works that he had obtained in Russia in 1935. From doing this he came 'to appreciate better the value of even the perversion of Marxism, subsequently branded as Marrism', and its demonstration of how prehistoric societies might be studied as functioning and developing organisms.[7] In particular he was impressed by the arguments of Kruglov and Podgayetskiy that collective tombs correlated with communal ownership of the means of production; that individual barrows were associated with pastoral, patriarchal societies, and that, as property became more important, the greed of heirs curtailed the burial of valuable possessions with the dead.[8] Childe did not necessarily accept all of these propositions as being true, but treated them as working hypotheses and as interesting examples of how archaeological data might be interpreted. He also continued to be intrigued by the manner in which Soviet archaeology had linked together the study of archaeology and ethnology.[9]

Of still greater importance for the development of Childe's thought was his increasing familiarity with American anthropology, which treated physical anthropology, archaeology, linguistics and ethnology as parts of a single discipline largely focused on the study of the American Indian. Its concern with historical problems, cultural diffusion and population movements was far more congenial to Childe than was the anti-historical social anthropology flourishing in Britain.

In September 1936 Childe had been one of approximately sixty distinguished scientists and men of letters from around the world invited to address a Conference of Arts and Sciences, organized by Harvard University to celebrate its Tercentenary. In his address, which he entitled 'A Prehistorian's Interpretation of Diffusion', Childe noted the work of American anthropologists, in particular the judicious studies of diffusion by the cultural historian R. B. Dixon.[10] Childe also received an honorary degree of Doctor of Letters from Harvard University. The following March he returned to America to attend a Symposium on Early Man, held to celebrate the 125th anniversary of the Academy of Natural Sciences of Philadelphia. Dorothy Garrod and Pierre Teilhard de Chardin also attended this conference, where some important correlations were worked out among Palaeolithic sequences from India, China and Java.[11] After being awarded an honorary Doctorate of Science from the University of Pennsylvania, Childe toured Arizona, visiting Tucson, Gila Pueblo in Globe, and the Grand Canyon, then on to Detroit, Michigan. In 1939, apparently at the suggestion of his friend Daryll Forde, he taught as Visiting Professor at the summer session of the University of California at Berkeley. He travelled across the United States by train, stopping in Chicago and Boston on the return journey. In addition to the anthropologists he encountered at Berkeley, Childe visited Robert Braidwood in Chicago, and Carleton Coon and E. A. Hooton at Harvard.

In the course of his three visits to America Childe had the opportunity to examine many archaeological collections and to gain a superficial familiarity with American archaeological material. He did not read much about American archaeology, the New World, like Africa and East Asia, lying beyond the confines of his geographical interests and outside what he regarded as the mainstream of history. Yet in 1945 he was involved in much correspondence with Robert Braidwood, helping him edit the portions of *Human Origins* dealing with Old World Archaeology in which Childe's own work received extensive coverage. It included a collection of papers written by the anthropology staff at the University of Chicago and was intended as an introductory, self-study syllabus for ex-soldiers who were coming back into the university as mature undergraduates. It was designed so that they could survey the whole of anthropology at their own pace and write examinations whenever they felt ready. Childe's reading of this material familiarized him with the findings and ideas of various New World archaeologists, and other prominent Chicago anthropologists, such as Fred Eggan, Robert Redfield, Sol Tax, and Sherwood Washburn.[12] Although efforts were made to appoint Childe a Visiting Professor at the University of Chicago and at other American universities at various times after World War II, problems with funding and the State Department, and later his concern with ill-health prevented these efforts from coming to fruition.[13]

Childe's observations in America had some direct influence on his interpretations of archaeological evidence. The parallels that he noted between the pottery of the Pueblo and Tripolje cultures, and between the Woodland pottery of eastern North America and the Kammerkeramik of northern Europe, suggested to him that convergence had played a more important role in cultural development than he had hitherto believed.[14] Knowledge of Kroeber's studies of the Indian cultures of California helped to undermine his faith in there necessarily being a close correlation between linguistic and cultural groupings, to the point where he stated that it would be rash to predict what sort of archaeological grouping might be expected to have had a distinct language.[15] Research by the physical anthropologist Aleš Hrdlička convinced him that stature and cranial indices were worthless as markers of different races.[16] It was also at this time that Childe learned from Coon about the distinction between part-time and full-time specialists.[17] Above all he began to be haunted by the Maya, whose metal-less, and therefore formally Neolithic civilization flagrantly contradicted his stereotype of what the technologies of early civilizations were like.

Numerous references to ethnographic facts and generalizations that were drawn from the work of American anthropologists began to appear in Childe's writings following his visits to America. He cited publications by R. B. Dixon, Alexander Goldenweiser, A. L. Kroeber, Robert Lowie, Margaret Mead and Leslie White. Yet he used their findings, as he had used ethnographic data previously, as illustrations rather than as crucial elements in his arguments. Childe now employed the term anthropology in its American usage, rather than restricting it as Europeans did to mean physical anthropology. He also started to designate as ethnology what, under the influence of Durkheim, he had formerly called comparative sociology. His prior acquaintance with British social anthropology had not produced any similar terminological changes.

Childe may have given his British colleagues the impression that he found American archaeology 'bizarre, unpalatable and irrelevant'.[18] Yet, even if he had no intrinsic interest in the New World, he drew lessons from the work of American archaeologists and ethnologists. In general, however, he derived concepts and facts piecemeal from American anthropology, whereas from Soviet archaeology he absorbed a broad approach, which he freely adapted for the interpretation of his data. This difference may partly reflect the fact that then as now Soviet social scientists used one 'grand theory' as the starting point for their investigations and for evaluating explanations, whereas Western scholars lack such uniformity and generally prefer to move from the particular to more modest generalizations.[19] The general orientation of American anthropology was also sufficiently close to that of Childe's culture-historical approach that it could be taken for granted by him.

ARCHAEOLOGY AS A SOCIAL SCIENCE

The combination of Soviet and American influences to which Childe had been exposed, and a strong desire for relevance that came to pervade the social sciences in wartime Britain, led him to define new goals for archaeology. Beginning in the early 1940s, Childe advocated a programme that in some important features resembled the New Archaeology that was to develop in America twenty years later. Unlike some British archaeologists, he had always regarded archaeology as a scientific discipline, a position that he had made clear in 1938 in his address as President of Section H of the British Association for the Advancement of Science.[20] In a note entitled 'Archaeology as a Science' published in *Nature* in 1943, he asserted polemically that 'the antithesis between history and science ... can be resolved by making history more archaeological and recognizing that archaeology is a science'.[21] He also agreed with R. G. Collingwood that archaeological excavations should be regarded as experiments, the primary aim of which is to test well considered hypotheses.[22]

The following year Childe argued that archaeology must develop as a science of man. He also suggested that it was more amenable to scientific generalization than was literary history. To become more scientific, archaeology had to ask not where a particular society had come from, but how it had developed.[23] In 1946, in his inaugural lecture to the Institute of Archaeology, which was entitled 'Archaeology as a Social Science', Childe argued that archaeological data can and must be a basic resource for studying the 'dynamics of social change' and 'long range trends in the life of societies'. These had recently been proposed as goals for all of the social sciences by the British Association Committee on the Scientific Study of Human Institutions. Hence, by advocating them as goals for archaeology, Childe was asserting his discipline's claim to be an integral part of the social sciences.[24]

Childe maintained that archaeology was a unique source of information about the material basis of life in prehistoric times and that it documented the transformation of cultures over long periods. It thus furnished data for studying the history of science and for the scientific examination of human institutions.[25] He later suggested that archaeology's three principal goals were to delineate *1* the standard behaviour patterns of prehistoric societies, *2* the history of these societies, and *3* their contributions to the pooled cultural tradition of which living human beings are the heirs.[26] He suggested that by comparing similar features and ignoring differences among various cultural traditions, it might be possible to abstract general laws of evolution from archaeological data.[27] This suggestion embodied a view similar to Julian Steward's later contrast between a scientific concern with cultural regularities and an unscientific interest in cultural differences and peculiarities.[28] Unlike Steward, who was intensely interested in ecology, Childe stressed that differences resulting from habitat were among those that should be ignored.[29]

Even prior to his inaugural lecture Childe had argued that archaeology and ethnology constituted complementary and inter-dependent branches of a unified science of man, the one treating the past, the other the present. He saw archaeology and ethnology as being related to the broader discipline of anthropology in a manner analogous to the relationship that palaeontology and zoology had to biology.[30] He also proposed that ethnology and archaeology both were, or had to begin as classificatory sciences.[31] Although this claim reflected his continuing preoccupation with artefact classification as the basis of his research, he was in this instance thinking primarily of the classification of whole cultures. He was criticized by M. C. Burkitt at this time for his alleged undue emphasis on the study of cultures at the expense of technology and typology.[32]

Childe urged that archaeologists must learn to study cultures not as static entities, but as systems changing through time.[33] He criticized British social anthropologists for generally viewing cultures as being functionally integrated and static, and for not emphasizing their comparative study. In his opinion the principal concern of a scientific discipline of anthropology should be to determine how different aspects of culture changed in relation to one another. To do this, anthropologists should attempt to arrange contemporary cultures at different levels of complexity in hierarchical sequences. This ought to reveal levels of cultural development, about which abstract evolutionary processes might next be inferred. Yet, to demonstrate how cultures really changed, it would be necessary to compare these hypothetical schemes with real sequences of cultural change, as the latter were determined for many different regions from the archaeological record.[34] Even if the archaeological record preserves evidence of only a few aspects of culture, archaeological data were indispensable to convert a sociological hierarchy into an historical classification. Childe argued that if archaeological and ethnological data were to be used for the same purpose, it was desirable that as far as possible both kinds of data should be classified in a similar manner. He believed that an alliance of archaeology and ethnology, based on a common system of classification, ultimately would reconcile the functionalist, diffusionist and evolutionary approaches in anthropology by means of a new, unified set of concepts and theories.[35] For example, he saw prophetically a common interest in population changes as helping to unite the various branches of anthropology.[36] While Childe's proposed methodology was reminiscent of nineteenth-century unilinear evolution, his concern with the study of structural change anticipated post-war developments in the social sciences.

Childe expressed concern from time to time with justifying archaeology in terms of its social value or utility. In 1944 he echoed Soviet colleagues by advocating that archaeologists should strive to produce practical results as a by-product of their research. For example, by studying prehistoric patterns of land use, they might facilitate the better location of modern settlements.[37] Nevertheless, a decade later, Childe seemed happy that no one had found a practical use for archaeology.[38] Yet he continued to maintain that the general conclusions of archaeology should help to answer broader social questions and guide society toward a better future.[39] He believed that the lack of a developed science of society was a major reason why human beings were so little able to control their social environment. He hoped that history and archaeology might help to create a 'science of progress' that would assist in filling such a need, even if it could not become an exact or mathematical science.[40]

THE NATURE OF CAUSALITY

It is clear that when Childe first spoke about general laws, he was thinking of explanations that would hold true, regardless of the historical tradition or stage of development to which a society might be assigned. The idea that human behaviour or its products could be explained in terms of laws that were universally valid implied that these laws were correlated either with a fixed human nature or with fixed principles of social organization. This concept had been borrowed from the physical sciences, and had been accepted as relevant for explaining human behaviour by most social scientists who sought to generalize about their subject matter. It remains the view that is held by the American New Archaeologists of how human behaviour is to be explained.

Yet as a Marxist Childe believed that human nature was not static, but that it tended to change as society itself was transformed. Thus, by the time he published *History* in 1947, he had ceased to believe in the existence of transcendental laws that governed human behaviour any time and anywhere. He adhered to an overall approach to the study of cultural change that was grounded in materialism and a dialectical mode of analysis. Hence he continued to believe in certain general laws of history such as the primacy of social relations of production, the periodic development of conflicts between the forces and relations of production and revolutions that adjusted these relations. On the other hand he regarded most explanations of human behaviour as being valid only for societies that shared a particular mode of production, and thus were at the same stage of development. For example, he considered that the laws of traditional political economy that had been designed to explain industrial societies could not be used to explain behaviour in other types of societies, or even major processes of related historical transformation. Historians must utilize a broader range of laws to explain such changes.[41]

Childe seems to have been assisted to reach this conclusion by reading Collingwood's *The Idea of History*, which had been recently published in 1946. Collingwood argued that medieval historians had wrongly divided the historical process into universal laws that determine the course of events and facts that are shaped by laws. Collingwood objected that this position isolated the universal process from the temporal and wrongly conceived of laws not as working through human consciousness, but as transcending the world of human action.[42] Although his idealistic view of the nature of historical investigation was rejected by Childe, his conceptualization of the relationship of man to history shared much in common with Childe's later work.

Childe characterized even the laws of history as short-hand

descriptions of the way in which historical changes had occurred, and denied the existence of external laws transcending empirical processes.[43] He sometimes referred to 'well-known patterns of human behaviour' and even inadvertently to 'universal laws' of behaviour.[44] As a Marxist, however, he viewed most of these as conditioned by specific circumstances and therefore as not eternally valid. He also pointed out that Marx had said that history would be mystical without accidents, such as the differing abilities of particular leaders.[45] More mundanely he noted that men often do things as ends in themselves, and that it is foolish to seek utilitarian answers for everything.[46]

As a result of his rejection of the notion of universal laws of human behaviour, Childe became as much opposed to cyclical theories of history, geographical and economic determinism as he already was to racial determinism. Like Collingwood, he regarded these self-styled naturalistic explanations of historical events as being teleological, and ultimately theological in nature. In particular he objected to theories that sought, by treating culture solely as an adaptation to environment, to turn society and culture into objects that could be studied by natural science methods. Explanations framed in terms of immutable laws could only explain recurrent events, and therefore could not account for genuinely novel changes in the archaeological record. The latter, he proposed, had to be explained as products of cumulative human experience.[47]

Childe considered history to be genuinely creative as well as unpredictable. In a letter to Braidwood he wrote, 'Any natural science must deny real change as much as theology since the limited aspect of reality it studies must and usefully can be reduced to eternal laws so that for it change is merely a phenomenal and passing manifestation of the unchangeable reality. But in the historical sciences it is precisely individual deviations from general laws and irreversible progressive change as against cyclical change that are interesting.[48] He remained convinced that innovations not only did, but had to occur in a particular order that was characterized by the increasingly rational control of nature by human beings. Yet he did not regard this order as being transcendental, that is as being predictable on the basis of general principles overriding the actual sequence.[49] For the same reason, economic history had to be empirical, not deductive. Only an empirical approach provided the basis for recognizing a genuinely historical order.[50]

Childe now spelled out the implications of his earlier declaration that evolution was what had happened in history.[51] He maintained that social scientists had mistaken cultural evolution 'for a sort of generalized magical force that does the work of the concrete individual factors that shape the course of history'.[52] He also observed that the historical character of evolution lies in its self-determination. He reiterated that Marx had not been an advocate of mechanical causation. While Marx had established that a particular technology can only function in the context of an appropriate economy, he had allowed that there might be considerable variation in the relations of production associated with that technology, and even more variation in the expression of religious beliefs and social values.[53]

Childe thus interpreted the work of Marx as providing the epistemological basis for viewing social reality as complex, and justifying a largely inductive approach to explaining it. No general formulae can disclose the total order of history – 'that can only be reproduced in the concrete whole of history itself, which no book and no library of books ... could contain'.[54] Laws are merely general descriptions of what is observed and, as such, statements of probabilities with varying degrees of applicability.[55] He had little sympathy for deductive explanations based on non-statistical covering laws, such as Spaulding and other New Archaeologists have proposed are the only form of scientific explanation suitable for archaeology.[56]

Nevertheless Childe believed that some of the basic factors that shaped the historical process were more evident than others, and that Marx had pin-pointed the most decisive of them. Even if history is free from transcendental laws, this does not mean that it is disorderly or that it is impossible to understand its main outlines. If scholars cannot predict the future in detail, an understanding of the past can still provide a basis on which to plan for the future.[57] Because archaeologists will never be able to specify in detail the nature of a particular prehistoric social system or ideology from knowing the associated technology, they must learn to reconstruct these other aspects, using the archaeological evidence that relates directly to them. In this way Childe believed that they could learn to interpret social structure in the same concrete fashion as they had already learned to understand prehistoric economies.

SCIENTIFIC HISTORY

Childe's views of causality led him to postulate a very different relationship between historicizing and generalizing activities in archaeology than was held by the empiricists of his day, or is now held by the New Archaeologists. For Childe there was no dichotomy between history and science.[58] Good history had to be based on explicit generalizations about human behaviour, but specific generalizations were not necessarily relevant outside of particular socio-economic contexts. Because it attempted to specify these contexts and to relate them to one another, scientific history became the keystone of the social sciences. Its comprehensiveness also made it a discipline that required laws of its own. Only within an historical framework (embracing prehistory) could the other social sciences be related to one another.

Childe saw historical disciplines as being scientific in that they sought to explain events not simply in terms of common sense, but as individual, and perhaps unique conjunctures of general and familiar processes and patterns.[59] He compared the explanation of a specific historical event with a geologist's explanation of the peculiarities of the particular location where a dam is to be built or a mine sunk. The geologist would have to consider the general characteristics of the minerals present, and the universally applicable processes of folding, faulting and erosion that they have experienced.[60] Yet, when studying human history, analogous generalizations could not be treated as universal constants. Reversing his earlier opinion, he condemned Soviet archaeologists for failing to explain the differences as well as the similarities among cultures, and especially for dismissing the differences as irrelevant. This, he wrote, made their history unhistorical. Archaeology can claim to be a science only insofar as it seeks to establish generalizations about human behaviour, and uses such generalizations to explain particular historical events.

Thus, unlike the New Archaeologists, Childe did not regard the search for laws governing human behaviour as constituting the ultimate goal of archaeology. Archaeology was pre-eminently a source of intelligible history rather than of generalizations claiming the dignity of natural laws. Although he accepted the search for laws concerning human behaviour as contributing to that goal, in his final books and articles he insisted that only an historical approach could provide the necessary framework for integrating and explaining all archaeological data.[61] Archaeology ought thus to align itself with history rather than with social science disciplines that were modelled on the naturalistic sciences. In this manner it would be able to exert the greatest influence among the social sciences.[62] Childe believed that once archaeologists had resolved the major problems of cultural chronology, perhaps through the application of radio-carbon dating, increasing emphasis on the economic and social interpretation of their data would help to produce better historical explanations, which were the ultimate goal of archaeology.[63]

Beginning in 1943 Childe attempted to develop a model of social change that would draw archaeology closer to the other social sciences. He decided that the most general goal of archaeological research was the explanation of cultural change. Yet, after considering a model of causality similar to that later developed in America by the New Archaeologists, he abandoned it in favour of one based on Marxist philosophy. The latter viewed cultural change as being an orderly process, but not one that was predictable in detail. It also saw the understanding of social change best achieved in an historical matrix. So far this sophisticated challenge to some of the basic premises of the New Archaeology has not received the detailed consideration it deserves. Childe's new model reconciled his Marxist beliefs with a largely inductive approach to the explanation of archaeological data. This allowed him to go on studying archaeology in much the same manner as he had done before. Yet it also directed his attention more forcefully to the two goals of archaeological research that he had delineated in *Man Makes Himself* and *What Happened in History*: understanding better the development of technology and of society.

CHAPTER VIII

The Prehistory of Science

IN THE 1940s CHILDE began to publish a series of papers dealing with the origin and diffusion of significant items of technology in Europe and the Near East. These included axes, adzes, tools employing rotary motion, bows, slings, wagons and carts, sickles and socketed celts.[1] These studies constituted the nucleus for a wide-ranging consideration of what archaeology might reveal about the development of science and technology.

Childe argued that tools bear the stamp of the different social and economic conditions under which they were manufactured, and hence can be made to yield information about these conditions.[2] He also noted that written records are so deficient that the history of applied science prior to the sixteenth century has to be based almost wholly on artefactual evidence.[3] Insofar as its method of manufacture and use can be determined, an archaeological tool-type can be studied as embodying the objective knowledge of the society that produced it, and an assemblage of tools the practical and scientific knowledge of a particular social tradition.[4] While decorative features may be more useful for working out cultural chronologies, a functional analysis of tools helps archaeologists to understand how prehistoric societies worked and to recognize the permanent contributions that each society has made to the world-wide development of technology.[5]

SOCIETY AND KNOWLEDGE

Childe agreed with Soviet archaeologists and other social scientists that the growth of technology cannot be studied as a self-contained, or even as a purely economic process. Innovation and the application of inventions required the development of new forms of thought that had ramifications throughout all parts of societies.[6] Childe considered that tools existed to fill human needs, but that the latter were not fixed. A Magdalenian harpoon served the needs of a small group of hunters as efficiently as a trawler serves those of a modern society. He continued to maintain that the relative importance of a tool or process cannot be measured by the efficiency with which it operates; succession alone demonstrates the relative efficiency of different tools and processes.[7] The biological function of knowledge is to ensure the survival and multiplication of the human species.[8]

Childe, like Julian Huxley and many social scientists during the 1940s and 1950s, was interested in determining the significance of parallels between organic and cultural evolution. At first he conventionally viewed culture as the equivalent of the somatic adaptation of other animals.[9] Yet his views changed as he perceived flaws in the Durkheimian analogy between societies and biological organisms. Childe came to describe cultural evolution as being a cumulative process, organic evolution as being a selective one.[10] He concluded that social and biological evolution had four mechanisms in common: natural selection, survival of the fittest, mutation or innovation and adaptation. He also concluded, however, that diffusion not only was a unique aspect of socio-cultural evolution, but also had played such an important role in it that no real analogy could be drawn between biological and cultural evolution.[11] He denied that taking account of diffusion introduced a random or irrational factor into the study of cultural evolution, since individual societies only adopt traits if these can be fitted into their existing cultural pattern.[12]

Childe defined knowledge as being a shared mental approximation of the real world that permitted human beings to co-operate in acting upon it.[13] This resembled the idealist view of culture held by American anthropologists such as Franz Boas, Cornelius Osgood and A. L. Kroeber, although in its materialist orientation it came closest to the views of Leslie White. Childe also began to assert that human beings adapt, not to real natural environments, but to their ideas about such environments.[14] Because of this, archaeologists must know something about the social structure and beliefs of prehistoric societies before they can hope to understand the environments to which these societies were adapting.[15] Advances in technology thus reflect the evolution of the total corporate knowledge (or what Childe called the 'social mind') of societies.[16]

Childe argued that the understanding of the world possessed by 'progressive' societies has continued to expand both spatially and temporally. By comparison with our own, primitive societies had only a vague and inaccurate knowledge of the past, and rarely knew what was happening a hundred kilometres beyond their borders.[17] He went further and accepted the arguments of Henri Frankfort and Lucien Lévy-Bruhl that past worlds of knowledge differed from our own in structure as well as comprehensiveness. Even something as seemingly axiomatic as mathematics was as specific to a particular culture as were that culture's tools and machines. Childe cited with approval C. G. Darwin's argument that formal logic had been compelled to change since the time of Aristotle in order to accommodate itself to new types of empirical data.[18] On this basis, Childe maintained that every society has its own logic, and that the thoughts of our ancestors followed patterns of logic that were totally different from our own. He argued that, because of this, it was fallacious to try to explain the actions of prehistoric peoples in terms of modern values and motives.[19]

Childe believed that accurate knowledge of pre-modern values and motives could only be derived from written historical data or the ethnographic study of modern small-scale societies. In spite of his mistrust of ethnographic analogy, he was prepared to use these data to produce some audacious generalizations about the systems of logic employed by societies that were technologically less evolved than our own. Some of these resemble his long abandoned ideas concerning the nature of 'primitive languages'. He maintained, for example, that peoples with simple technologies do not distinguish between animate and inanimate; instead they see nature and society as being coterminous, and use social relationships as categories for organizing their experience of the natural world.[20] He maintained that the notion of a separate natural order was unclear even to the Sumerians, who spoke of the flint they knapped as if it were a person.[21] He also argued that modern languages had developed in the Stone Age, and still embody many of the categories of thought of that period. Survivals, such as the Indo-European gender system, reflect the ideology of the Stone Age and to that degree hinder modern thought.[22]

Childe also considered that speculative thought and theoretical (as distinguished from practical) science first appeared among the clerks of the ancient civilizations. In these societies the dichotomy between a privileged managerial class that was exempt from manual labour and a lower class consisting of craftsmen and peasants was reflected in a differentiation between thinking about nature and acting upon it. This also produced hitherto unknown dichotomies between mind and matter, subject and object, and still later between society and nature. Causality was now interpreted as a personal and verbal process. The gods were thought of as creating and managing the world by giving orders, as an official might give orders to his workmen.[23]

Childe also derived from the psychologist Jean Piaget the argument that science and magic remained undifferentiated so long as nature was not distinguished from society. Primitive science was thus a mixture of technical skills and magic, resembling the practical lore of modern sailors. In the early civilizations specialized technical processes were riddled with ceremonies and magical precautions that were designed to keep them esoteric and restricted to a small group of adepts. Magic was also patronized by clerks and rulers, who owed their power largely to their control of religious and military activities. Because of its importance to these officials, far more magical lore was set down in writing than craft lore.

Childe believed that modern science arose by extracting craft lore from magic.[24] Yet he saw notions of causality remaining personal or animistic until the growing use of inanimate power to work machines engendered the idea of mechanical causality embodied in the work of Newton. More recently the development of electronic machines that are not cyclical in their operation had encouraged the development of a more probabilistic view of causality.[25]

Childe also elaborated his view of knowledge in terms of the Marxist dichotomy between true and false consciousness. He identified true consciousness as the operational correspondence of views of reality with external reality itself. False consciousness was the absence of such a correspondence. The members of an individual society for the most part may be unable to distinguish between true and false consciousness. Yet Childe believed that a decline in cholera ultimately should reveal that burning garbage is more effective than burning witches.[26] He thus agreed with Collingwood that the only test of truth is an operational one; ideas cannot be tested by theory divorced from practice. The ultimate function of true knowledge is to provide rules for action. Mankind's biological success to date is proof that useful knowledge is both attainable and cumulative.[27]

Childe continued to maintain that all archaeological data must be studied as expressions of human thoughts and purposes. If not, they could only be valued for their own sakes, and would have no more scientific value than a collection of postage stamps.[28] It did not matter to him that unexpressed thoughts and unexecuted intentions were not recorded archaeologically, since they had no historical significance. History for him was concerned only with socially effective acts.[29]

Yet Childe had long acknowledged that what he regarded as 'false consciousness', and therefore as not normally being of long-term importance, was abundantly recorded in the archaeological record alongside evidence of developments that had increased mankind's control of nature. He also allowed that the archaeologist cannot be a complete materialist, since archaeological data contain expressions and symbols of human thought and volition that are eminently immaterial.[30] In addition he doubted that individual thoughts and purposes (which are surely the only ones that can have any objective existence) are by themselves of historical or archaeological significance. He argued that, because of the complexity of society, the final outcome of any social process is the resolution of a conflict between numerous individual wills, and is thus a natural event in the sense that no one person has willed it.[31] He also argued that it was sociologically and historically meaningless to interpret tool-production in terms of individual psychology. The standardized tool-type is the fossilized embodiment of an idea that transcends any one individual. In short, it is a social concept.[32] Thus it was inferred natural events and social concepts, rather than the actual thoughts and purposes of individual human beings, that were seen by Childe as shaping the overall pattern visible in the archaeological record.

CULTURAL RELATIVISM

Childe was led by his concern with evolution and progress to reject the cultural relativism that characterized the anthropology of his day and which, to a considerable degree, still does today. Cultural relativism posits that there is no absolute scale of values applicable to all cultures, and that each culture must be judged in terms of its own value system. Childe, on the contrary, argued that the smaller a society is, the less internally heterogeneous it can be and the less freedom it can grant to its members.[33] The system of knowledge at the disposal of our contemporary industrial civilization is more comprehensive and coherent than any previously known. By contrast, the knowledge available to a tribe of Australian aborigines systematized the pooled experiences of only a few hundred people who possessed no records from the past. Because it is more comprehensive and coherent, a more complex system works better than theirs, in the sense that it provides reliable rules for a far greater number of actions.[34] On this ground he had no qualms about declaring his own civilization superior to all preceding ones.

Childe saw the expansion of knowledge trending towards the realization of a universal society that ultimately might transcend the limitations of even current humanistic ideals.[35] This was not a reference, as some reviewers have concluded,[36] to a Marxist millennium, but to a society in which human beings would acknowledge a duty to non-human nature by regarding the latter as having rights in respect of human use. It might be concluded that, at the same time that Childe explicitly rejected cultural relativism, his thinking foreshadowed the currently popular notion of a conserver society. He was probably thinking, however, of Marx's prediction that the study of the reciprocal relationship between man and nature eventually would give rise to a single discipline in which the natural sciences and the science of man would be fused.[37]

By rejecting cultural relativism, he set up a new basis for his interpretation of cultural evolution. He now analysed the development of scientific knowledge as a dialectical process, in which true knowledge was achieved through the negation of error. False beliefs, by which Childe meant those that did not allow human beings to manipulate the material world, were viewed as 'corrigible in theory though not by theory divorced from practice'.[38] He viewed the divorce of intellectual pursuits from practical application as the principal impediment to the growth of knowledge. By extension he maintained that knowledge that is not applicable to practical problems is not true knowledge.

ARCHAEOLOGICAL IMPLICATIONS

Childe had yet to determine what significance these ideas had for the analysis of archaeological data. He admitted that archaeologists can discover nothing directly about the knowledge or world view of prehistoric societies. Unlike ethnologists they cannot hear or witness the beliefs, hopes, intentions, or emotions of the people they study. The thoughts of prehistoric man are therefore subject to analysis only insofar as they produced actions that left traces in the archaeological record.[39]

In *Society and Knowledge*, published 1956, Childe argued that a prehistorian must treat artefacts and monuments 'always and exclusively as concrete expressions and embodiments of human thoughts and ideas – in a word of knowledge'.[40] Insofar as artefacts are concrete expressions of thoughts, tool development was seen as constituting a 'very good index' of the development of knowledge.[41] Knowledge, however, had acquired a very restricted meaning. He admitted that religious beliefs, magic and superstition leave their mark on the archaeological record, no less conspicuously than does practical knowledge. Yet, because the variations in the detail of magical and religious conceptions are infinite and the thoughts of different peoples follow different systems of logic, the archaeologist has no hope of ever being able to infer the content of these beliefs with any degree of precision. By contrast the number of practical solutions to any technological problem is strictly limited. This allows the archaeologist to infer such processes with a high degree of accuracy and detail. The study of prehistoric knowledge must therefore be restricted to technical knowledge, and be framed in terms of the practical results of such knowledge, not the subjective goals and purposes of those who possessed it.[42]

Childe was thus proposing that archaeology can provide the basis for studying the evolution of technical knowledge, free from the error, delusions and superstitions that characterized individual societies, and which by their very nature are non-cumulative. While erroneous beliefs and superstitions leave abundant traces in the archaeological record, he advocated that archaeologists should ignore this aspect of their data. They should seek to determine the 'real historical function' of their material rather than the subjective intentions of its makers. This meant that they should try to determine what scientific knowledge was embodied in their material, as well as the social and economic roles that had been played by it. He went so far as to suggest that it was fitting that the motives of prehistoric people, like their emotions, were lost forever, since they were illusions.[43] By contrast, any concept that objectively assisted human beings to adjust better to their environment remains perpetually intelligible, precisely because it has contributed to human advancement. In this sense, the best thoughts of the past remain alive and influential in modern societies.[44] It was in this carefully qualified sense that Childe proclaimed that archaeologists could reconstitute the genuine science of an age, and offer authentic documents to the history of science.[45]

Childe's most important substantive demonstration of how such an approach might be applied was in an article entitled 'The Artifacts of Prehistoric Man as Applications of Science'. This was prepared for the International Commission for a History of the Scientific and Cultural Development of Mankind, and was published in two parts in the *Journal of World History* in 1954.[46] In this study he sought to delineate the processes by which technological knowledge had developed in prehistoric times.

Childe's recommendation that one of the principal goals of archaeology should be to study the prehistoric development of science was the culmination of his career-long interest in technology. Because of his distrust of ethnographic analogy, his approach to the study of technology remained more sociological and economic than ethnological. Commentators have seen this as depriving him of an awareness of cultural differences that would have allowed him to exploit this approach more adequately.[47] Yet Childe was scarcely more interested in the details of technological change for their own sake than he was in studying environments and ecology. He was first and foremost interested in social and political problems, and tended to investigate technology primarily in relationship to these areas of behaviour. In spite of this Childe's concern with technology indicated one direction in which archaeological research might develop. Yet he regarded this as only one archaeological endeavour among several, and he was in the vanguard as regards exploring alternatives.

CHAPTER IX

Societal Archaeology

PURSUING HIS EARLIER commitment to some of the common features of both a Marxist and Durkheimian analysis of society, Childe equated Reality and Society. He argued that nothing of which human beings are conscious can be conceived as existing apart from society, which is a completely self-contained and self-sufficient entity. If there can be no society without people, it is equally true that no individual could exist without society. Every society possesses its own social traditions, which are cumulative and transmitted from one generation to the next. It is these traditions that the archaeologist seeks to study and explain.[1]

SOCIETY AND TECHNOLOGY

In order to study society as a self-contained and self-sufficient creative process, Childe argued the need for a classificatory system that could be shared by all of the social sciences, and in particular be used by them to compare the ways of life of all peoples, past and present. Yet as early as 1944 he had rejected the Soviet classification of prehistoric cultures. This scheme was formulated in terms of the property relations that were alleged to have governed the manner in which different types of tools were used, rather than on the basis of the tool-types themselves.[2] He considered that the archaeological record was vague about the social organization of preliterate communities; hence it was potentially misleading for the Russians to attempt to pigeon-hole archaeological findings in terms of pre-clan, clan and class society. He also pointed out that certain aspects of the Soviet scheme, such as its assumption of a universal priority of matrilinear over patrilinear kinship, were erroneous and that Soviet archaeologists could not agree on what basis particular archaeological cultures should be assigned to a specific stage of development.[3] More generally, however, he objected that 'the Russian scheme of classification assumes in advance precisely what archaeological facts have to prove'.[4] Childe argued that the conventional system of classification based on technology was preferable because it made it possible for archaeologists to search for contradictions between the artefacts, or material forces of production, and the relations of production.[5] He also maintained that, because it is principally by means of tools that people act upon and alter their environment, it is appropriate that tool-types should serve as the basis of a classification of different types of society.[6] Thus he persisted in a twenty-year struggle to demonstrate that the traditional ages of Stone, Bronze and Iron retained their social and economic significance, and to harmonize them with the Morgan–Engels' scheme of Savagery, Barbarism and Civilization. While Childe was primarily interested in economic development, the material correlates that Morgan had proposed for his original scheme, however untenable they may have been, made the idea of them archaeologically attractive to him.[7]

Childe experienced endless difficulties in attempting to fit these unilinear technological and economic schemes to the archaeological data. Neither system yielded subdivisions that could be shown to follow each other in a consistent way in different parts of the world. He squarely acknowledged that Morgan's nine sub-divisions did not work, and that his three main periods were valid only in the trivial sense that no society appeared ever to have passed directly from Savagery to Civilization.[8] Even in his most general schemes of social development, Childe could not resist being multilinear. In 1954 he postulated the 'Temple City', ruled by a corporation of priests, and the 'Conquering City', ruled by a divine king, as alternative forms of early civilizations.[9] Childe also noted that a Bronze Age had not everywhere intervened between the use of stone and iron tools, and that when Thomsen's technological ages were subdivided the resulting typologies were valid only for a single archaeological province.[10] He maintained that technological development was divergent rather than unilinear and that individual sequences contained surprises.[11] In spite of this, he was reluctant to acknowledge that Thomsen's technological ages were wholly arbitrary.[12] In the 1940s he still saw cutting tools as being important enough to mold or determine social organization, and the development of metallurgy as signalling the separation of handicraft production from agriculture.[13]

Childe was slowly but inexorably compelled to acknowledge that it was imposible to correlate technological ages with economic stages. Already, in *Man Makes Himself*, he had argued that, while in the Near East the invention of bronze-working had led to the rise of cities, it had required the introduction of iron-working to produce the same result in Europe.[14] From this he concluded that the invention of bronze-working was not equal in importance to that of agriculture.[15] In *What Happened in History* he further noted that, while all Palaeolithic societies could be equated with Morgan's stage of Savagery, his Barbarism included some societies that had a Neolithic and others that had a Bronze or Iron Age technology, while civilizations were founded upon the use of both bronze and iron.[16] He later noted that the Maya civilization had been based on a lithic technology. While Childe maintained that the institutions of Iron Age civilizations differed in certain crucial respects from those of Bronze Age ones, he did not see technological criteria providing a basis for the subdivision of Barbarism.[17]

In his 1944 Huxley Memorial Lecture Childe made a valiant effort to demonstrate that the traditional archaeological ages represented significant stages in the development of the forces of production.[18] In particular, he sought to defend the integrity of the Bronze Age against T. A. Rickard's proposal that the Bronze and Iron Ages should be treated as a single Metallic Age. He also sought to refute Glyn Daniel's argument that economic changes did not follow immediately in the wake of technological ones, and that the real break between an essentially Neolithic economy and the significant use of metal was at the beginning of the Late Bronze Age. To rehabilitate the concept of the Bronze Age, Childe defined four 'modes' of copper-bronze usage: mode 0, a Neolithic one in which copper was treated as a type of stone, and three numbered Bronze Age modes (1, 2, and 3), in which the metal was used first for weapons and ornaments, then also for handicraft tools, and finally also for agricultural and other heavy implements. He divided the Iron Age into two modes. In the first, heavy iron tools replaced previous stone and bronze ones; during the second, new types of tools, such as tongs, hammers, shears, planes and augers, were added to the repertoire. He noted that specific modes were not everywhere synchronous, and that individual cultural sequences did not have to evolve from one mode to another in a fixed sequence. In northern Italy, for example, the use of bronze passed directly from mode 1 to mode 3. Modes were also not systadial; that is, they did not everywhere correlate with the same level of over-all cultural development. Bronze 2 equated with the civilization of the Old and Middle Kingdoms in Egypt, but with barbarian societies in Europe. Childe noted that mode 3 had begun at about the same time in Egypt, Anatolia, the Aegean and central Europe, and suggested that this had resulted from a general reduction in the cost of metal throughout this region, which in turn was related to a complex series of interrelated historical events.[19] Diffusion was assigned a major role in explaining the sequences and correlations of modes found throughout Europe and the Near East.

Childe continued to correlate the use of bronze and iron with the genesis of completely different kinds of civilization. Bronze Age civilization was characterized by an archaic social order that was not transcended in Mesopotamia, Egypt and China, even when iron was introduced there. In those civilizations, the 'relations of production, adequate to a Bronze technology had turned into [what Marx called] "fetters on the development of new forces" '. This left the serfs of the Egyptian nobleman, Petosiris, to shatter their wrists with the miserable equipment of Bronze 2 two centuries after an Iron 1 technology had been introduced into Egypt.[20] Only in hitherto marginal areas was Iron Age technology free to create a new type of civilization. Childe argued that the development of the Mediterranean city state would have been impossible without the more efficient transport facilities that iron tools alone could provide.

In *Social Evolution*, published 1951, Childe assembled data on the specific cultural sequences through which barbarian societies had evolved into civilizations in various parts of temperate Europe, the Mediterranean region, Egypt and the Near East. Each sequence was scanned to determine what was known about trends in food production, technology, transport, trade, warfare, settlement, population, family structure, ritual, ownership of property, chieftain-ship and slavery. For each of these categories he sought to determine what specific features had appeared in each area and in what order. He concluded that all of these societies had developed from essentially the same Neolithic base, and that the spread of this economy into different regions had resulted in cultural divergence, which was later offset by convergence.[21] Given his ideological predilections, Childe might have been tempted to attribute the latter process to a strain towards an ideal fit between the economic institutions of each society and its social organization and ideology. Instead he rested the main weight of his explanation on diffusion. Indeed he maintained that the processes of change were too rapid to permit diffusion to effect the total integration of societies into stable configurations.[22] He allowed that the civilizations that he saw as the end product of these sequences of development had in common certain features of an abstract structural variety that might have evolved in a parallel fashion, but he attributed more specific cultural similarities to diffusion.

In 1954 Childe asserted for the last time that all societies might be assigned to a few abstract types constituting a unilinear sequence that was valid both hierarchically and chronologically. Yet the specific sequence that he proposed was a gross one that distinguished only food-gathering, Neolithic and urban societies.[23] After 1950 he abandoned his efforts to correlate stages of technology with social development. He was constrained to do this principally by what he had learned concerning the Maya of Central America. Thus he recognized the existence of a fully developed civilization that lacked irrigation, metallurgy, ploughs, sails, wheels, or domestic animals – all of which he had interpreted as prerequisites of civilization for the Near East.[24] None of these criteria could henceforth be regarded as marking a definite stage on the road to civilization. As a result his criteria of urbanism and civilization became increasingly generalized and functional instead of technological.[25] Long before he had accepted that, because of their scarcity, copper and bronze had never been as economically important as their technological potential suggested they should have been.[26] He later concluded that he had over-estimated the technological importance of bronze-working altogether, when he discovered that the Polynesians had carved wood very elaborately, using only stone tools and sharks' teeth.[27]

Thus Childe gradually learned to live with the implications of an argument that he had advanced in his inaugural address to the Institute of Archaeology: that technological criteria can be misleading when one seeks to use archaeological data to understand social evolution. He suggested that there were two reasons for this. First, cutting tools do not exhaust the forces of production, which also include such elements as means of transport. Second, it is the mode of production, rather than the specific forces of production, that determines social structure.[28] Childe continued to advocate the need for a new and less superficial classification of societies that was based on criteria perceptible to archaeologists, but also meaningful to ethnologists and historians. The formulation of such a scheme was an ambition that he was never to realize. Instead he was to focus his research more specifically on trying to delineate social change.

SOCIETAL APPROACHES

In an attempt to come to grips with the problems of social evolution, Childe began to inventory what archaeologists could hope to learn about individual prehistoric societies. He had continued to cling to his own version of Kossinna's dictum that a distinctive archaeological culture is always the product of a single people. Yet he had long found it difficult to equate protohistoric cultures with historically known peoples. He grew increasingly aware of the difficulties that were involved in determining what sort of social or political groupings were associated with a particular archaeological culture and in assuming that a single culture was congruent with a single society.[29] He observed that in historical times one material culture might be shared by a number of separate tribes or states, while in other examples a single state might embrace several different cultures, or its frontiers might cut across various cultural boundaries. He was forced to conclude that the boundaries of various aspects of culture did not necessarily coincide. If prehistorians were to delineate the development of societies, they must first attempt empirically to clothe their cultures with social institutions.[30]

Thus Childe grew increasingly preoccupied with the societal interpretation of data.[31] Like Christopher Hawkes, he believed that archaeologists could reconstruct an adequate, although always incomplete picture of the technology and subsistence economy of a prehistoric group. This permitted them to understand the mode, as well as the means of production. He also thought that they could learn something about the division of labour (although he thought that the sexual division of labour would remain obscure), trade (which he still recognized as a covering term for a host of different processes), and the concentration and distribution of social surpluses.[32]

Childe further believed that archaeologists could profitably investigate the density and distribution of population, but he regarded social institutions as more illusive.[33] He thought that archaeologists might detect the existence of economic differences among households, and on this basis infer the existence of hierarchical social divisions, including classes.[34] Informed guesses might be made concerning the existence of slavery, the status of women and the inheritance of property, and some clues might be found relating to the form of government and the nature of the family, ranking systems and warfare. He was less certain that anything significant could be learned about residence patterns, descent systems and justice.[35] At one point he believed that it might be possible to distinguish the burial or residence of a king from that of a mere chief, but in his 'Valediction' he was uncertain about this.[36]

Childe thought that even ideologies might be made the subject of 'cautious hypotheses'. Nevertheless both art and religion were capricious in their expression, and there was too much latitude to permit the confirmation of detailed interpretations.[37] He dismissed speculations about the possible significance of 'mother goddess' figurines as a harmless outlet for the sexual impulses of old men.[38] He believed that nothing significant could be learned from archaeological evidence about prehistoric customs, laws, language, or myth.[39] Yet, in spite of his general pessimism, no less a contemporary than Julian

Steward described Childe's efforts to wring sociological meaning from archaeological data as being 'very impressive'.[40] This indicates the innovative character of what Childe was trying to do.

One way in which Childe sought to gain more detailed insights into the nature of prehistoric societies was through the study of archaeological settlement patterns. This grew naturally out of his earlier work at Skara Brae and other habitation sites in Scotland. In 1949 he published a paper summarizing what was known about Neolithic house types in central Europe, and the following year another one describing Russian excavations of Palaeolithic dwellings.[41] In *Prehistoric Migrations*, published 1950, he argued that the transition from longhouses to single family dwellings marked the break-up of the clan as a basic social unit.[42] In spite of his reservations about the value of quantitative approaches in archaeology, he also proposed some quantitative generalizations concerning prehistoric settlements on the basis of archaeological data. He suggested that where settlements are known to have been occupied simultaneously, half the distance between them would give an indication of the size of their respective territories.[43] He also estimated that the majority of Neolithic villages in Europe covered 1.5 to 6.5 acres and had a population of between 8 and 35 households, or 110 to 600 persons.[44] On this basis he suggested that Pueblo Indian villages with over 1,000 inhabitants, such as he had visited in the south-western United States, might have evolved beyond the Neolithic level.[45] He failed, however, to take note of the impact that different patterns of warfare and ecological adaptation had on Neolithic communities outside of Europe. He proposed that the first cities were ten times as large as any known European Neolithic village.[46]

Yet Childe made little progress in using the archaeological record to gain a deeper understanding of prehistoric social organization. He did not draw any significant conclusions from his studies of settlement patterns, and failed to pursue these investigations in a rigorous or comprehensive manner, in spite of the obvious value of his initial findings. Nor did he extend his quantitative observations to other aspects of culture. Many of Childe's efforts to infer social structure from archaeological data, such as his casual but repeated references to female figurines as possible evidence of a matriarchate, or to alleged instances of *sati* as evidence of patriarchal society, were regarded with much scepticism by his contemporaries, and ultimately so by himself.[47] In other instances he was strangely reluctant to draw conclusions from his data. In *Social Evolution* he stated that the limited archaeological evidence concerning hunting and gathering cultures in Europe could not support enough sociological inferences to justify generalizations concerning the institutions and forms of social organization proper to Savagery in general.[48] But the data he presented demonstrated that increasingly sophisticated technology and the utilization of a broader range of resources were correlated with larger and more sedentary groups, and with increasing status differentiation. In this case Childe was perhaps inhibited by his lifelong reluctance to admit significant cultural change among societies that had hunting and gathering economies.

Scotland Before the Scots

The main trend in Childe's sociological concerns during this period was his effort to explain cultural change in terms of its relationship to evolving social systems. In this he was influenced by the spirit rather than by the letter of the Soviet archaeology of the 1930s, as well as by various aspects of British social anthropology. *The Story of Tools* and *Scotland Before the Scots* mark Childe's first major steps in this direction, the former being in many respects a trial piece for the longer and more important work.

The Story of Tools was a pamphlet written for the Young Communist League in 1944. Its express purpose was to demonstrate that the general ideas Engels had set forth in *The Origin of the Family, Private Property and the State* were confirmed by the archaeological record. This work enjoyed the approval of the British Communist Party, and in due course was translated into Hungarian, Polish and Chinese. In it Childe stressed changes in the ownership of the means of production as a key variable in social development. Societies in which tools were owned by the people who used them remained creative and flexible, while societies in which expensive machines were owned by capitalists and craftsmen were reduced to wage labour became hierarchical and fossilized.[49] He interpreted the work that Neolithic women did in the fields as enhancing their status, so long as the crops they grew remained a primary source of food.[50] He agreed with Engels that the barbarian conquest of the Roman Empire had rejuvenated Europe. Because the conquerors lacked usury, industrial slavery and private ownership of land, they were able to revive the creativity that had been stifled by Roman totalitarianism.[51]

Scotland Before the Scots, which was based on Childe's Rhind Lectures delivered to the Society of Antiquaries of Scotland in 1944, proclaimed itself to be a trial application of Soviet methods of archaeological interpretation to the prehistory of Scotland. This book aroused more controversies than did any of Childe's other writings. It has been described as a parting insult to the Scots and an attempt to offend conventional propriety. Yet if so, it is unclear who was being fooled or how. Childe examined six phases of Scottish prehistory in terms of their economy, houses, instruments of production, trade and inferences about the related development of society. He interpreted the earliest phase of Scottish Neolithic society as characterized by egalitarian clans, whose members held herds and tombs in common.[52] Increasing specialization and commodity production encouraged individual ownership as a means of facilitating a growing number of economic transactions. As a result clans were broken apart to form individual extended families, the cattle becoming the property of their heads. Yet the surplus production was so small that local chiefs were required to concentrate the surpluses of many such families in order to support visiting craftsmen. Childe speculated that these chiefs derived their authority from their seniority, or the role they played in trade and war. He followed Durkheim in suggesting that the power of chiefs was consecrated by them absorbing the 'soul substance' of their clans to become the prototypes of divine kings. Their tombs, no longer collective, became clan shrines, and the cult of dead chiefs formed a major component of tribal fertility rituals. In spite of this the power of chiefs was still restrained by important kinship obligations.[53]

Childe saw the expanding bronze industry as being utilized, not to release new forces for the production of wealth, but to produce gear for warriors and ornaments for their wives. It therefore failed to provide a growing population either with more food or with more jobs in industry and commerce. As a result population pressure led to increasing warfare.[54] Iron Age technology was characterized as more efficient, but as also failing to transform the social order in any fundamental way. Increased productivity was channelled into the erection of larger forts and the production of more elaborate ornaments. War chiefs and charioteers acquired rank by force of arms, replacing the earlier sacred chiefs and, in some parts of Scotland, republican governments composed of councils of landowners emerged. This social order lasted until, under the aegis of the Normans, an entrepreneurial class was able to develop, which in time bought out the landed aristocracies.[55]

Childe stated that in *Scotland Before the Scots* he had attempted to demonstrate the superiority of the Soviet developmental approach to the explanation of archaeological data over the sort of migrationary explanations that were popular in Britain. Yet the book is riddled with explanations of change that are couched in terms of migration and diffusion. Concerning the first appearance of agriculture in Scotland, Childe wrote: 'It cannot be unMarxian to assert that the first cultivated plants and domestic food animals were brought to Scotland ... not by the wind or waves, but by actual human cultivators and herdsmen who came and settled on our soil'.[56] Had this not happened, cultural development in Scotland might have remained static for centuries. The Beaker-folk, whose arrival Childe saw as putting an end to egalitarian clan society, are credited with accelerating change 'that was indeed logically necessary but that might have been indefinitely postponed'.[57] The dissolution of tribal society was attributed to successive incursions of 'Goidels', Norsemen, Saxons and Normans.[58]

British archaeologists had good reason to question Childe's cavalier and clearly experimental use of Soviet developmental stages to reconstruct various aspects of prehistoric Scottish social organization and religion. Yet, in whatever spirit these lectures had been planned, the book turned out to be at least as much a critique as a demonstration of the merits of the Soviet method. His main conclusion was that 'the internal development of Scottish society in accordance with "universal laws" simply could not explain the archaeological data from Scotland'.[59] The unflattering picture that he painted of Scotland as a peripheral and backward region had nothing to do with Soviet ideas, which emphasized the importance of internal development. On the contrary, it reflected his rejection of such views in favour of one emphasizing diffusion and migration from the Near East as major forces promoting cultural change. It is ironic that this book should so long have been regarded by many British archaeologists as a doctrinaire exposition of Marxism.

Childe's conclusion was in accord with his public rejection, a few years later, of the Soviet scheme of unilinear development on which the interpretations of prehistoric society and religion offered in *Scotland Before the Scots* were based.[60] This, together with Childe's privately luke-warm opinion of Engels' *Origin of the Family, Private Property and the State*, may explain why he never found time to produce a joint edition of it with R. Palme Dutt, which was to have been supplied with notes by Childe, designed to bring Engels' text 'up to date'.[61]

Childe's strongest and most influential denunciations of the Soviet unilinear scheme of cultural evolution, as well as his most outspoken criticisms of Soviet archaeology generally, followed the publication in 1950 of Stalin's *Concerning Marxism in Linguistics*, in which the Soviet leader denounced Marr's linguistic theories, pointing out that the same Russian language was spoken in the Soviet Union as had been spoken in tsarist Russia. Peter Gathercole has noted that this essay unintentionally pricked the bubble of monolithic restraint among Communist intellectuals in western Europe.[62] He suggests that it offered Childe an opportunity to criticize some of the fundamental concepts of Soviet archaeology by identifying them with Marrism, while at the same time it freed him to develop and express an alternative view of the significance of Marxism for archaeology. It must not be forgotten, however, that Childe had publicly criticized aspects of Soviet archaeology as early as 1938.[63]

FURTHER PROGRESS

Childe made progress towards a societal explanation of archaeological data in his *Prehistoric Migrations in Europe*, which was published in 1950. This book was based on a series of lectures that he had delivered in Oslo in the autumn of 1946, as part of a symposium on folk movements in prehistoric and protohistoric Europe. In it he returned to his original quest to locate the homeland of the Indo-Europeans; although he was later to note ruefully that his then plausible identification of the first Indo-Europeans in Europe with the Urnfield-folk was refuted within ten years by the identification of the language of the Linear B script as an early form of Greek and by the discovery of still earlier wheeled vehicles north of the Alps.[64] As in his previous syntheses of European prehistory, Childe considered climatic change, population growth and technological development as factors promoting social and economic change. He also emphasized the importance of diffusion and migration; arguing, for example, that the economic revolution of the Late Bronze Age could hardly have occurred without a fresh (though archaeologically undocumented) incursion of miners and bronze-workers from the Near East.[65]

Yet the conception of this book was more compact than that of *The Dawn of European Civilization*. This may have encouraged Childe to emphasize the social characteristics that were shared by related cultures rather than the cultural detail that distinguished them. Once again he sought to see in the archaeological record a chronicle of the break-up of egalitarian clans into natural families, and the development of tribes and chiefdoms whose leaders began to concentrate the social surplus and to augment their share of it by warfare and trading.[66] Childe hailed the development of pastoral tribes in late Neolithic times as a confirmation of Engels' 'almost prophetic' assertion that 'pastoral tribes had separated out from the mass of barbarians'.[67] The Bronze Age was characterized by the improvement of mining, further development of trade and crafts, and the emergence of affluent chiefdoms in some areas. Although iron weapons were far more common than bronze ones had been, they did not produce a more egalitarian society. Instead they allowed a growing population to wage war more effectively, which led to a further concentration of political power in the Iron Age.[68] The whole of European prehistory was interpreted in terms of much the same model that Childe had applied to Scotland in *Scotland Before the Scots*.

In a paper on 'The Urban Revolution', published in *The Town Planning Review* in 1950, Childe attempted to distinguish the earliest cities from Neolithic villages. He defined them, and by implication civilization, in terms of ten criteria: *1* size, *2* type of inhabitant, most of whom in some cities may have been peasants but all cities contained craftsmen, merchants, officials and priests who were supported by the surpluses of primary producers, *3* primary producers paying surpluses to a deity or a divine ruler, *4* monumental architecture, *5* a ruling class exempt from manual labour, *6* a system for recording information, *7* the development of exact but practical sciences, *8* monumental art, *9* the regular importation of raw materials, both as luxuries and as industrial materials, and *10* resident specialist craftsmen, politically as well as economically under the control of secular or religious officials.[69] It is now generally agreed that Childe erred in suggesting that writing was a necessary prerequisite for civilization, although this belief was shared by most archaeologists at that time. This was the most specific of his criteria. He hedged his bets by referring to 'systems of recording' in place of 'writing' in some places. This more ambiguous expression might cover Peruvian *quipu* records and Dahomean pebble-counting, although it does not appear that Childe had such devices in mind.

In general Childe's criteria were of a broad, often societal nature. He clearly believed that these common features, including writing, had evolved in a parallel or convergent fashion, rather than resulting from historical connections. In support of this he observed that while secondary civilizations had been built on the cultural capital of a small number of primary ones, each normally differed from its ancestor more than the latter did from each other.[70] It was clear to him that most features shared in common by civilizations were abstract ones that were functionally inherent in any social system at that level of complexity. Thus they served to define a stage of social development. The concrete detail associated with each of these civilizations, and the nature of their social institutions, were highly divergent. Similarities at that degree of specificity were best explained historically.[71]

In *Social Evolution* Childe's interest in societal development was overshadowed by his preoccupation with diffusion. Yet he attempted to survey in broad terms what archaeology might reveal about the nature of prehistoric societies. He also began to distinguish, hesitatingly and for the first time, between the concept of society and that of culture. He argued that, as a network of self-perpetuating social relations, a society had a self-contained, organic quality that cultural traits, with their susceptibility to diffusion, did not. While the duty of the archaeologist, as prehistorian, was to distinguish and describe as many archaeological cultures as possible, an approach modelled on comparative sociology would seek to reduce this multiplicity by ignoring minor cultural differences and assigning cultures, on the basis of similarities in their social systems, to a smaller number of types. Childe feared that the abstraction involved in the latter approach might overlook significant concrete differences, but he argued that it was preferable that this should result from a deliberate selection among adequate data than from a blind acceptance of the shortcomings of the archaeological record. Like social anthropologists, he was coming to regard social relations as the structured aspect of human behaviour and culture as fragmentary elements that were functionally interrelated through their relationship to the behavioural systems of specific societies.[72]

In 1952 Childe contributed a brief survey of trade and industry in barbarian Europe until Roman times to *The Cambridge Economic History of Europe*. Although he dealt mainly with items that were well attested in the archaeological record, such as *spondylus* shells, he attempted to treat the development of long-distance trade in the context of regional economic and social change. This tended to emphasize social factors involved in economic change.[73]

Childe was later to decry as 'incredibly bad' his book-length synthesis of the relationship between the development of culture in Europe and the Near East that was published in 1954 as part of *The European Inheritance*. His main objection was that this essay 'was dominated by an old-fashioned over-estimation of the Orient's role, and utterly missed the individuality of prehistoric Europe'.[74] Yet in many respects it offered the broadest and most integrated perspective that he produced of cultural development in the western part of the Old World. Because of its conciseness, it too stressed social structure rather than cultural detail. Although Europe's roles as a field for Neolithic colonization and a supplier of raw materials to the expanding markets of the Near East were major themes of this study, its view of the relationship between Europe and the Near East did not differ markedly from Childe's position in other publications since the late 1930s. It also foreshadowed his final effort to differentiate

European from Near Eastern civilization, on the basis of the greater freedom from state control that he believed artisans and the economy in general had long enjoyed in Europe.[75]

When he revised *The Dawn of European Civilization* for its sixth edition in 1955, Childe renounced the 'dogmatically Orientalist attitude' of the third edition. He denied that Europeans had ever been the passive recipients of cultural influences from the Near East. In his preface he credited this change to criticisms that the Soviet archaeologist Alexander Mongait had made of his work in the introduction to a Russian translation of *The Dawn of European Civilization*, published four years earlier.[76] Childe was more critical than he had been prior to this time in his assessment of possible Near Eastern influences on Europe. He had come to doubt that trade with the Near East had been the main stimulus for the development of the megalithic cultures of Western Europe.[77] He also devoted more space to Soviet theories of *in situ* cultural evolution.[78] Yet, while he attached more historical importance to possible survivals of Mesolithic cultures than he had done before, he continued to maintain that migrating shepherds and cultivators must have brought a Neolithic economy to Europe from the Near East.[79] He also still thought it worthwhile to suggest that refugees who fled from the Nile Delta at the beginning of the First Dynasty might have contributed to the development of civilization in the Cyclades.[80] He characterized the Near East as a region where aridity necessitated conformity and rigid discipline in areas that could support a high population density, while the dispersal of population in Neolithic Europe encouraged independence and cultural divergence among relatively small-scale societies. Because of this, European groups were unable to concentrate a large enough social surplus to permit a metallurgical revolution. It was the surpluses produced by Near Eastern societies, and their demands for raw materials, that effected the introduction of a metallurgical industry into Europe, without European peoples experiencing the same need for political unification, and developing the rigid class divisions, that had stultified the Near Eastern heartland.[81] Childe rather naively maintained that the development of prehistoric Europe had depended as much on Near Eastern capital as the development of Japan had depended on that of Europe and America in the nineteenth century.[82]

The Prehistory of European Society

The societal approach reached its climax in Childe's last and posthumously published book, *The Prehistory of European Society*. In it he returned to the questions that he had posed and tried to answer in *The Dawn of European Civilization* and *The Aryans*: how did European barbarians come to outstrip their oriental masters and Europe eventually achieve world pre-eminence in science and technology?[83] He stated that, while preparing the final editions of *The Dawn of European Civilization* and *New Light on the Most Ancient East*, he realized that Christopher Hawkes had been right when he had insisted in *The Prehistoric Foundations of Europe*, published in 1940, that many progressive and already distinctly European features had already been apparent in the Bronze Age.[84] In a letter that he wrote to R.J. Braidwood in October 1956 Childe asserted that he now believed that he could explain why this was so, and that he hoped to write a short book that would answer the questions that Hawkes' observations had posed.[85] In his preface to *The Prehistory of European Society* Childe castigated all of his previous publications, except the final edition of *The Dawn of European Civilization*, for giving the impression that European Bronze Age cultures were nothing more than primitive and debased copies of the Near Eastern civilizations, the vast achievements of which he had extolled in *New Light on the Most Ancient East* and *What Happened in History*.[86] Childe had evidently forgotten that the 'Orientalism' in the 1939 edition of *The Dawn of European Civilization* had been a reaction against National Socialism, which he said had made him lose sight of the positive aspects of all European barbarisms. In all likelihood Hawkes had derived much of his appreciation of the novelty and creativity of prehistoric European cultures from Childe's own earlier works, including the first edition of *The Dawn of European Civilization*, where one of its principal themes was praise for the originality of Europeans in prehistoric times. At the most Hawkes and Mongait had stimulated Childe to return unwittingly to a position that he had adopted at the beginning of his career and later lost sight of.

Childe proposed that the unique features of European civilization could best be explained by the historical fact that the Urban Revolution took place earlier in the Near East than in Europe: 'All follows from that posteriority'.[87] He regarded it as inevitable that totalitarian concentrations of wealth and power had developed in the large river valleys of the Near East, because of the high productivity and circumscribed distribution of their soils, the ease with which those soils could be worked, and the dependence of civilization in those areas upon imported materials.[88] Where rainfall was more abundant, the solution for an expanding Neolithic population was to seek fresh land elsewhere through warfare or migration. Only in the Near East was a different solution found but, in Childe's opinion, at frightful social cost.[89] Kings arose who were able to amass sufficient concentrations of surplus resources (especially foodstuffs) to ensure that full-time metallurgists had the security and materials necessary to exercise and perfect their skills. Yet the circumstances under which the new technology had to develop reduced these craftsmen to a state of economic servitude, and forced both them and the peasantry who supported them to surrender the right to plan their lives to the priests and warriors who were their rulers.[90]

In a teleological perspective, Childe viewed the inequality and exploitation that were required to establish a metallurgical industry and civilization in the Near East as a necessary evil, if people in other regions were to gain effective control over their environment. He continued to believe that the technology of the Near East had been transferred to Europe by the younger sons of craftsmen seeking their own clientele or new sources of raw materials for which there was a demand in the Near East.[91] Childe thought that because it was impossible to concentrate surpluses on a sufficiently large scale in Europe, a metallurgical industry was even less likely to have evolved indigenously there than among the North American Indians, who failed to develop one although they had access to large amounts of native copper.[92] In Europe craftsmen were not bound to totalitarian masters. On the contrary, they were compelled to move from one tribal centre to another in order to sell their produce to chieftains, who lacked the resources to employ them full time. As a result of this experience, European craftsmen became used to selling their skills to the highest bidder. Hence, even after the productivity of Europe increased to the point where individual chiefs could employ artisans on a full-time basis, merchants and craftsmen were able to remain independent of political control.[93]

The difficulties of coping with the forests and heavy soils of Europe also made the people who lived there appreciate labour-saving devices, while the multiplicity of small, often warring societies stimulated a demand for improved weapons. The resulting competition for better quality goods and more skilled craftsmen encouraged technological development in Europe on a scale unseen in the Near East since the growth of the first civilizations in that area.

Childe considered that European craftsmen and scholars had preserved their freedom of movement in a supra-national economy from the Bronze Age to modern times, even though slavery and totalitarianism had temporarily distorted this pattern under the Hellenistic monarchies and the Roman Empire, and peasantries often had been reduced to a worse serfdom than they had experienced in the ancient Near East. In a curious apotheosis of free enterprise he claimed that the metics at Athens, the journeymen of the Middle Ages and the migrant unionists of the nineteenth century were the spiritual descendants of his putative Bronze Age metallurgists. Likewise since Classical times scholars had been free to exchange ideas by means of publications, correspondence and visits, a pattern that he protested had been disrupted in an unprecedented and wholly unEuropean manner by the Cold War.[94]

Childe gave rather contradictory accounts of what he had sought to accomplish by writing *The Prehistory of European Society*. In his preface he suggested that it outlined in simpler terms, and without abstruse and often inconclusive archaeological documentation, the arguments that he had developed in the final edition of *The Dawn of European Civilization*.[95] This suggested that it was merely a summary or popularization of the latter. On the other hand, in 'Retrospect' Childe stated that *The Prehistory of European Society* 'exemplifies better than any other work I know how what everyone will accept as history could be extracted from archaeological finds'.[96] He also regarded it as the 'final answer' to those who overrated the role played by the Near East in the development of Europe.

The Prehistory of European Society was much more than a synopsis of *The Dawn of European Civilization*. In it Childe differentiated with greater clarity than he had done before between the concept of society and that of culture. He developed the idea of society as the structural matrix in terms of which individual items of culture acquired their functional significance. He also made it clear that functional constraints severely limited the range of variation in political systems, kinship behaviour and other forms of social relations. As a result, social structures tended to conform to a rather narrow range of types that could be classified and compared relatively easily. On the other hand, the specific detail of cultures was far greater. From the point of view of societal analysis, much of the latter could be regarded as an historical accident, in the sense that the presence of one trait as opposed to another was often the result of a culture's particular antecedents and the specific groups with which it had come into contact. Because of this, social systems may be defined and studied cross-culturally far more easily than cultural patterns can be.

Thus Childe, apparently quite independently, arrived at a view of how archaeological data might be studied in terms of their relationship to social systems that in many ways resembled what had been achieved a few years earlier by Gordon Willey in his *Prehistoric Settlement Patterns in the Virú Valley, Peru*.[97] The latter study marked the beginning of formal settlement pattern analysis in American archaeology, and also the beginning of the societal interpretation of archaeological data. The principal use that Willey made of the concept of culture was to distinguish successive phases in the development of the Virú Valley and thus to group together sites that were known to belong to approximately the same period of time. Cemeteries, habitation sites, temples, forts and irrigation systems belonging to the same period provided a basis for attempting to reconstruct the social and political organization of the Virú Valley at different stages in its history. Instead of viewing social and political systems as attributes of individual archaeological cultures, Willey tried to interpret the cultural remains of the Virú Valley as parts of an evolving social system. While Childe was not proposing a form of settlement archaeology, the societal approaches that he and Willey had developed were virtually identical. It is perhaps not coincidental that a concern with settlement patterns had played a role in the evolution of Childe's thinking in this direction.

Yet, in spite of this major accomplishment, *The Prehistory of European Society* had its shortcomings. Its discussion of aims and methods is riddled with doubts concerning what can be learned about prehistoric societies, which seemed to be limited to certain aspects of the division of labour, social hierarchies and government.[98] Childe seems to have been more preoccupied with detailing the problems and limitations of this approach than with demonstrating its potential. His strong emphasis on outlining rather than documenting his arguments also revealed more clearly than did his other late works the extent to which his thought was now burdened with concepts that he had formulated long ago, but had never subjected to rigorous testing. He had accepted these concepts for so long that he could no longer evaluate them critically. He still described hunters and gatherers as parasites and, without solid evidence, invoked immigrant prospectors and craftsmen from the Near East as an essential element in the transmission of Near Eastern technology to Europe. He also assumed that experienced metallurgists came to Europe in search of raw materials and, having minimally satisfied local demand, shipped their surplus production to the eastern Mediterranean.

The spread of craftsmen from the Near East might have been expected to produce widespread stylistic uniformities in pottery and metallurgy over much of Europe. Childe attempted to explain away the absence of such uniformity by claiming that these craftsmen quickly adapted their output to suit local taste.[99] He also retreated to an earlier position when he described the metallurgical industry as necessarily constituting 'the first step towards escape from the rigid limits of neolithic barbarism', and as the main factor that had overturned the barbarian social order and evoked a new population of full-time specialists.[100] By doing this he abandoned his hard-won conclusion that cutting tools did not exhaust the forces of production. Childe laid more stress than ever before on the independence of craftsmen in Bronze Age Europe, and on their freedom to move from place to place, an idea largely based on his understanding of the behaviour of free craftsmen in Classical Greece and on Homer's description of bards and craftsmen in earlier times.[101] He was troubled by Leonard Palmer's claim that in the Linear B texts craftsmen were assigned to the lowest rank of Mycenaean society, and that in some texts they appeared to be mentioned as cultivators, which implied that they were not full-time specialists. He countered this argument only feebly by asserting that in Mycenaean times craftsmen likely had been as free as they were in the Homeric epics, upon which he would continue to rely.[102] Childe also continued to toy with such arguments as that the clay phalli, and the prominence of bulls in the plastic art of the Tripolje culture, foreshadowed the transition to a patriarchal order. While he now recognized that evidence of *sati* was often dubious, it was on the basis of such evidence that he concluded that the Battle-axe peoples were patriarchal.[103] He argued also that the expansion of Bronze Age civilization was analogous to the colonialism of modern times, especially insofar as both involved the export of capital from the main centres of development. His uncritical adherence to these theories not only limited his creativity but seems to have reached the point where it blinded him to the significance of evidence or new theories that ran contrary to them.

CLIMBING MOUNT NEBO

Childe's early work had been based on an intimate knowledge of artefact types, and their temporal and geographical distribution in the archaeological record of Europe. This formalist approach antedated Childe, having been evolved in the heyday of evolutionary archaeology, but it had retained its universal respectability into the post-evolutionary period, as a result of its use and refinement by archaeologists such as Oscar Montelius and Joseph Déchelette. Childe spent the rest of his life reading archaeological reports and visiting museums and archaeological sites throughout Europe and the Near East. To satisfy his curiosity about the stratigraphy at Mersin, in Turkey, he spent several weeks there digging with John Garstang over the Christmas holidays in 1946. Childe's notebooks are filled with crude, but effective sketches of pottery, bronze objects and stone tools. His unrivalled knowledge of this material facilitated his culture-historical syntheses, but did not provide a wholly satisfactory basis for his economic studies. Even less did it suffice to allow him to study prehistoric social organization, scientific knowledge and ideology. His desultory examinations of settlement pattern data were clearly designed to remedy this deficiency, but they did not produce methodological breakthroughs. To have explored the social significance of archaeological data would have required a far more systematic knowledge of ethnographic material than he had at his disposal. Moreover Childe was not alone in his reticence. Only recently have systematic ethnographic perspectives on metal-working been considered in interpreting the archaeological record for Bronze Age Europe.[104] In addition, as Grahame Clark clearly understood, the application of such knowledge to further an understanding of the archaeological record could not take place without innovations in field work. While Childe urged excavators to record additional categories of data, such as whether there were oval or bolster-shaped depressions on querns,[105] his lack of interest in innovative field work and his preoccupation with a typological approach ill-equipped him for this type of research.

The increasing fossilization of Childe's creative imagination is also evident in his attitude towards quantification. In *Man Makes Himself*, he had praised quantification as a means to overcome the personal biases of a researcher.[106] He also suggested, as many American archaeologists had already done, that the concept of the archaeological culture was largely a statistical one.[107] Yet, in spite of this, Childe remained anti-quantitative. He argued that the need to understand archaeological material from a functional point of view ruled out the use of mathematical formulae to define cultures. Too few specimens of most classes of artefacts were found for them to be treated statistically, while the need for narrowly defined types of artefacts introduced an arbitrary element into any statistical classification.[108] Childe cited some even less convincing difficulties, such as the alleged impossibility of plotting the distribution of frequencies of artefacts on maps.[109] While he allowed that statistics might be useful for comparing artefacts from different levels of a single stratified site, he believed that, for general purposes, statistical methods were unlikely to replace typological ones.[110]

It seems symptomatic of a growing impasse in Childe's thought during the last years of his life that at the same time he was failing to produce significant new interpretations of the course of European prehistory, he was also experiencing serious doubts about whether archaeological data could be shown to support many of his favourite ideas. Childe had long been aware that explanations in archaeology tended to be determined by *a priori* assumptions and subjective prejudices.[111] Now, however, he sought to examine and publicize more systematically the assumptions on which his work had been based, and to demonstrate that he could defend these assumptions as being probable, even if he could not prove them to be true.[112] An important manifestation of this concern was *Piecing Together the Past*, published in 1954, which was based on his lectures dealing with archaeological classification, terminology and the concepts he had used to extract history from archaeological data.[113]

As Childe once more began to emphasize the innovativeness of prehistoric European cultures, he admitted that the Orientalist view of European cultural development, upon which he still relied, was only an assumption, and that alternative assumptions would produce radically different interpretations of what had happened.[114] As a result of his growing awareness of functional limitations on structural variation, he also began to doubt that all similarities between the barbarian societies of Europe and the civilizations of the Near East could be explained as diffusions from the Near East.[115] This was very different from his assertion in 1935 that new archaeological findings were tending to confirm both the Orientalist hypothesis and his own short chronology. More recent developments had convinced Childe that even the most solidly based archaeological interpretations were tentative at best.[116] He was prepared to admit that a not inadmissible shift in dating might suggest that copper-working had been independently reinvented in Hungary. That would allow the shapes of the earliest copper celts in that region to be interpreted as metal copies of local implements that had formerly been manufactured of stone or antler. Nevertheless he felt that such 'independent invention of casting is hard to admit'.[117]

The discovery of pre-pottery Neolithic cultures in the Near East had posed unexpected complications for understanding the beginnings of agriculture in Europe.[118] It also seemed possible that pottery had been separately invented by the Mesolithic Ertebølle culture of Scandinavia, rather than having diffused there from the Near East.[119] The disintegration of the assumed correlation between the invention of pottery and beginnings of agriculture compelled archaeologists for the first time to base their studies of the origins of food-production solely upon palaeobiological data. Childe accepted this as inescapable, although, given his preference for a typological approach, he can scarcely have regarded it as welcome.

Childe also recognized as fallacious the idea that the Chalcolithic pottery of Iberia was of Mycenaean inspiration.[120] He noted that no artefact, undoubtedly manufactured in the eastern Mediterranean area prior to 1800 BC, had been found in an archaeological context in the western Mediterranean. If prospectors from the east had visited the latter region, they had imparted 'hardly anything of their lore to native apprentices'.[121] He also saw that the failure to associate metal objects with the construction of megalithic tombs in western Europe was a serious blow to his view of 'megalithic religion' as an ideological distortion of an Early Aegean quest for tin, amber and gold. Yet, in spite of this, he clung to the belief that 'actual colonization by East Mediterranean people does seem the best explanation' for these phenomena.[122] He admitted, however, that archaeological evidence now indicated that the urbanization of Palestinian sites, such as Ai and Jericho, had been achieved without Egyptian capital, and that it had not obviously been expanded as a result of trade being opened up with Egypt.[123] Robert McC. Adams recalls that, when he visited Childe in the spring of 1956, they had a long discussion, in the course of which Childe expressed the deepest despair about the lasting value of any interpretation of archaeological data, and maintained that the only genuine increment to knowledge was new data.[124] A similar opinion dominates his final assessment of *The Prehistory of European Society*: 'My whole account may prove to be erroneous; my formulae may be inadequate; my interpretations are perhaps ill-founded; my chronological framework – and without such one cannot speak of conjunctures – is frankly shaky.' But nevertheless he felt that the result was worth publishing.[125]

Childe's doubts about his interpretations of European prehistory were clearly related to his realization that most of them were linked to assumptions he had made about chronological relationships. The invention of radio-carbon dating offered the hope that the chronology of prehistoric Europe might some day be established independently of archaeological postulates.[126] While he was cautious in his assessment of the potential significance of radio-carbon dating,[127] the prospect of an imminent judgment of this sort may have made him fearful for the survival of his interpretations of European prehistory. This, in turn, may have led him to hope that his interpretative concepts rather than his specific interpretations would be recognized as his most original and lasting contributions. Childe clearly did not view these two aspects of his work as being so closely linked that they had to stand or fall together. It may not stretch inference too far to suggest that he was also depressed by a growing awareness of the inadequacy of his typological methods for dealing with the problems of societal analysis and prehistoric knowledge that were now of major interest to him.

In 1956 Childe retired a few months ahead of time in order to facilitate the relocation of the Institute of Archaeology to its present quarters in Gordon Square. He accepted an invitation from the Government of India to attend a Science Congress in Calcutta in January 1957; then returned to England briefly.[128] In April that year, he went back to Australia for the first time since 1922, and travelled about the country, visiting friends and relatives. He encouraged an interest in prehistoric studies by giving two lectures at Melbourne University and a radio broadcast on that theme. In June he delivered a set of lectures before the Australian National University in Canberra covering the material that was to appear in his forthcoming *The Prehistory of European Society*. He carefully summarized these lectures in a paper titled 'The Bronze Age', which reached the editor of *Past and Present* in October.[129] Childe received the honorary degree of Doctor of Letters from the University of Sydney.

Childe deplored the lack of interest in museums and local prehistory in Australia, as well as the continuing indifference of his countrymen to what he regarded as the vital affairs of their society. F. B. Smith recalls Childe 'shocking an audience of *bien pensants* in Melbourne with a merciless comparison between the tepid suburban life of Australia and the vital culture of Ireland in the tenth century'.[130] Childe spent part of his time finishing *The Prehistory of European Society* and writing his autobiographical sketch 'Retrospect'. He also spent much time hiking and studying rock formations in the Blue Mountains near Sydney, an area associated with happy memories of his youth. It was understood that he was planning to write a book about the area.[131] Childe complained about poor health, giddiness and failing eyesight. He was also said to be prone to take risks when mountaineering.[132] On 19 October 1957, he did not return from a hike, and was found fallen to his death 1,000 feet below Govett's Leap, near Katoomba.

Various explanations of the circumstances of Childe's death have been offered. He feared sickness and loss of independence in his old age, but his half-sister Ethel stated that he was looking forward to his return to England,[133] even though to many of his colleagues he appeared to have packed up there. Some people have tried to link his death to his disillusionment with the Soviet Union or with Marxism, which, it is alleged, he finally realized was a bankrupt philosophy. The evidence is overwhelmingly against this. Latterly he had become more outspoken about the shortcomings of Soviet archaeology, in spite of his desire not to endanger contacts with his Soviet colleagues. Nevertheless, while he had relished citing Stalin as an authority in his writings and public addresses as late as 1951, he had long before revealed in private correspondence that he was aware of the evils of totalitarianism, as practised both in Germany and the Soviet Union.[134] The impact of even such a tragic event as the Soviet invasion of Hungary in 1956, however much it dismayed him about Soviet foreign policy and however sorry he felt for the Hungarian people (he had visited Hungary in 1955), was lessened by the fact that it seemed not unlike Britain's behaviour during the Suez crisis.

Since his youthful excursion into Australian politics, Childe had learned to co-exist with unpalatable political situations, and what he regarded as a very imperfect world.[135] He does not appear to have been more distressed by the Cold War than he was by the post-war economic ills of Britain (about which he complained greatly) and by what he regarded as the over-generous treatment of a defeated Germany by the West.[136] John Morris was correct when he observed that to Childe Marxism was a way of thought, not a set of dogmas.[137] It is also clear that for Childe Marxism and the Soviet Union were not synonymous. His attack on Marrism in his 'Valediction' was a reaffirmation rather than a repudiation of Marxism, as he understood it.[138] Far from playing him false, Childe's liberal interpretation of Marxism had inspired much of his most creative work during the post-war years. Childe the Marxist and Childe the archaeologist had never been closer.

Yet Childe clearly treated the last few years of his life as a summing-up. In his 'Valediction' and 'Retrospect' he self-consciously reviewed his life's work with modesty and considerable objectivity. *The Prehistory of European Society* was also a summing-up in that it attempted to answer problems about the nature of European society that he had first raised in *The Dawn of European Civilization*. But this book revealed that the typological skills on which most of Childe's archaeological analysis had been based did not provide an adequate foundation for coping with the problems of knowledge and society that were now central to his interests. He was past the stage where a major reorientation of his methods of analysis could be expected. Hence, while *The Prehistory of European Society* was a milestone pointing towards some important future developments in archaeology, it also marked the limits beyond which its author was unable to progress. Like Moses, Childe had been able to survey the Promised Land from the summit of Mount Nebo; it was left to others to enter and take possession of it.

CHAPTER X

Beyond the New Archaeology

CHILDE'S REPUTATION during his lifetime was based primarily on his interpretations of the archaeological record of Europe and the Near East. He was able to read meaning and significance into this record more convincingly than were any of his contemporaries. Yet in recent years, and especially since radio-carbon dates have been subject to tree-ring calibrations, Childe's reconstruction of European prehistory has been severely challenged, and with it many of the concepts upon which this reconstruction was based. Present trends suggest that Childe may remain significant to archaeologists (as he thought he would) more as a general theorist than as either a prehistorian or a field worker. While some of the concepts that he utilized in his interpretations of archaeological data, particularly during the early stages of his career, are probably as antiquated as the interpretations themselves seem to be,[1] his creative theoretical work did not end in the 1930s, as some have claimed, but continued to the end of his life.

To understand the ideas that shaped the development of Childe's later thought, his writings must be considered as a whole. In spite of a tendency for the interpretations found in his culture-historical works not to keep abreast of the development of his theoretical concepts, there is no evidence of a split between Childe as a humanist and as a Marxist or social scientist. To a large degree his early theoretical orientation was derived from the archaeological tradition in which he was trained and worked. An examination of his references and surviving notebooks[2] indicates that during these years he relied both for data and for ideas mainly upon literature published by other archaeologists. Finally, while the development of Childe's thought can be conceptualized in terms of certain rather arbitrary stages, there is no warrant for believing that there was ever a major crisis or break in this process. The nearest to a crisis was his reaction to the coming to power of Adolf Hitler in 1933. Yet even this served largely as a catalyst that hastened the broadening of an earlier concern with prehistoric economies into an interest in a wider range of social issues. It also may have encouraged a greater concern with the study of cultural progress than he might otherwise have developed.

Childe's interests gradually shifted from trying to understand major trends in European and Near Eastern prehistory to trying to account for cultural development in more general terms (though not in a broader geographical context). He struggled to understand archaeological data in relationship to increasingly holistic and functional patterns. This led him to investigate aspects of prehistoric cultures that are more difficult to understand than is technology; first the economy and later social organization and the development of scientific knowledge. In his efforts to cope with these problems, he utilized the ideas of Durkheim, the schools of American anthropology that were based on the work of Franz Boas and Leslie White, and various concepts he had acquired from philology, sociology, and the philosophy of history and of science. He also made more systematic use of Karl Marx's materialist approach, with which he identified both emotionally and intellectually. Although these ideas never overpowered Childe's fundamental commitment to his data and to the professional concerns of archaeology as a discipline, they endowed his writings with an intellectual richness that did not characterize the work of any contemporary archaeologist, except R. G. Collingwood.

The principal strength of Childe's work lay in his detailed knowledge of the archaeological record for Europe, and to a lesser degree for the Near East. This knowledge, like that of Oscar Montelius, consisted of intimate familiarity with artefacts and artefact types. Such an approach was derived from the evolutionary archaeology of the nineteenth century. Childe's main weakness, recognized (if at all) too late in his career to be remedied, was his lack of knowledge of comparative ethnography, especially as it related to processes such as metallurgy that featured prominently in his theorizing. While this stifled his awareness of how broad was the range of variation in human behaviour, it may have encouraged him to try to derive more information about economy, society and ideology directly from a study of the archaeological record than he would have had he relied uncritically, as an older generation of archaeologists had done, upon the more lavish application of ethnographic analogy.

EARLY WORK

Childe's first major accomplishment was to demonstrate how the concept of the archaeological culture could be used in place of, or alongside, the older concept of unilinear developmental stages to reconstruct European prehistory beginning in Upper Palaeolithic times. *The Dawn of European Civilization* convinced British archaeologists of the value of attempting to analyse data systematically in terms of such units. According to Glyn Daniel, it marked 'a new starting-point for prehistoric archaeology'.[3] Childe had borrowed the concept of the archaeological culture from Kossinna, but he made it respectable in western Europe by ridding it of Kossinna's racist and nationalistic biases. He did this by replacing Kossinna's emphasis on migration from Germany as the principal explanation of cultural change in Europe with Montelius' scheme stressing the diffusion of more developed culture to Europe from its point of origin in the Near East. The latter interpretation had been popular among British archaeologists for some time.

The adoption of the concept of the archaeological culture by Kossinna and Childe reflected a widespread conviction that the archaeological record could (and ought to) be used to trace the origin and prehistoric development of specific peoples, in addition to the general evolution of technology as had been done formerly. This interest appears to have led independently to the formulation of something closely resembling this concept in various parts of the world. Archaeologists working in the Ohio Valley had begun to organize their data in terms of archaeological cultures (which they named as such) as early as 1903.[4] They were led to adapt the ethnographic concept of cultural units to archaeological usage when a growing awareness of chronological variation in the archaeological record began to enrich a long-standing concern with studying geographical variation in American archaeological assemblages. This was, of course, precisely the opposite way from which the notion of the archaeological culture had evolved in Europe. There a growing interest in geographical variation in artefact assemblages gradually complemented a long-standing concern with temporal and evolutionary variation. In the 1920s and 1930s American archaeologists working in the south-western United States and the Mississippi Valley developed cultural unit concepts that were similar to what had been formulated in the Ohio Valley, and these soon came into general use for analysing North American archaeological data. The new units were labelled 'focus' or 'phase' on the ground that the term 'culture' was already used in too many ways. These developments took place in the United States at a time when Childe's work either had not begun or was virtually unknown to American archaeologists.[5]

From the beginning Childe's concept of the archaeological culture differed from American ones – particularly that of the Midwestern Taxonomic Method – in that Childe viewed the data he was studying functionally.[6] American archaeologists, on the other hand, were preoccupied with typology, and tried to define cultural units by measuring similarities and differences quantitatively. Later, however, as they grew more aware of the limitations of such pseudo-objectivity and of the importance of a functionalist approach, they paid increasing attention to Childe's work.[7]

Yet, after Childe had published *The Dawn of European Civilization* and *The Aryans*, he decided that a concern with ethnic history was essentially non-explanatory. He also wholly repudiated the idea that qualitative differences among languages might be a significant force shaping prehistory. It might have been expected that this development would have aligned his thinking more closely with the ecological and economic concerns of Cyril Fox, O. G. S. Crawford, Mortimer Wheeler, Grahame Clark and Stuart Piggott, whose work was revolutionizing British prehistory. Yet Childe never warmed to this approach, although he incorporated many of its findings into his interpretations of European prehistory.

This appears to have been because Childe continued to view the typological study of artefacts as being the most important archaeological activity. This method had originally been applied to the study of museum specimens, often with only minimal reference to their archaeological context. Because of this he was also not inclined to play an active role in the application of new techniques of analysis, such as palynology, to the interpretation of archaeological data or to be greatly interested in the development of new techniques for excavating sites and recording archaeological information. Between 1920 and 1940 developments along these lines radically expanded the kinds of data that were available to archaeologists.[8] Excavations, such as that at Star Carr, also highlighted the limitations of data that had been collected earlier. Clark has noted in respect of his own book, *Prehistoric Europe*, the disadvantages that were involved in using old data to investigate new problems.[9] That Childe's research lacked a basis in innovative field work must be seen as both a cause and a consequence of the channelling of his interests along different lines from those of his most prominent British contemporaries.

Another reason is that, although Childe was a materialist, he was much more interested in what Christopher Hawkes has called 'the more specifically human' rather than in 'the more generically animal' side of human behaviour.[10] As someone who had actively engaged in politics as a young man, he was perhaps naturally attracted to studying ideas and social relationships rather than to the details of how prehistoric people had fed and clothed themselves. This attitude may also be reflected in his treatment of technology as a system of ideas, rather than as components in an adaptive strategy, an orientation that is otherwise hard to reconcile with Childe's functional rather than normative view of culture. His lack of more than a superficial interest in adaptation also found expression in his view of hunter-gatherers as all being much alike: 'parasitic', poor and dependent on nature. Even when he later took note of 'rich' hunting and gathering societies, he dismissed them as irrelevant dead-ends. Nor did he venture beyond conventional generalities about slash and burn cultivation and irrigation agriculture to consider the details of specific regimes. The only handicrafts that he examined closely were bronze-working and to a lesser degree carpentry. Even in his treatment of these, his emphasis was more sociological than technological.

Childe's original contributions to the study of prehistoric economies were very limited, although his work drew more attention to certain theories, such as the desiccation hypothesis, than these might otherwise have received. The main value of his economic approach was that it encouraged archaeologists to believe that their data could serve as a basis for understanding the economic, and perhaps even the social and ideological aspects of prehistoric societies. This had been an ambition of early evolutionary archaeologists such as Daniel Wilson, but had been lost sight of, as these archaeologists became increasingly preoccupied with treating artefacts as index fossils that could be used to define specific evolutionary stages and with using loose ethnographic analogies, rather than archaeological data, to define the cultural content of these stages.

EVOLUTION

Today, especially in the United States, much of the interpretation of archaeological data is geared to an evolutionary perspective that once again assumes certain types of social organization and belief systems to be correlated with particular modes of subsistence. It is, however, an evolutionism that, following a brief period of optimism at the end of World War II, no longer takes endless progress for granted.[11] This pessimism has much in common with the particularistic, antievolutionary attitudes that prevailed in the social sciences during the first half of the twentieth century, and that Childe at first largely accepted. Yet it was Childe's works asserting cultural progress in the 1930s and 1940s that brought him world fame as an interpreter of archaeological data. *Man Makes Himself* and *What Happened in History* were born out of Childe's concern with a deepening political crisis that he, as well as many others, feared might destroy Western civilization.

His desire to establish the pathological and transient character of National Socialism led him to draw more deeply than hitherto upon Marxism, a philosophy that had preserved more elements of the rationalism and optimism of the Enlightenment (and of early evolutionary archaeology) than any other system of analysis had done.

Childe's efforts to rekindle belief in the reality of progress won him a following among American archaeologists who were dissatisfied with the manner in which their discipline was concerned only with cultural chronologies and problems of artefact classification. Either directly or indirectly his writings helped to inspire American archaeologists interested in the Near East, such as Robert Braidwood and Robert McC. Adams, or in the New World, such as Richard MacNeish, to undertake major projects of research aimed at shedding more light on the origins of food-production and the rise of urban societies. In the 1950s, as Childe's work became more widely known in America, he was accorded respect, along with Julian Steward and Leslie White, as one of the key figures promoting the development of evolutionary anthropology.[12] In spite of this, Childe's position on cultural evolution was and remains misunderstood in the United States.

Childe was a materialist, but unlike White he was not a technological determinist. He occasionally toyed with the idea that the means of production, or even something as narrow (but accessible to archaeological recovery) as cutting tools, might ultimately determine social evolution. Yet he always ended up assigning a creative role to the mode rather than to the means of production. He also did not minimize the importance of social and ideological factors, at least when it came to thwarting or retarding progressive development.

Childe differed from his popular stereotype as an evolutionist by treating diffusion as an integral part of evolution. He saw diffusion as helping to offset the divergence that resulted from cultural drift and adaptation to new environments. Yet, while he treated Europe and the Near East as a single diffusion area, he stressed that the social impact of particular technologies was different in Europe from what it had been in the Near East. He also viewed technologies as affecting the societies into which they diffused very differently from those in which they were invented. This is a problem of understanding cultural variation to which contemporary evolutionists have paid very little attention.

Yet today there is some evidence of renewed awareness of the important role that cultural contact has played in shaping the archaeological record, and cultural development generally. It is once again being questioned whether any surviving hunting and gathering societies are so untouched by neighbouring, more advanced peoples that they can provide an example of what hunting and gathering cultures were like, prior to Neolithic times.[13] Morton Fried has argued that tribes, as generally understood by ethnologists, are products of acculturation to expanding state systems.[14] It is also being realized that the native cultures of eastern North America not only cultivated plants of Mesoamerican origin, but also shared with that region a variety of political and religious traits, including a human sacrificial complex, the origins of which remain obscure. It has not yet been determined how these influences shaped the development of the indigenous societies of North America, and made them different from what they would have been had they shared only food crops with Mesoamerica.[15] Finally the distinction between primary and secondary civilizations, maintained by many evolutionists, tacitly acknowledges the importance of culture contact and diffusion. Thus Childe's concerns remain with us, despite the best efforts of a new generation of extreme unilinear evolutionists.

Childe was at least as interested in why societies did not change or evolve in a progressive manner as with why they did. He saw culture as developing in a series of surges and recessions that could be explained largely in societal terms. Undue emphasis on religion was treated as both a symptom and a cause of social decline. Childe's views of social change incorporated many facets of Marxism. But his concern with the forces impeding social change had grown out of the romantic pessimism that had influenced the social sciences in Europe since the 1880s.

Childe has been wrongly characterized as a unilinear evolutionist.[16] Yet he divided both hunter-gathering and Neolithic societies into progressive and dead-end types, and contrasted the temple cities of Mesopotamia with the divine monarchy of Egypt. His differences with Henri Frankfort did not concern whether or not Egypt and Mesopotamia were examples of parallel evolution, but whether, as Frankfort claimed, the evident differences between them resulted from unconscious and largely unchangeable archetypes, a proposition that Childe as a Marxist was unable to accept. When we consider Childe's even more radical differentiation of cultural development in Europe from what had occurred in the Near East, it becomes clear that his view of evolution was at least as multilinear as was that of Julian Steward. Childe himself saw it as being multilinear to the point of being historical. There is no straight line connecting Childe's work with the unilinear stages of Soviet archaeology.[17] Nor is there any substance to Steward's suggestion that Childe sought only to formulate cultural development in terms of universal stages, rather than, like Steward, seeking to determine the causes of cultural change.[18]

Childe was widely criticized for calling the transitions between his major stages of social development 'revolutions'. He defined a revolution as the 'culmination of a progressive change in the economic structure and social organisation of communities that causes, or was accompanied by, a dramatic increase in the population affected'.[19] He admitted that he generally assumed prehistoric changes in population, rather than demonstrating them from the archaeological record. Nevertheless he valued the concept of revolution as according with Engels' principle of quantitative change giving rise to qualitative change that resolved previous contradictions. American archaeologists admitted to being influenced by Childe's concept of revolution, but in general rejected the notion of radical social transformations in favour of a gradualist view of social change, such as was expressed in Robert Redfield's concept of transformation.[20] American archaeologists also criticized Childe for failing to pay sufficient attention to archaeological data from the New World, which suggested that the Urban Revolution had been slow and gradual there.[21] Childe countered American objections by arguing that he did not regard revolutions as being 'sudden violent catastrophes',[22] yet he continued to treat them as events involving accelerated change. Today his concept of revolution seems less out-of-date than it did a decade ago. Robert McC. Adams has criticized archaeologists for viewing all processes of change as taking place in graceful, uninterrupted and irreversible trajectories. He points out that in the early civilizations changes often took place in 'dizzyingly abrupt shifts'.[23] Colin Renfrew has attempted to come to grips with the same problem by applying to archaeology the 'Catastrophe Theory' developed by the French mathematician René Thom.[24]

While Childe cited many instances of social change as responses to what he called contradictions, he disappointed some Marxists by failing to analyse even the hierarchical early civilizations in terms of overt class conflict. In general he tended to view societies as being socially integrated, and avoided discussing social change in terms of conscious conflicts of interest. This may have been the result in part of his desire as an archaeologist to avoid formulating explanations in terms of human actors and their subjective intentions. Yet class has been described as Marx's most important concept for mediating the subjective and objective sides of the dialectic.[25] Although Childe was interested in change, like contemporary British social anthropologists, he found the idealization of the functionally integrated society, as proposed by Durkheim, and later by Malinowski and Radcliffe-Brown, a congenial concept, as presumably did many Fabian socialists. Thus he tended to conceive of his revolutions as mechanisms for resolving economic contradictions in the absence of overt class conflict.

CAUSALITY

The last fifteen years of Childe's life were dominated by a continuing dialogue between Childe the Marxist and Childe the archaeologist. To a large degree this dialogue centred on two main topics that he had first clearly defined in *Man Makes Himself* and *What Happened in History*: the development of scientific knowledge and the evolution of society. Although this dialogue was pursued in a series of published books and papers, it was essentially a private one, which most contemporary British archaeologists did not try to understand and often refused to take seriously. The main criticism that contributed to the further refinement and development of Childe's ideas came in the form of reviews and comments by American anthropologists, and these were limited in scope.

Childe viewed his work of this period as an attempt to understand the dynamics underlying social change, especially long-range trends in society. Julian Steward described as appallingly naive Childe's claim that social evolution had eliminated the possibility of assuming that supernatural interpositions were necessary to explain the evolution of culture.[26] What Steward did not understand was that in previous studies Childe had included under the rubric of the supernatural any deterministic explanation of cultural change, including environmental and technological determinism. Childe insisted that history was a self-determining process. It was a product of orderly and explicable patterns of behaviour, but ones that were capable of producing genuine novelties, and which therefore could not be accounted for by the application of a few formulae. Because of this it was also possible to explain the past without being able to predict (in any significant sense) the future. Childe had no sympathy for views that equated explanation and prediction, at least in respect of human behaviour.

In 1946 Childe believed that one of the aims of archaeology was to search for universal laws that would explain human behaviour and cultural change. This implied that these laws should correlate with human nature, universal properties of social systems, or in modern terminology with properties of systems generally. As a Marxist, however, he was committed to believing that human nature was not fixed, but that it and the rules governing society changed as society experienced fundamental alterations. Because of this, he came to view the search for universally valid laws as unacceptably teleological.

Archaeologists have been unable to agree about the nature of causality. Some of them may still deny that human behaviour can be explained with reference to any sort of laws. Yet this extreme version of the doctrine of free will now has few vocal champions. In America archaeological opinion is divided between 'law and order' evolutionists, who argue that the crucial variables affecting human behaviour are few in number and can easily be identified, and those who view causality as being much more complex and its underlying regularities less easily discernable. It has been observed that the latter tend to prefer a systems theory approach to the analysis of archaeological data.[27] Both of these groups have in common that they are searching for universally valid laws. Yet, if Childe's analysis is even partially correct, the search for such laws may have limited value for the social sciences. His thinking, and the Marxist analysis on which it is based, deserve more careful consideration than they have received so far. He was proposing not only a more inductive approach to the explanation of human behaviour, but also an alternative to the assumptions about causality on which all of the thinking of the New Archaeology has been based.

Although Stalin's repudiation of Marrism in 1950 may have encouraged Childe to interpret Marxism in a freer and more personal fashion, he had begun to reassess a Marxist approach to archaeological analysis in print at least three years earlier.[28] His dissatisfaction with Soviet archaeology, far from indicating disenchantment with Marxism, represented a renewed and more perceptive interest in it. His earlier Marxism had not been mechanical or dogmatic as some critics have suggested. Instead he had applied it only perfunctorily to his interpretation of the archaeological record. His thinking had remained coloured to a large degree by the particularizing, antievolutionary attitudes of the social sciences of his day. Ravetz has shrewdly observed that the keynote of Childe's renewed effort to apply Marxism to the study of archaeological data was his insistence that these data must constitute the starting point of archaeological theory.[29] Childe criticized Soviet archaeologists for assuming in advance what archaeological facts have to prove.[30] He also defended German archaeologists of the National Socialist period who reported their archaeological findings accurately, in spite of the conclusions they attempted to draw from them.[31]

Childe increasingly came to treat the development of society as being the central focus of historical and archaeological explanations. He viewed social organization and social relationships as the structural matrix in relation to which all cultural change had to be explained.

Although Marxist in origin and concerned with explaining change, the structuralist basis of this conceptualization and the terminology that he used to express it were close enough to those of British social anthropology to be acceptable to non-Marxist readers. The position that he adopted in *The Prehistory of European Society* was similar in many respects to that evolved by Willey in his study of settlement patterns in the Virú Valley. Both archaeologists interpreted cultural remains in terms of their relationship to a changing social system, rather than viewing social and political organization as aspects of culture, as archaeologists normally had done prior to that time. Their work helped to lay the foundations for the societal approach that has since been adopted by Robert McC. Adams, Colin Renfrew and many other archaeologists.[32] Thus, having established the archaeological culture as the key operational concept in archaeology in 1925, at the end of his career Childe helped to initiate a movement that sought to remedy the deficiences of that concept by supplementing or replacing it with the concept of society.

Childe was criticized in his lifetime for adopting a 'rational-utilitarian' viewpoint that over-simplified his subject matter. Thorkild Jacobsen complained that Childe wrote 'as if the invention and introduction of writing were a measure proposed by a pan-Mesopotamian congress of priests and adopted ... in consideration of its present and future utility'.[33] Adams also objected to Childe inferring 'utilitarian motives' that were not supported by written evidence in his explanations of the rise of civilization in Egypt and Mesopotamia.[34] Yet, however much Childe was inclined to prefer utilitarian explanations, his position was not a naive one. After due consideration he concluded that magic and religion were manifestations of false consciousness, that scientific knowledge (both practical and theoretical) constituted true consciousness, and that the latter alone could be understood to any significant degree using archaeological data. He attempted, perhaps with a certain element of conscious sophistry, to rationalize the apparent inability of archaeology to understand the nature of individual systems of religion and magic by claiming that only true consciousness was cumulative, and therefore relevant for understanding how past developments had contributed to shaping the present.

Peter Gathercole has argued that by adopting this position Childe forsook the methods of both anthropology and Marxism.[35] There can be little doubt that Childe's desire to use archaeological data to study the prehistoric development of scientific knowledge by determining the economic, social and utilitarian significance of innovations is far removed from the ethnologist's desire to study cultures in their entirety. An important objective of the latter approach is to determine the meaning that such cultures had for their members. Yet studying the prehistoric development of scientific knowledge was only one of the goals that Childe proposed for archaeology. Moreover, as Gathercole points out, some Marxists acknowledge that information and skills that permit the modification and control of the material world by their very nature transcend the limitations of class interests.[36] Childe evidently regarded what he was doing in this light rather than as a repudiation of Marxist theories of knowledge. He not only demonstrated that archaeological data might constitute a major element in an expanded and enriched history of science, but also carried out more substantive research in this area than in any other. While prehistoric archaeology in general has not developed closer links with the history of science since Childe's time, his proposal remains worthy of further consideration, especially as a result of the development of industrial archaeology.

Though Childe's Marxist orientation might have inclined him to believe in the essential similarity of societies at the same level of development, he never relinquished his suspicions about the validity of broad ethnographic analogies. These suspicions had been characteristic of archaeology since the abandonment of nineteenth-century concepts of unilinear evolution. Childe's early knowledge of ethnology was derived from Durkheimian sociology and from reading Hobhouse, Wheeler and Ginsberg's *The Material Culture and Social Institutions of Simpler Peoples*. Childe's contacts with American anthropology came too late for its demonstration of the value of ethnographic information for interpreting archaeological data to stimulate more than a superficial interest in ethnology. Although his growing awareness of the implications of a functionalist analysis of society convinced him that the free variation between different facets (or sub-systems) of culture was less than social scientists formerly had believed, he continued to use ethnographic data only occasionally and informally to infer aspects of prehistoric cultures that were not attested directly in the archaeological record. Steward hoped in vain that Childe's search for regularities in human behaviour would lead him to pay more attention to anthropologists who post-dated L. H. Morgan, and to undertake more comparative studies using archaeological data from East Asia and the New World, as well as from Europe and the Near East.[37] For many reasons Childe was not to be poured into the mould of American neo-evolutionists.

From the outset of his career Childe had been more aware than had most archaeologists that an axe was an instrument for felling trees as well as the expression of an historical tradition. Or, as Braidwood put it, he never forgot the 'Indian behind the artifact'. This view found new force and direction when his first direct contact with Soviet archaeology in 1935 led him to expand his functional view of artefacts to become a functional view of cultures. For the rest of his career Childe endeavoured to use the skills that he had at his disposal to 'extort' information about as many facets of culture as possible from the archaeological record. His original concern with prehistoric movements of peoples was supplemented by an attempt first to analyse their prehistoric economic behaviour, and then to study their social organization and practical knowledge. Although his functional interests were reflected in his assembling data about settlement patterns and trying to calculate population sizes, they did not lead him to collect new kinds of information in the context of his field work, such as might have helped to answer the questions he was posing. Instead his pan-European orientation compelled him to rely on an existing corpus of data, much of which concerned artefacts and remained typological; and hence was no longer adequate to his needs. Eventually this led him to believe that archaeological data might be inadequate to answer many of the questions he was asking.

Throughout his working life Childe's reputation rested on broad syntheses rather than on the depth of research in any one area. Of the many archaeological projects that he carried out in Scotland, only Skara Brae played a significant role in his intellectual development. As Irving Rouse has pointed out, Childe kept his conceptual tools as simple as possible and was inclined to work intuitively, a tendency that in general has been more characteristic of British than of American archaeologists. Childe's key concept remained that of the archaeological culture, which was temporally aligned with other cultures by means of synchronisms. He made no use of more complex integrative concepts, such as horizon and tradition.[38] He also espoused only a limited number of explanations of cultural processes, some of which tended to become *idées fixes*. These were often based on feeble evidence, and were never tested against ethnographic data. Perhaps the most influential of these explanations was his concept of the independent, itinerant metallurgists of Bronze Age Europe.

In spite of recent challenges to Childe's interpretations of European prehistory and a growing realization of the weaknesses of the concepts upon which many of these interpretations were based, much of Childe's view of the orientation of archaeology remains central to the research of the discipline. Although he was not the only archaeologist who, by the 1930s, had realized the importance of viewing archaeological evidence not merely as isolated fossils from the past, but as parts of functioning social and cultural systems,[39] his writings played a major role in expounding and disseminating this approach. Because Childe was a Marxist, and because he understood that the main strength of the archaeological record was its time perspective, he rejected the analysis of these systems as if they were static entities. This ran counter to the practice of social anthropology at that time. He made the explanation of how systems change central to his later work. Some of his explanations anticipated the systems formulations that are now fashionable in archaeology. In this, and in his pervasive materialism, Childe realized some of the key concepts, and even the nomenclature, that have revolutionized American archaeology since 1962. While Lewis Binford's ideas developed independently out of the American archaeological tradition, some of Childe's programmatic writings (such as 'Archaeology and Anthropology' published in the *Southwestern Journal of Anthropology*), and his better known evolutionary treatises helped to direct that tradition at least to a limited degree in the direction of the New Archaeology.

On two related topics Childe's thinking diverged from that of the New Archaeology. He hoped, as many New Archaeologists do, that archaeological generalizations would contribute, along with those from the other social sciences, to what he thought of as the more rational control of our social environment. In spite of this he did not accept as valid for the social sciences the positivist equating of explanation and prediction that underlies the deductive approach advocated by many New Archaeologists. Childe frequently used a deductive mode of explanation but, as a matter of principle, opted for a 'mixed strategy' in which inductive and deductive approaches were both employed. He saw archaeological data as providing a basis for understanding human behaviour and the dynamics of social change. Yet in his 'Valediction' he pronounced that the future of archaeology lay with history rather than with the production of generalizations claiming the dignity of natural laws.[40] His rejection of the principle that generalizations about human behaviour could be achieved apart from their historical context did not signify his rejection of the attempt to explain human behaviour and human history. Childe did not view history and the social sciences as antithetical pursuits; rather he saw history as an integral part of the social sciences, just as palaeontology was seen as an integral part of the biological sciences. The scientific approach to the study of history that he espoused was based on the premise that all human behaviour, though modifiable, was also potentially explainable. History remained a study of the particular, insofar as the individual events that it sought to account for were sufficiently complex that each constituted a unique concurrence of lawful processes.

Childe's assertion in his 'Valediction' that he regarded the explanation of history as an ultimate goal, to which the formulation of laws of human behaviour was subordinate and contributory, was the opposite of the position adopted by American archaeologists, such as W. W. Taylor, Gordon Willey and Philip Phillips, who saw historical reconstruction as only one step towards the ultimate goal of explaining human behaviour.[41] The explanation of these diametrically opposed positions involves more than the fact that American archaeologists have equated history with chronology and hence regard it as descriptive, while Childe viewed it as scientific and explanatory. As we have already noted, the Americans view ultimate knowledge about human behaviour as taking the form of a series of generalizations about human behaviour that are valid regardless of time and place. Childe, as a Marxist, strongly doubted that anything about human nature was fixed except change itself; hence he regarded such generalizations with great scepticism. In his view, in attempting to explain how historical changes occur, history became an independent science with its own laws. These transcend the laws of most of the other social sciences, which usually apply only to one mode of production or to one stage of social development. They may also be generically akin to the sorts of regularities now discussed under the rubric of general systems theory. Childe defined laws as being shorthand descriptions of real processes. This led him to argue that, while the most decisive aspects of historical processes may be isolated and explained, no general formula can disclose the order of history fully; 'that can only be reproduced in the concrete whole of history itself which no book and no library of books, however vast, could contain'.[42]

While Childe's critique of universal laws remains undeveloped, it was based on a philosophical tradition as venerable as that of logical positivism. It represents a powerful alternative to the view of causality held by the New Archaeologists and one which has strong methodological implications. Its significance is highlighted by the failure of New Archaeologists to agree about higher level generalizations and by Binford's recent advocacy of middle-range ones.[43] Whether Childe saw beyond the New Archaeology or mere mirages in the Promised Land remains to be determined.

Throughout his career Childe sought to answer what he regarded as being an historical question of major importance: what was unique about European society that even in prehistoric times made it a peculiar and individual manifestation of the human spirit? One may or may not regard this as a significant, or even a valid question. Yet it gave unity to Childe's work, and led him to investigate many questions. During the first half of the twentieth century, narrow concerns with defining archaeological cultures and explaining the relationships among them by mechanically invoking concepts, such as diffusion and migration, came to threaten both European and American archaeology with total irrelevance for understanding broader social and intellectual problems. Childe realized this, and reacted against it by trying to interpret in functional terms what could be learned about the economy, society and practical knowledge of prehistoric cultures. His work was in the forefront of developments that have transformed archaeology.

Yet today American archaeology, in spite of its remarkable accomplishments during the past two decades, is threatened by a new form of irrelevance. Elsewhere I have noted that the New Archaeology 'consists of widely scattered individuals and groups of individuals innovating along many lines, and in respect of problems that are very different from one another. They are united by certain common perspectives, but as an act of conviction or faith rather than from focusing on common problems. In Durkheimian terms, the unity of the New Archaeology is mechanical not organic'.[44] This has come about as a result of archaeologists seeking to study in detail isolated aspects of the archaeological record, either as an exercise in technical or theoretical virtuosity, or in order to establish general 'laws' concerning fragments of human behaviour. These disparate studies threaten archaeology with intellectual as well as social inconsequence. This situation is made worse by the fact that, when used only to generalize about human behaviour, archaeological data suffer by comparison with ethnographic or sociological data. The argument frequently used to justify such an approach – that archaeology is what archaeologists do – begs the question. If archaeology is to be more than intellectual butterfly-collecting, it must adopt goals that are both appropriate to its data and relevant for understanding the human condition.

In his later work Childe concentrated on two goals of this sort: understanding the development of technology and of social organization. He studied these problems, not by analysing isolated fragments of archaeological data, but by trying to understand historical sequences of development in terms of their social, economic, political and ecological implications. At the present time, archaeological research expends more economic and human resources than ever before. Although not without its shortcomings, Childe's work challenges modern archaeologists to shape goals for their discipline that in the long run will enable archaeology to make a distinctive contribution to the social sciences. It is surely a measure of Childe's intellectual stature that, in spite of the buffeting of two decades, the major questions that he dealt with at the end of his career are now more critical to the future of archaeology than they were when he first raised them.

Chapter I

1 Renfrew 1969: 169; Spriggs 1977: 5–9.
2 Daniel 1958: 66.
3 Braidwood 1958: 736.
4 Steward 1953a.
5 Clark 1976: 6.
6 Piggott 1958a: 312.
7 Movius 1957: 42.
8 Braidwood 1958: 733.
9 Piggott 1958a: 312.
10 Wheeler 1957.
11 Mulvaney 1957: 93.
12 Ravetz 1959; Allen 1967; Gathercole 1971, 1976; Clark 1976; unpublished studies known to me include Gathercole 1974, 1975; Green 1976; Wheatley 1972.
13 Gathercole 1976: 5.
14 Kuhn 1970.
15 Piggott 1958a: 309.
16 Piggott 1958b: 77.
17 Ravetz 1959.
18 Gathercole 1976.
19 Childe 1958b: 69.
20 Renfrew 1969: 167.
21 Childe 1936a: vii.
22 Childe 1935a: xi.
23 Childe 1928: xiii–xiv.
24 Daniel 1965: x.
25 Piggott 1958a: 308.
26 Ravetz 1959: 56.
27 Daniel 1965: xi.
28 Braidwood 1958: 734.
29 Rouse 1958: 82.
30 Daniel 1958: 66.
31 Artsikhovskii 1973: 247.
32 Miller 1956: 151.
33 Thomson 1949; Ravetz 1959: 66.
34 Morris 1957.
35 Dutt 1957a, b.
36 Gathercole 1976: 5.
37 Gathercole 1974.
38 Ravetz 1959: 65–66.
39 Wheeler 1957.
40 Piggott 1958a: 311–12; 1971: 219.

41 Daniel 1958: 66–67.
42 Daniel 1977b.
43 Clark 1976: 3.
44 Spriggs 1977: 5–7.
45 Rouse 1958: 82.
46 Ravetz 1959.
47 Mulvaney 1957: 94.
48 Gathercole 1971: 231–32.
49 Gathercole 1976: 5.
50 Cf. Piggott 1958a: 310 and Clark 1976: 1.
51 Piggott 1958a: 310; Mallowan 1977: 235.
52 Lindsay 1958: 136.
53 Clark 1976: 2–3.
54 Piggott 1958a: 310–11.
55 Clark 1976: 3; Gathercole 1976: 5.
56 Lindsay 1958: 135–36.
57 Daniel 1977b.
58 Wheeler 1957.
59 Braidwood 1958: 735.
60 Piggott 1958a: 312.
61 Green 1976.
62 Piggott 1958a: 311.

Chapter II

1 Daniel 1975: 13–40.
2 Harris 1968: 34.
3 Klindt-Jensen 1975: 49–52.
4 Daniel 1975: 78, 92.
5 Nilsson 1868.
6 Wilson 1851.
7 Daniel 1975: 89–93; cf. Childe 1955a. Daniel's material was originally published in 1950.
8 Daniel 1975: 45.
9 Childe 1932a: 207.
10 Daniel 1975: 57–67, 85–121.
11 Harris 1968: 144.
12 Lubbock 1882, 1913.
13 Pitt-Rivers 1906.
14 Trevelyan 1949, Volume IV: 119.
15 Collingwood 1946: 146.
16 G. E. Smith 1933: 235.
17 Myres 1911: 9.

18 Petrie 1939.
19 Reisner 1906: 5–6.
20 Montelius 1899.
21 Kossinna 1911, 1926; Klejn 1974.
22 Rouse 1972: 72.
23 G. E. Smith 1923; Perry 1923, 1924.
24 Wilson 1851: 353, 359.
25 Chantre 1875–76.
26 Daniel 1975 (1950): 110–11; cf. Childe 1953a: 8.
27 Daniel 1975: 108, 125.
28 A. J. Evans 1890; Childe 1953a: 9; Abercromby 1902.
29 Daniel 1975: 149–50.
30 Ratzel 1882–91.
31 Kossinna 1911.
32 Daniel 1975: 78, 100.
33 Gradmann 1906.
34 Childe 1958b: 70; J. Evans 1956: 372.
35 Daniel 1975: 305–8.
36 Pumpelly 1908: 65–66.
37 Childe 1953a: 13–14.
38 Daniel 1975: 180.
39 *Ibid.*
40 A. J. Evans 1896; Myres 1933: 284; Daniel 1975: 180–81.
41 Myres 1911.

Chapter III

1 Piggott 1958a: 305. For other biographical data, see Piggott 1971 and *Times* Obituary 1957.
2 Childe 1958b: 69; J. Evans 1977.
3 Clark 1976: 4.
4 Childe 1958b: 69.
5 Daniel 1975: 233–34.
6 Childe 1915.
7 Dutt 1957a.
8 Lindsay 1958: 134–35.
9 F. B. Smith 1964: v.
10 Childe 1923.
11 F. B. Smith 1964: viii.
12 *Ibid.*, vii.

13 Gathercole 1974: 3.
14 Childe 1923: xi.
15 *Ibid.*, 179.
16 F. B. Smith 1964: v.
17 Dutt 1957a.
18 F. B. Smith 1964: ix.
19 Childe 1958b: 70.
20 Childe 1929: v.
21 Childe 1956e: 5.
22 Delaporte 1925; Moret and Davy 1926; Homo 1926. Childe also translated Borovka's *Scythian Art* from German (I. F. Smith 1956: 296).
23 Childe 1922a.
24 Childe 1922b.
25 Childe 1925b.
26 Childe 1925a, 1926.
27 Childe 1925a: xiii.
28 Cf. Childe 1958b: 69 and 1958c: 2.
29 Fraser 1926.
30 Crawford 1926.
31 Piggott 1958b: 76.
32 Fox 1923: 18; Peake 1922; Peake and Fleure 1927a, b, c, d.
33 Daniel 1958: 66.
34 Clark 1976: 5.
35 Childe 1930a: 42.
36 Childe 1932a: 207.
37 Cf. Childe 1929: 414 and 1937a: 11.
38 Childe 1950a: 4; Childe and Burkitt 1932: 187.
39 Clark 1976: 10.
40 Childe 1929: 417.
41 *Ibid.*, v–vi.
42 Binford 1965.
43 Childe 1929: 248.
44 *Ibid.*, vii; Childe 1930a: 42–43.
45 Childe 1956a: 33.
46 Childe 1929: vi–vii.
47 Childe 1930a: 43–45.
48 Childe 1935b: 1–2; 1956a: 33–34, 38.
49 Childe 1929: following p. 418.
50 Childe and Burkitt 1932.
51 Rouse 1972: 116–18.
52 Childe 1929: vii.
53 Childe 1935b: 7.
54 Childe 1922a.
55 Childe 1929: v–vi.
56 Fox 1923: 18, 67, 236, 317, 318.
57 Peake 1922: 31, 32, 66; Crawford 1921: 78–79.

58 Myres 1923a: 2.
59 Myres 1923b: 67, 71.
60 Daniel 1975: 247.
61 Childe 1958b: 70.
62 Childe 1956a: 28.
63 Childe 1935b: 3.
64 Childe 1929: vi.
65 Childe 1925a: 216; 1926: 167.
66 Piggott 1958b: 77.
67 For an example, see Henri Berr's 'Foreword' to Moret and Davy 1926.
68 Childe 1928: 227; 1930a: 10, 12
69 Childe 1925a: 150.
70 Childe 1922a: 255.
71 Childe 1926: 149.
72 Childe 1926: 200; 1929: vii.
73 Childe 1938a, 1939b.
74 Childe 1939a; cf. Renfrew 1973a; 39–41.
75 Renfrew 1973a: 36–37.
76 Childe 1925a: 216; Letter of V. G. Childe to R. J. Braidwood, 1 August 1945.
77 Childe 1926: 198–200.
78 Childe 1925a: 226.
79 *Ibid.*, xiii.
80 *Ibid.*, 132–37; Childe 1926: 193.
81 Childe 1926: 193.
82 Childe 1958b: 70.
83 Childe 1926: 101. Childe cites Peake 1922: 55–60. See also Childe 1946c and 1948.
84 Childe 1925a: 285.
85 *Ibid.*, 271–301.
86 Daniel 1975: 343; the concept of Four Empires is also discussed by Collingwood 1946: 57.
87 Childe 1925a: 137, 171, 195, 200.
88 *Ibid.*, xiv–xv.
89 *Ibid.*, xiv, 29.
90 *Ibid.*, 151.
91 *Ibid.*, 302.
92 *Ibid.*, 108.
93 Childe 1926: 116.
94 *Ibid.*, 210, 136.
95 Childe 1925a: 242, 259.
96 Peake 1922: 61.
97 Childe 1926: 143–44.
98 *Ibid.*, 3.
99 *Ibid.*, 3–4.
100 *Ibid.*, 4.
101 *Ibid.*, 5.
102 *Ibid.*, 4.
103 *Ibid.*, 211.

104 *Ibid.*
105 *Ibid.*
106 Childe 1925c; see also Childe 1933a: 417.
107 Childe 1940a: 3.
108 Childe 1958b: 70.
109 McKern 1939.
110 Childe 1926: 3–4.
111 Childe 1929: v, 413.

CHAPTER IV

1 Childe 1930a: 240–47.
2 Childe 1958b: 70.
3 Childe 1928, 1929, 1930a, 1934a.
4 Green 1976.
5 Notebook No. 53 of V. G. Childe deposited at the Institute of Archaeology, University of London.
6 Childe 1929: 1, 9.
7 *Ibid.*, 20–21, 414.
8 *Ibid.*, 392.
9 *Ibid.*, 314.
10 E.g., *ibid.*, 68–97.
11 Cf. *ibid.*, vi and pp. 34–35.
12 Renfrew 1973a: 97.
13 Childe 1958b: 70; see also Childe 1925a: 13, 20.
14 See Chapter II.
15 Childe 1929: 3, 161.
16 Childe 1930a: 225. This principle was first enunciated in print in Fox 1926.
17 E.g., Childe 1925a: 193, 200.
18 Childe 1929: 31.
19 *Ibid.*, 97, 215–22, 414–15.
20 *Ibid.*, 109–10.
21 *Ibid.*, 240.
22 *Ibid.*, 238.
23 *Ibid.*, 246.
24 Childe 1944a: 62.
25 Childe 1929: 247.
26 *Ibid.*, 413.
27 Daniel 1977a: 3–4. About Abercromby's quarrel with the Society of Antiquaries of Scotland, see Piggott and Robertson 1977, item 91.
28 Piggott 1958a: 307.
29 Childe 1947b: 49; 1953a: 9.
30 Piggott 1958a: 307.
31 Hall 1930.
32 Childe 1951a: 22.
33 Childe 1935b: 7; cf. Peake 1927, and Peake and Fleure 1927c.
34 Childe 1928: 2.
35 Childe 1944a: 12.

36 Childe 1928:41.
37 Peake and Fleure 1927c:14.
38 Childe 1928:42.
39 Perry 1924: 29–32. Cherry's paper was published in 1921 in the *Journal of Agriculture* of the State of Victoria.
40 Childe 1928:42–44.
41 *Ibid.*, 46.
42 *Ibid.*, 105.
43 *Ibid.*, 170.
44 *Ibid.*, 197, 221.
45 *Ibid.*, 9–10.
46 *Ibid.*, 218–19.
47 Frankfort 1956.
48 Childe 1928:169.
49 *Ibid.*, 170; cf. Adams 1972.
50 Childe 1928:221.
51 *Ibid.*, 222.
52 Childe 1950a:40–41.
53 Childe 1928:221.
54 *Ibid.*, 221–22.
55 *Ibid.*, 221.
56 *Ibid.*
57 *Ibid.*, 3.
58 *Ibid.*, 11.
59 Childe 1929:274; 1930a:239
60 Childe 1928:2–3,
61 *Ibid.*, 10–11.
62 Childe 1940a:41.
63 Childe 1928:46.
64 *Ibid.*, 234–35.
65 *Ibid.*, 120, 144–45; cf. Emery 1961.
66 Childe 1928:120.
67 *Ibid.*, xiii.
68 Childe 1930a:60.
69 Childe 1958b:71.
70 Childe 1930a:xi.
71 Childe 1951a:24–25.
72 Childe 1930a:23–24.
73 *Ibid.*, 10.
74 *Ibid.*, 24–27.
75 *Ibid.*, 4; Childe 1936a:136.
76 Childe 1951a:25.
77 Childe 1930a:10.
78 Childe 1942a:163.
79 Childe 1930a:12.
80 *Ibid.*, 10.
81 *Ibid.*, 39.
82 *Ibid.*, 8–11.
83 *Ibid.*, 17.
84 Childe 1951a:26.
85 Childe 1930a:3–7.
86 *Ibid.*, 1–2.
87 *Ibid.*, 18.
88 *Ibid.*, 146.
89 *Ibid.*, 168.
90 *Ibid.*, 193.
91 Fox 1923; Childe 1935b:8.

92 Childe 1930a:167.
93 *Ibid.*, 14–15.
94 *Ibid.*, 238.
95 Childe 1934a:xv.
96 Childe 1958b:71.
97 Childe 1934a:42.
98 *Ibid.*, 41.
99 *Ibid.*, 296–97.
100 *Ibid.*, 284.
101 *Ibid.*, 298–301.
102 *Ibid.*, 150, 181.
103 *Ibid.*, 284.
104 *Ibid.*, 184.
105 *Ibid.*, 285, 287–88.
106 *Ibid.*, 291–92.
107 *Ibid.*, 300–1.
108 *Ibid.*, 290.
109 *Ibid.*, 292–93.
110 Hawkes 1954.
111 Trevelyan 1949, Volume III: 48–51.
112 Childe 1934a:186.
113 Hobhouse *et al.* 1915.
114 Rowlands 1971.
115 Childe 1940a:163, 180.
116 Childe 1958b:71.
117 Crawford 1921.
118 Childe 1934a:300–1.
119 *Ibid.*, 301.

CHAPTER V

1 Piggott 1958a: 307–8; Braidwood 1958: 734; Mulvaney 1957:94.
2 Letter of V. G. Childe to Mrs H. V. Evatt, 23 June 1931 (Flinders University Library, Adelaide, Australia).
3 Piggott 1958a:308.
4 Childe 1952c, 1956d.
5 Piggott 1958a:308.
6 Letter of V. G. Childe to Mrs H. V. Evatt, 23 June 1931.
7 Anderson 1886.
8 Childe 1935a:1.
9 *Ibid.*, xi.
10 Letter of V. G. Childe to R. J. Braidwood, 28 March 1945.
11 Childe 1931a.
12 For more detailed parallels, see Curwen 1938.
13 Mulvaney 1957:94.
14 Marwick 1932.
15 Childe 1931a:104, 181.
16 *Ibid.*, 163.
17 Piggott *et al.* 1936.
18 Childe 1938d.
19 Childe and Grant 1939, 1947.
20 Childe 1940a:84.

21 Childe 1943c.
22 H. Kilbride-Jones, personal communication, 2 April 1978.
23 Childe and Forde 1932; Childe 1933d, 1933e, 1936b, 1941b, 1941c.
24 Childe 1935d.
25 Childe 1935c; Childe and Thorneycroft 1938.
26 Childe 1938c.
27 Childe 1937d, 1954g.
28 Childe 1936c, 1938e.
29 Childe 1930c, 1931b, 1932b, 1933c, 1934b, 1937c.
30 Childe 1952c, 1956d.
31 Childe 1942d; cf. Renfrew 1973a: 132–37.
32 Piggott 1958a: 308; Clark 1976: 2.
33 Childe 1935a:xi.
34 Childe 1940a:v.
35 *Ibid.*, 9.
36 Childe 1935a:1.
37 Childe 1940a:252.
38 *Ibid.*, 1–2.
39 *Ibid.*, 7–11.
40 *Ibid.*, 42.
41 *Ibid.*, 206–7.
42 *Ibid.*, 30, 81.
43 Cf. Chapter IV, note 7.
44 Childe 1945b: 9.
45 Childe 1940a: 141–45.
46 *Ibid.*, 176–78.
47 Childe 1935a: 18, 116.
48 *Ibid.*, 113.
49 *Ibid.*, 56–57.
50 *Ibid.*, 24.
51 Childe 1934c.
52 Childe 1935a: 49–50.
53 Renfrew *et al.* 1976.
54 Childe 1935a: 52.
55 Childe 1940a: 46–47, 52–53, 69.
56 Childe 1935a: 60–61, 77–78.
57 *Ibid.*, 78.
58 *Ibid.*, 59–60.
59 Childe 1940a: 78.
60 Childe 1935b: 13–14.
61 Childe 1936a: 127–30.
62 Childe 1939a: 301–2.
63 Childe 1954a: 69.
64 Childe 1957a: 220.
65 Childe 1940a: 180.
66 *Ibid.*, 178–80.
67 *Ibid.*, 187.
68 *Ibid.*, 194.
69 Hawkes 1940.
70 Clark 1940.
71 Childe 1937a: 4.

72 Childe 1933a: 417.
73 Childe 1940a: 80.
74 Childe 1933a.

CHAPTER VI

1 Childe 1933b.
2 Childe 1933a.
3 Childe 1937a: 15.
4 Childe 1958b: 71–72. The same archaeologists are listed as having influenced Childe in Childe's letter to R.J. Braidwood, 1 August 1945.
5 Miller 1956: 73–84.
6 *Ibid.*, 75–89.
7 Tallgren 1936.
8 Clark 1936; Anonymous 1939.
9 Childe 1940b.
10 Miller 1956: 108–11.
11 Childe 1958b: 72.
12 Cf. Childe 1928: 11 and 1930a: 2.
13 Letter of V. G. Childe to R.J. Braidwood, 1 August 1945. On Engels' modifications of Morgan, see Leacock 1972: 13–14.
14 Childe 1958b: 72.
15 Farrington 1936, 1939.
16 Childe 1935b.
17 See also Childe 1946b: 246; 1951a: 167; 1956a: 157–58.
18 Childe 1958b: 72.
19 Childe 1946b: 250.
20 Childe 1944a: 78.
21 Childe 1935a: 21; 1935b: 12; 1942a: 15; 1946a: 47–50.
22 Childe 1946b: 250.
23 Childe 1936a: 9; 1947a: 65, 72.
24 Childe 1936a: 35–36; 1944a: 78–79; 1945a: 13.
25 Childe 1946b: 250.
26 Childe 1956a: 53.
27 Childe 1936a: 9.
28 Childe 1936a: 7; 1944c: 23; 1946b: 250; 1956a: 53.
29 Childe 1935b: 14.
30 Childe 1936a: 110.
31 Childe 1935b: 14.
32 Childe 1942a: 130.
33 Childe 1935b: 14; 1942a: 9–10.
34 Childe 1954a: 102, 118.
35 Childe 1947a: 75.
36 Childe 1942a: 11.
37 Childe 1936a: 146.
38 Childe 1942a: 11–12, 124.

39 Childe 1942a: 10.
40 *Ibid.*
41 Childe 1936a: 112.
42 Childe 1942a: 11–12; 1956b: 103.
43 Childe 1947a: 73.
44 Childe 1936a: 181.
45 Childe 1950c: 16.
46 Childe 1936a: 14–16, 39–41.
47 *Ibid.*, 51–53, 110–11.
48 *Ibid.*, 52–53.
49 Childe 1942a: 38.
50 Childe 1956a: 49–51.
51 Childe 1946b: 250.
52 Childe 1942a: 77.
53 Curwen 1938; Clark 1951.
54 Childe 1936a: 82.
55 Childe 1958c: 6.
56 Childe 1936a: 145–46; 1950a: 10.
57 Childe 1946a: 41.
58 Childe 1937a: 18.
59 Childe 1936a: 146–47.
60 Childe 1950a: 10.
61 Childe 1936a: 74.
62 Cf. *ibid.*, 105 with Childe 1942a: 51–52 and 1944b: 9.
63 Childe 1937a: 4.
64 Childe 1947a: 12.
65 *Ibid.*, 10–11.
66 Childe 1936a: 118.
67 Childe 1956a: 154.
68 Childe 1937a: 4; 1951a: 167.
69 Childe 1937a: 18; 1944a: 76–77; 1944d.
70 Childe 1937a: 14–18.
71 Childe 1942a: 16–17.
72 Childe 1945b: 6.
73 Childe 1944d; 1956a: 152–53.
74 Childe 1958c: 5.
75 Childe 1945b: 6.
76 Childe 1940b.
77 Childe 1951a: 36–37.
78 Childe 1957a: 173–74.
79 Letter of V. G. Childe to R.J. Braidwood, 1 August 1945.
80 Childe 1958b: 73; cf. Heichelheim 1958: 1 (originally published 1938, in German).
81 Childe 1936a: 1–2.
82 Childe 1935b: 11.
83 Childe 1936a: 270; 1942a: 11.
84 Childe 1942a: 26.
85 *Ibid.*, 37–38; Childe 1941a: 128; 1944a: 16.
86 Childe 1942a: 41.
87 Childe 1936a: 110.

88 *Ibid.*, 112–16.
89 *Ibid.*, 113–16, 260.
90 Childe 1942a: 53.
91 Childe 1936a: 118–19.
92 *Ibid.*, 123; Childe 1942a: 63.
93 Childe 1936a: 126–27.
94 *Ibid.*, 153.
95 *Ibid.*, 176, 183, 187–88; Childe 1937a: 14.
96 Childe 1936a: 98–99.
97 *Ibid.*, 146.
98 *Ibid.*, 256.
99 *Ibid.*, 251.
100 *Ibid.*, 248.
101 *Ibid.*, 212–13.
102 Childe 1942a: 189.
103 Childe 1936a: 259–60; 1942a: 123–24.
104 Childe 1936a: 262–66.
105 *Ibid.*, 260–62.
106 *Ibid.*, 267–68.
107 *Ibid.*, 145–46.
108 Childe 1958b: 72.
109 Gathercole 1976: 5.
110 Childe 1958b: 73; 1942a: 1.
111 Letter of V. G. Childe to O. G. S. Crawford, 3 January 1941 (Western Ms Collection, Bodleian Library, Oxford).
112 Childe 1958b: 73.
113 Childe 1942a: 83–96, 107–12, 123.
114 *Ibid.*, 59–61.
115 *Ibid.*, 62; 1950a: 157.
116 Childe 1942a: 123.
117 Childe 1944a: 35.
118 Childe 1942a: 94.
119 *Ibid.*, 104.
120 *Ibid.*, 92.
121 *Ibid.*, 132–37.
122 *Ibid.*, 116–17, 267–68.
123 *Ibid.*, 272.
124 Childe 1936a: 268.
125 Childe 1942a: 144–45, 148, 273.
126 *Ibid.*, 247–53.
127 *Ibid.*, 275.
128 Childe 1958b: 72–73.
129 Childe 1950c: 16.
130 Childe 1944a: 115.
131 *Ibid.*, 1–2.
132 *Ibid.*, 109–13.
133 *Ibid.*, 16.
134 *Ibid.*, 24.
135 Childe 1957b: 212.
136 Childe 1954g.
137 Childe 1944a: 48.
138 Childe 1942a: 260.
139 Childe 1944a: 71.

140 *Ibid.*, 58.
141 *Ibid.*, 67–70.
142 Winters 1968.
143 Childe 1944a: 78–97; 1945a.
144 See also Childe 1946: 75–76.
145 Childe 1944a: 107–8.
146 *Ibid.*, 1.
147 Kroeber 1919; Kroeber and Richardson 1940.
148 Childe 1944a: 109–14.
149 Childe 1936a: 4; 1946b: 250.
150 Childe 1943a.
151 Childe 1941a.
152 Childe 1950b.
153 Childe 1939a: xiii.
154 Childe 1958b: 72.
155 Childe 1939a: 220.
156 Childe 1936a: 95–96.
157 Childe 1958b: 72.
158 Childe 1939b: 10.
159 Childe 1939a: 327.
160 Childe 1935b: 14.
161 Childe 1939a: 265–66; 1942a: 140–41.
162 Childe 1936a: 200.
163 Childe 1939b: 25–26.
164 Childe 1939a: 265–66.
165 *Ibid.*, 321.
166 Childe 1947a: 65, 81.
167 *Ibid.*, 75.
168 *Ibid.*, 83.
169 *Ibid.*, 76.
170 Childe 1944a: 25.
171 Ravetz 1959: 66.

Chapter VII

1 Childe 1958b: 73; Rouse 1958: 83.
2 Childe 1958b: 73.
3 Letters of V.G. Childe to R.J. Braidwood, 1 August 1945 and 22 November 1945.
4 Miller 1956: 110–12, 133–46.
5 Daniel 1958: 66
6 *Ibid.*; see also Childe 1958a: 140.
7 Childe 1958b: 73; 1944d.
8 Childe 1942b; 1944a: 74–75.
9 Childe 1944d.
10 Childe 1937a.
11 Childe 1937b.
12 Letters of V.G. Childe to R.J. Braidwood, 24 July 1945, 1 August 1945, 9 January 1946; Letters of Braidwood to Childe, 14 July 1945, 5 November 1945, 18 July 1946.

13 Letter of R.J. Braidwood to V.G. Childe, 18 July 1946; Letter of Childe to Braidwood, 4 October 1956.
14 Childe 1937b.
15 Childe 1942a: 14–15.
16 Childe 1950a: 1.
17 Childe 1958b: 71.
18 Daniel 1975: 343.
19 Dragadze 1978: 119.
20 Childe 1938a: 182–83.
21 Childe 1943a: 22.
22 *Ibid.*; cf. Collingwood 1939: 122–27.
23 Childe 1944d.
24 Childe 1947b: 51.
25 *Ibid.*, 53–56.
26 Childe 1956a: 13.
27 Childe 1947a: 61.
28 Steward 1955: 209.
29 Childe 1951a: 35.
30 Childe 1946b: 243; see also Childe 1949b: 57 and 1951a: 15–16.
31 Childe 1950a: 2–3; 1953a: 3–5; 1956c: 13.
32 Childe 1944d: 19.
33 Childe 1958c: 5.
34 Childe 1951a: 16.
35 Childe 1946b: 247–50; 1949a: 4; 1951a: 9, 16.
36 Childe 1944d.
37 *Ibid.*
38 Childe 1956b: 5.
39 Childe 1946b: 250; 1947b: 60.
40 Childe 1947a: 1–3.
41 *Ibid.*, 43–59.
42 Collingwood 1946: 54–55.
43 Childe 1947a: 82.
44 Childe 1958b: 74.
45 Childe 1947a: 80.
46 Childe 1956a: 43.
47 Childe 1949a: 23; 1956b: 123.
48 Letter of V.G. Childe to R.J. Braidwood, 1 August 1945.
49 Childe 1947a: 11.
50 *Ibid.*, 59.
51 Childe 1946b: 248.
52 Childe 1951a: 1.
53 Childe 1956a: 53.
54 Childe 1947a: 69.
55 *Ibid.*, 3; Childe 1958b: 74.
56 Spaulding 1968.
57 Childe 1947a: 68–69.
58 *Ibid.*, 3.
59 Childe 1958c: 6–7; cf. Childe 1958b: 74.
60 Childe 1958b: 74.

61 Childe 1956a: 1.
62 Childe 1947a: 60; 1958c: 7.
63 Childe 1958c: 2, 6–7.

Chapter VIII

1 Childe 1942c, 1943b, 1950e, 1951b, 1953d, 1954c, 1954d, 1954e, 1954f, 1954g.
2 Childe 1944b: 1.
3 Childe 1956a: vi.
4 *Ibid.*, 10.
5 *Ibid.*, 38.
6 Childe 1936a: 132.
7 Childe 1951a: 8–9.
8 Childe 1956b: 9.
9 Childe 1944a: 56–57.
10 Childe 1947a: 2; 1949b: 62.
11 Cf. Childe 1944a: 56–57; 1947a: 64–65; 1950a: 1; 1957b: 213.
12 Childe 1949b: 60.
13 Childe 1956b: 54.
14 Childe 1949a: 6–7; 1956a: 163; 1958b: 73.
15 Childe 1949a: 19.
16 *Ibid.*, 5.
17 *Ibid.*, 11.
18 Darwin 1938.
19 Childe 1949a: 16–18; 1950b: 18; 1958c: 4.
20 Childe 1953c: 13–14; 1956b: 86–87.
21 Childe 1956a: 170.
22 Childe 1956b: 94.
23 Childe 1949a: 20–22; 1953c: 13.
24 Childe 1950b: 7–9, 13, 18; 1953c: 13, 17, 21.
25 Childe 1956b: 79–80.
26 *Ibid.*, 59–60, 106.
27 *Ibid.*, 1949a: 25, 64, 68, 107, 113, 119.
28 Childe 1947b: 60; 1956c: 11.
29 Childe 1956c: 10.
30 Childe 1958c: 8.
31 Childe 1947a: 80.
32 Childe 1954e.
33 Childe 1956c: 18.
34 Childe 1956b: 111–12.
35 *Ibid.*, 131.
36 Rouse 1958: 83.
37 McLellan 1975: 36.
38 Childe 1956b: 119.
39 Childe 1949a: 24; 1950b: 3, 18; 1953c: 13.
40 Childe 1956b: 1.
41 Childe 1949a: 25; 1954a: 8.
42 Childe 1938b; 1950b: 4, 18; 1956a: 45.

43 Childe 1956a: 172.
44 Childe 1949a: 26.
45 Childe 1958c: 5.
46 Childe 1954e, 1954f.
47 Gathercole 1971: 231; Rowlands 1971.

CHAPTER IX

1 Childe 1956a: 8; 1956b: 97, 130-31.
2 Childe 1944c: 23.
3 Childe 1951a: 28-29.
4 *Ibid.*, 29.
5 Childe 1944c: 23.
6 Childe 1944a: 25.
7 Childe 1951a: 6-7.
8 *Ibid.*, 26-27; 1949b: 58. The development of civilization along the coast of Peru may constitute an exception to Childe's generalization that a food-producing stage must always intervene between food-collecting and civilization (Moseley 1975).
9 Childe 1954f: 47-49.
10 Childe 1953a: 6.
11 Childe 1956a: 54, 164.
12 Childe 1951a: 22.
13 Childe 1944b: 10-11.
14 Childe 1936a: 40-41.
15 Childe 1935b: 7.
16 Childe 1942a: 17-19; 1950c: 3.
17 Childe 1951a: 26-27.
18 Childe 1944c.
19 *Ibid.*, 17.
20 *Ibid.*, 23.
21 Childe 1951a: 163-69.
22 *Ibid.*, 173.
23 Childe 1954b: 40.
24 Childe 1950c: 9; 1951a: 26-27.
25 Cf. Childe 1950c: 9-16 and 1930a: 2.
26 Childe 1944a: 35.
27 Childe 1946a: 56.
28 Childe 1947b: 59.
29 Childe 1956c: 19.
30 Childe 1951a: 38-41.
31 *Ibid.*, 54.
32 Childe 1946b: 249; 1949b: 61; 1951a: 34; 1958a: 12-14.
33 Childe 1946b: 249.
34 Childe 1958c: 3.
35 Childe 1951a: 34, 54-71.
36 Cf. Childe 1958a: 12-13 and 1958c: 4.
37 Childe 1946b: 249; 1951a: 33-34.

38 Childe 1958c: 4.
39 Childe 1946b: 249.
40 Steward 1953b: 240.
41 Childe 1949c, 1950d.
42 Childe 1950a: 98.
43 Childe 1951a: 56.
44 Childe 1942a: 52; 1950c: 5; 1953b: 201; 1953c: 15; 1958a: 50.
45 Childe 1950c: 5-6.
46 *Ibid.*, 8.
47 Steward 1953b: 240; Childe 1958a: 14.
48 Childe 1951a: 84.
49 Childe 1944b: 18-19, 24.
50 *Ibid.*, 8.
51 *Ibid.*, 22.
52 Childe 1946a: 32-33, 37-38.
53 *Ibid.*, 41, 48-50.
54 *Ibid.*, 78.
55 *Ibid.*, 95-96.
56 *Ibid.*, 24.
57 *Ibid.*, 41.
58 *Ibid.*, 96.
59 Childe 1958b: 73.
60 Childe 1946b: 250; 1947b: 60; 1951a: 29.
61 Dutt 1957a.
62 Gathercole 1974.
63 Childe 1938a: 182.
64 Childe 1958b: 73.
65 Childe 1950a: 204.
66 *Ibid.*, 92, 98, 107, 109, 157.
67 *Ibid.*, 133.
68 *Ibid.*, 222.
69 Childe 1950c: 9-16.
70 *Ibid.*, 17.
71 See also Childe 1951a: 161, 170.
72 Childe 1951a: 41, 167-68.
73 Childe 1952b.
74 Childe 1958b: 73.
75 Childe 1954a: 131-32.
76 Childe 1957a: iii.
77 *Ibid.*, 220.
78 *Ibid.*, 173-74.
79 *Ibid.*, 14.
80 *Ibid.*, 52-53.
81 *Ibid.*, 343-345.
82 *Ibid.*, 342; 1958a: 110-11.
83 Childe 1958a: 7.
84 *Ibid.*, 8; Childe 1958b: 74.
85 Letter of V. G. Childe to R. J. Braidwood, 4 October 1956.
86 Childe 1958a: 7-8.
87 Letter of V. G. Childe to R. J. Braidwood, 4 October 1956.
88 Childe 1958c: 7.
89 Childe 1958a: 76-77.
90 *Ibid.*, 95-97.

91 *Ibid.*, 103, 111.
92 Childe 1957c: 5.
93 Childe 1958a: 113-14.
94 *Ibid.*, 172-73.
95 *Ibid.*, 8.
96 Childe 1958b: 74.
97 Willey 1953.
98 Childe 1958a: 12-14.
99 *Ibid.*, 104; cf. 1950a: 166; 1954c: 204.
100 Childe 1958a: 78.
101 *Ibid.*, 113-14.
102 *Ibid.*, 157; for a review of Palmer's work, see Childe 1955b.
103 Childe 1958a: 63, 74, 141.
104 Rowlands 1971.
105 Letter of V. G. Childe to R. J. Braidwood, 17 November 1941.
106 Childe 1936a: 2.
107 Childe 1956a: 34.
108 *Ibid.*, 36-38, 80-82.
109 *Ibid.*, 121-22.
110 Concerning Childe's 'limited understanding of the nature of statistics', see Spaulding 1957.
111 Childe 1938a.
112 Childe 1950a: 2.
113 Childe 1956a: v-vi.
114 Childe 1950a: 6.
115 Childe 1956a: 107.
116 Childe 1958a: 14.
117 Childe 1957a: 122-23.
118 Childe 1958a: 43.
119 Childe 1957a: 13.
120 Childe 1958c: 6.
121 Childe 1958a: 122.
122 *Ibid.*, 123.
123 Childe 1952a: 237.
124 R. McC. Adams, personal communication, 12 March 1977.
125 Childe 1958b: 74.
126 Childe 1958c: 1-2.
127 Childe 1950f.
128 Letter of V. G. Childe to Alexander Gordon, 20 November 1956. A copy of this letter was provided to me by G. Munster.
129 Childe 1957c.
130 F. Smith 1964: ix.
131 Letter of Ethel Childe to the Vice-Chancellor of the University of London, 1 November 1957; cf. Lindsay 1958: 135-36.
132 Case 1957.

133 Letter of Ethel Childe, *op. cit.*, note 131.
134 Cf. Childe 1937a: 15; 1956b: 22, 41 and his letter to O. G. S. Crawford, 1940.
135 Letter of V. G. Childe to Mrs H. V. Evatt, 26 June 1931.
136 Letter of V. G. Childe to R. J. Braidwood, 29 May 1946.
137 Morris 1957.
138 Spriggs 1977.

CHAPTER X

1 Cf. Renfrew 1973a: 20–119.
2 Cf. Childe's reading outside of archaeology, as recorded in his notebooks deposited in the Institute of Archaeology, University of London, especially notebooks 44–48.
3 Daniel 1975: 247.
4 Mills 1903.

5 Trigger 1978: 75–95.
6 Braidwood 1958: 734.
7 Steward 1955: 181.
8 Sieveking 1976: xvi.
9 Clark 1974.
10 Hawkes 1954: 162.
11 See, e.g. Harris 1977.
12 Steward 1953a.
13 Wobst 1978.
14 Fried 1975.
15 H. Martin Wobst, personal communication, 18 March 1978.
16 Steward 1955: 12.
17 Klejn 1973.
18 Steward 1955: 5.
19 Childe 1950c: 3.
20 Haury 1962: 117.
21 Braidwood and Willey 1962: 352.
22 Childe 1950c: 3.
23 Adams 1974: 249.
24 Renfrew 1978.
25 McLellan 1975: 43.

26 Steward 1953b: 241.
27 Leone 1975: 197; see also Flannery 1973.
28 Childe 1947a.
29 Ravetz 1959: 62.
30 Childe 1951a: 29.
31 Childe 1938a: 182; 1945b: 6.
32 Adams 1966; Renfrew 1973b.
33 Cited from *Human Origins* in Braidwood 1958: 736.
34 Adams 1958: 1241.
35 Gathercole 1974.
36 *Ibid.*
37 Steward 1953b: 241.
38 Rouse 1958: 84.
39 Clark 1939.
40 Childe 1958c: 6.
41 Taylor 1948: 41; Willey and Phillips 1958: 5–6.
42 Childe 1947a: 69.
43 Binford 1977: 6–7.
44 Trigger 1978: 17.

BIBLIOGRAPHY

For an almost complete bibliography of the archaeological publications of V. Gordon Childe to 1956, see I. F. Smith 1956. Major works which appeared later include Childe 1956d,e; 1957a,b,c; 1958a,b,c. Smith's reference for Childe 1954a includes only part of this work. Works omitted from Smith's bibliography include Childe 1923, 1941d, 1952d, 1953b.

ABERCROMBY, JOHN, 'The Oldest Bronze-Age Ceramic Type in Britain: Its Probable Origin in Central Europe', *Journal of the Royal Anthropological Institute*, vol. 32: 373–97. 1902.

——*A Study of the Bronze Age Pottery of Great Britain and Ireland and its Associated Grave Goods*. 2 vols. Oxford, Oxford University Press, 1912.

ADAMS, R. McC., 'Review of V. G. Childe, *The Prehistory of European Society*', *American Anthropologist*, vol. 60: 1240–41. 1958.

——*The Evolution of Urban Society*. Chicago, Aldine, 1966.

——'Patterns of Urbanization in Early Southern Mesopotamia', in *Man, Settlement and Urbanism*, P. J. Ucko *et al.* (eds), 735–49. London, Duckworth, 1972.

——'Anthropological Perspectives on Ancient Trade', *Current Anthropology*, vol. 15: 239–58. 1974.

ALLEN, JIM, 'Aspects of Vere Gordon Childe', *Labour History*, no. 12: 52–59. 1967.

ANDERSON, JOSEPH, *Scotland in Pagan Times*. Edinburgh, Douglas, 1886.

ANONYMOUS, 'Science and Political Theory under the Soviets', *Nature*, vol. 144: 971–72. 1939.

ARTSIKHOVSKII, A. V., 'Archaeology', *Great Soviet Encyclopedia: A Translation of the Third Edition*, vol. 2, 245–50. New York, 1973.

BINFORD, L. R., 'Archaeological Systematics and the Study of Cultural Process', *American Antiquity*, vol. 31: 203–10. 1965.

——'General Introduction', in *For Theory Building in Archaeology*, L. R. Binford (ed.), 1–10. New York, Academic Press, 1977.

BRAIDWOOD, ROBERT J., 'Vere Gordon Childe, 1892–1957', *American Anthropologist*, vol. 60: 733–36. 1958.

BRAIDWOOD, R. J. and G. R. WILLEY, 'Conclusions and Afterthoughts', in *Courses Toward Urban Life*, R. J. Braidwood and G. R. Willey (eds), 330–59. Chicago, Aldine, 1962.

CASE, H. J., 'V. Gordon Childe', *The Times*, 13. 13 October, 1957.

CHANTRE, E., *L'Age du Bronze*. 3 vols. Paris, Baudry, 1875–76.

CHILDE, V. G., 'On the Date and Origin of Minyan Ware', *Journal of the Hellenic Society*, vol. 35: 196–207. 1915.

——'The East European Relations of the Dimini Culture', *Journal of the Hellenic Society*, vol. 42: 254–75. 1922a.

——'The Present State of Archaeological Studies in Central Europe', *Man*, vol. 22: 118–19. 1922b.

——*How Labour Governs: A Study of Workers' Representation in Australia*. London, Labour Publishing Company, 1923.

——*The Dawn of European Civilization*. London, Kegan Paul, 1925a.

——'When Did the Beaker-folk Arrive?' *Archaeologia*, vol. 74: 159–78. 1925b.

——'National Art in the Stone Age (review of M. Hoernes, *Urgeschichte der bildenden Kunst in Europa*)', *Nature*, vol. 116: 195–97. 1925c.

——*The Aryans: A Study of Indo-European Origins*. London, Kegan Paul, 1926.

——*The Most Ancient East: The Oriental Prelude to European Prehistory*. London, Kegan Paul, 1928.

——*The Danube in Prehistory*. Oxford, Oxford University Press, 1929.

——*The Bronze Age*. C.U.P., 1930a.

——'The Early Colonization of North-eastern Scotland', *Proceedings of the Royal Society of Edinburgh*, vol. 50; 51–78. 1930b.

——'Excavations in a Chambered Cairn at Kindrochat, near Comrie, Perthshire', *Proceedings of the Society of Antiquaries of Scotland*, vol. 64, 264–72. 1930c.

——*Skara Brae: A Pictish Village in Orkney*. London, Kegan Paul, 1931a.

——'The Chambered Long Cairn at Kindrochat, near Comrie, Perthshire', *Proceedings of the Society of Antiquaries of Scotland*, vol. 65: 281–93. 1931b.

——'Chronology of Prehistoric Europe: A Review', *Antiquity*, vol. 6: 206–12. 1932a.

——'Chambered Cairns near Kilfinan, Argyll', *Proceedings of the Society of Antiquaries of Scotland*, vol. 66: 415–25. 1932b.

——'Is Prehistory Practical?' *Antiquity*, vol. 7: 410–18. 1933a.

——'Races, Peoples and Cultures in Prehistoric Europe', *History*, vol. 18: 193–203. 1933b.

——'Trial Excavations at the Old Keig Stone Circle, Aberdeenshire', *Proceedings of the Society of Antiquaries of Scotland*, vol. 67: 37–52. 1933c.

——'Excavations at Castlelaw Fort, Midlothian', *Proceedings of the Society of Antiquaries of Scotland*, vol. 67: 362–88. 1933d.

——'Excavations at Castlelaw, Midlothian, and the small Forts of North Britain', *Antiquaries Journal*, vol. 13: 1–12. 1933e.

——*New Light on the Most Ancient East: The Oriental Prelude to European Prehistory*. London, Kegan Paul, 1934a.

——'Final Report on the Excavation of the Stone Circle at Old Keig, Aberdeenshire', *Proceedings of the Society of Antiquaries of Scotland*, vol. 68: 372–93. 1934b.

——'Neolithic Settlement in the West of Scotland', *Scottish Geographical Magazine*, vol. 50: 18–25. 1934c.

——*The Prehistory of Scotland*. London, Kegan Paul, 1935a.

——'Changing Methods and Aims in Prehistory (Presidential Address for 1935)', *Proceedings of the Prehistoric Society*, vol. 1: 1–15. 1935b.

——'Excavation of the Vitrified Fort of Finavon, Angus', *Proceedings of the Society of Antiquaries of Scotland*, vol. 69: 49–80. 1935c.

——'Notes on some Duns in Islay', *Proceedings of the Society of Antiquaries of Scotland*, vol. 69: 81–84. 1935d.

——*Man Makes Himself*. London, Watts, 1936a.

——'Carminnow Fort; Supplementary Excavations at the Vitrified Fort of Finavon, Angus; and Some Bronze Age Vessels from Angus', *Proceedings of the Society of Antiquaries of Scotland*, vol. 70: 341–62. 1936b.

——'A Promontory Fort on the Antrim Coast', *Antiquaries Journal*, vol. 16: 179–98. 1936c.

——'A Prehistorian's Interpretation of Diffusion', in *Independence, Convergence and Borrowing in Institutions, Thought and Art*, 3–21. Harvard Tercentenary Publications. Cambridge, Harvard University Press, 1937a.

——'Symposium on Early Man, Philadelphia', *Antiquity*, vol. 11: 351. 1937b.

——'A Round Cairn near Achnamara, Loch Sween, Argyll', *Proceedings of the Society of Antiquaries of Scotland*, vol. 71: 84–89. 1937c.

——'On the Causes of Grey and Black Coloration in Prehistoric Pottery', *Man*, vol. 37: 43–44. 1937d.

——'The Orient and Europe: Presidential Address to Section H (Anthropology)', *Report of the British Association for the Advancement of Science*, 1938: 181–96. 1938a.

——'The Oriental Background of European Science', *The Modern Quarterly*, vol. 1: 105–20. 1938b.

——'The Experimental Production of the Phenomena Distinctive of Vitrified Forts', *Proceedings of the Society of Antiquaries of Scotland*, vol. 72: 44–55, 1938c.

——'Excavations Carried out by H.M. Office of Works in the Bronze Age Levels at Jarlshof in 1937', *Proceedings of the Society of Antiquaries of Scotland*, vol. 72: 348–62. 1938d.

——'Doonmore, a Castle Mound near Fair Head, Co. Antrim', *Ulster Journal of Archaeology*, 3rd Series, vol. I: 122–35. 1938e.

——*The Dawn of European Civilization*. 3rd edition, revised. London, Kegan Paul, 1939a.

——'The Orient and Europe', *American Journal of Archaeology*, vol. 44: 10–26. 1939b.

——*Prehistoric Communities of the British Isles*. London, Chambers, 1940a.

——'Archaeology in the USSR', *Nature*, vol. 145: 110–11. 1940b.

——'War in Prehistoric Societies', *The Sociological Review*, vol. 32: 127–38. 1941a.

——'The Defences of Kaimes Hill-fort, Midlothian', *Proceedings of the Society of Antiquaries of Scotland*, vol. 85: 43–54. 1941b.

——'Examination of the Prehistoric Fort on Cairngryfe Hill, near Lanark', *Proceedings of the Society of Antiquaries of Scotland*, vol. 85: 213–18. 1941c.

——'Man and Science from Early Times', *University Forward*, vol. 6(5): 4–7. 1941d.

——*What Happened in History*. Harmondsworth, Penguin Books, 1942a. (all page numbers cited from the first American edition of 1946).

——'Prehistory in the USSR. II. The Copper Age in South Russia', *Man*, vol. 42: 130–36. 1942b.

——'The Antiquity and Function of Antler Axes and Adzes', *Antiquity*, vol. 16: 258–64. 1942c.

——'The Chambered Cairns of Rousay,' *Antiquaries Journal*, vol. 22: 139–42. 1942d.

——'Archaeology as a Science', *Nature*, vol. 152: 22–23. 1943a.

——'Rotary Querns on the Continent and in the Mediterranean Basin', *Antiquity*, vol. 17: 19–26. 1943b.

——'Another late Viking House at Freswick, Caithness', *Proceedings of the Society of Antiquaries of Scotland*, vol. 77: 5–17. 1943c.

——*Progress and Archaeology*. London, Watts, 1944a.

——*The Story of Tools*. London, Cobbett, 1944b.

——'Archaeological Ages as Technological Stages', *Journal of the Royal Anthropological Institute*, vol. 74: 7–24. 1944c.

——'The Future of Archaeology,' *Man*, vol. 44: 18–19. 1944d.

——'Directional Changes in Funerary Practices During 50,000 Years', *Man*, vol. 45: 13–19. 1945a.

——'Introduction to the Conference on the Problems and Prospects of European Archaeology', *University of London, Institute of Archaeology, Occasional Paper*, no. 6: 6–12. 1945b.

——*Scotland Before the Scots*. London, Methuen, 1946a.

——'Archaeology and Anthropology', *Southwestern Journal of Anthropology*, vol. 2: 243–51. 1946b.

——'The Distribution of Megalithic Cultures and their Influence in Ancient and Modern Civilization', *Man*, vol. 46: 97. 1946c.

——*History*. London, Cobbett, 1947a.

——'Archaeology as a Social Science', *University of London, Institute of Archaeology, Third Annual Report*: 49–60. 1947b.

——'Megaliths,' *Ancient India*, vol. 4: 4–13. 1948.

——*Social Worlds of Knowledge* (L. T. Hobhouse Memorial Trust Lecture, no. 19). London, Oxford University Press, 1949a.

——'Organic and Social Evolution', *The Rationalist Annual*, 1949: 57–62. 1949b.

——'Neolithic House-types in Temperate Europe', *Proceedings of the Prehistoric Society*, vol. 15: 77–86. 1949c.

——*Prehistoric Migrations in Europe*. Oslo, Aschehaug, 1950a.

——*Magic, Craftsmanship and Science*. Liverpool, Liverpool University Press, 1950b.

——'The Urban Revolution', *The Town Planning Review*, vol. 21: 3–17. 1950c.

——'Cave Men's Buildings', *Antiquity*, vol. 24: 4–11. 1950d.

——'Axe and Adze, Bow and Sling: Contrasts in Early Neolithic Europe', *Schweizerische Gesellschaft für Urgeschichte, Jahrbuch*, vol. 40: 156–62. 1950e.

——'Comparison of Archaeological and Radiocarbon Datings', *Nature*, vol. 166: 1068–69. 1950f.

——*Social Evolution*. New York, Schuman, 1951a.

——'The Balanced Sickle', *Aspects of Archaeology in Britain and Beyond: Essays Presented to O.G.S. Crawford*, W.F. Grimes (ed.), 39–48. London, Edwards, 1951b.

——*New Light on the Most Ancient East*. 4th edition, revised. London, Routledge and Kegan Paul, 1952a.

——'Trade and Industry in Barbarian Europe till Roman Times', in *The Cambridge Economic History of Europe*, vol. 11, M. Postan and E. Rich (eds), 1–32. Cambridge, Cambridge University Press, 1952b.

——'Re-excavation of the Chambered Cairn of Quoyness, Sanday, on behalf of the Ministry of Works in 1951–52', *Proceedings of the Society of Antiquaries of Scotland*, vol. 86: 121–39. 1952c.

——'Archaeological Organization in the USSR', *Anglo-Soviet Journal*, vol. 13(3): 23–26. 1952d.

——'The Constitution of Archaeology as a Science', in *Science, Medicine and History. Essays on the Evolution of Scientific Thought and Medical Practice, written in Honour of Charles Singer*, vol. 1, E.A. Underwood (ed), 3–15. Oxford, Oxford University Press. 1953a.

——'Old World Prehistory: Neolithic', in *Anthropology Today*, A. L. Kroeber (ed.), 193–210. Chicago, University of Chicago Press, 1953b.

——'Science in Preliterate Societies and the Ancient Oriental Civilizations', *Centaurus*, vol. 3: 12–23. 1953c.

——'The Significance of the Sling for Greek Prehistory', in *Studies Presented to David Moore Robinson*, G. E. Mylonas and D. Raymond (eds), 1–5. Washington University, 1953d.

——'Prehistory', in *The European Inheritance*, E. Barker, G. Clark and P. Vaucher (eds), 3–155. Oxford, Oxford University Press, 1954a.

——'Early Forms of Society', in *A History of Technology*, vol. I, C. Singer, E. J. Holmyard and A. R. Hall (eds), 38–57. Oxford, Clarendon Press, 1954b.

——'Rotary Motion', *A History of Technology*, vol. I, C. Singer, E. J. Holmyard and A. R. Hall (eds), 187–215. Oxford, Clarendon Press, 1954c.

——'The Diffusion of Wheeled Vehicles', *Ethnographisch-Archäologische Forschungen*, vol. 2: 1–16. 1954d.

——'Archaeological Documents for the Prehistory of Science (I)', *Journal of World History*, vol. 1: 739–59. 1954e.

——'Archaeological Documents for the Prehistory of Science (II)', *Journal of World History*, vol. 2: 9–25. 1954f.

——'The Socketed Celt in Upper Eurasia', *University of London, Institute of Archaeology, Tenth Annual Report*, 11–25. 1954g.

——'The Significance of Lake Dwellings in the History of Prehistory', *Sibrium*, vol. 2, pt 2: 87–91. 1955a.

——'The Sociology of the Mycenaean Tablets', *Past and Present*, vol. 7: 76–77. 1955b.

——*Piecing Together the Past: The Interpretation of Archaeological Data*. London, Routledge and Kegan Paul, 1956a.

——*Society and Knowledge: the Growth of Human Traditions*. New York, Harper, 1956b.

——*A Short Introduction to Archaeology*. London, Muller, 1956c.

——'Maes Howe', *Proceedings of the Society of Antiquaries of Scotland*, vol. 88: 155–207. 1956d.

——'The Past, the Present, and the Future (Review Article)', *Past and Present*, vol. 10: 3–5. 1956e.

——*The Dawn of European Civilization*. 6th edition, revised. London, Kegan Paul, 1957a.

——'The Evolution of Society', *Antiquity*, vol. 31: 210–13. 1957b.

——'The Bronze Age', *Past and Present*, vol. 12: 2–15. 1957c.

——*The Prehistory of European Society*. Harmondsworth, Penguin, 1958a.

——'Retrospect', *Antiquity*, vol. 32: 69–74. 1958b.

——'Valediction', *Bulletin of the Institute of Archaeology, University of London*, No. 1: 1–8. 1958c.

CHILDE, V. G. and M. C. BURKITT, 'A

Chronological Table of Prehistory', *Antiquity*, vol. 6: 185–205. 1932.

CHILDE, V. G. and C. D. FORDE, 'Excavations in Two Iron Age Forts at Earn's Heugh, near Coldingham', *Proceedings of the Society of Antiquaries of Scotland*, vol. 66: 152–82. 1932.

CHILDE, V. G. and W. G. GRANT, 'A Stone-age Settlement at the Braes of Rinyo, Rousay, Orkney (First Report)', *Proceedings of the Society of Antiquaries of Scotland*, vol. 73: 6–31. 1939.

——'A Stone-age Settlement at the Braes of Rinyo, Rousay, Orkney (Second Report)', *Proceedings of the Society of Antiquaries of Scotland*, vol. 81: 16–42. 1947.

CHILDE, V. G. and W. THORNEYCROFT, 'The Vitrified Fort at Rahoy, Morvern, Argyll', *Proceedings of the Society of Antiquaries of Scotland*, vol. 72: 23–43. 1938.

CLARK, J. G. D., 'Russian Archaeology: The Other Side of the Picture', *Proceedings of the Prehistoric Society*, vol. 2: 248–49. 1936.

——*Archaeology and Society*. London, Methuen, 1939.

——*Prehistoric England*. London, Batsford, 1940.

——'Folk Culture and the Study of European Prehistory', *Aspects of Archaeology in Britain and Beyond*, W. F. Grimes (ed.), 39–48. London, Edwards, 1951.

——'Prehistoric Europe: The Economic Basis', in *Archaeological Researches in Retrospect*, G. Willey, (ed.), 31–58. Cambridge, Mass., Winthrop, 1974.

——'Prehistory Since Childe', *Bulletin of the Institute of Archaeology, University of London*, no. 13: 1–21. 1976.

COLLINGWOOD, R. G., *An Autobiography*. Oxford, Oxford University Press, 1939.

——*The Idea of History*. Oxford, Oxford University Press, 1946.

CRAWFORD, O. G. S., *Man and his Past*. London, Oxford University Press, 1921.

——'Review of *The Dawn of European Civilization*', *The Antiquaries Journal*, vol. 6: 89–90. 1926.

CURWEN, E. C., 'The Hebrides: A Cultural Backwater', *Antiquity*, vol. 12: 261–89. 1938.

DANIEL, GLYN, 'Editorial', *Antiquity*, vol. 32: 65–68. 1958.

——'Preface' to the 4th edition of *Man Makes Himself*, ix–xii. London, Watts, 1965.

——*A Hundred and Fifty Years of Archaeology*. London, Duckworth, 1975.

——'Editorial', *Antiquity*, vol. 51: 1–7. 1977a.

——'Of Archaeology and of Agatha, review of *Mallowan's Memoirs*', *The Times Literary Supplement*, No. 3940, 30 September, 1103. 1977b.

DARWIN, C. G., 'Logic and Probability in Physics', *Report of the British Association for the Advancement of Science*, 21–34. 1938.

DELAPORTE, L. J., *Mesopotamia*. London, Kegan Paul, 1925.

DRAGADZE, TAMARA, 'A Meeting of Minds: A Soviet and Western Dialogue', *Current Anthropology*, vol. 19: 119–28. 1978.

DUTT, R. PALME, 'Tribute to Memory of Gordon Childe', *Daily Worker*, 3. 22 October 1957a.

——'Prof. V. Gordon Childe', *The Times*, 14. 24 October, 1957b.

EMERY, WALTER B., *Archaic Egypt*. Harmondsworth, Penguin, 1961.

EVANS, A. J., 'Late-Celtic Urn-field at Aylesford, Kent', *Archaeologia*, vol. 52: 317–88. 1890.

——'"The Eastern Question" in Anthropology', *Proceedings of the British Association for the Advancement of Science*, 906–22. 1896.

EVANS, JOAN, *A History of the Society of Antiquaries*. London, The Society of Antiquaries, 1956.

——'Early Memories of Oxford', *Antiquity*, vol. 51: 179. 1977.

FARRINGTON, BENJAMIN, *Science in Antiquity*. London, Home University Library, 1936.

——*Science and Politics in the Ancient World*. London, Allen and Unwin, 1939.

FLANNERY, K. V., 'Archaeology with a Capital "S"', *Research and Theory in Current Archaeology*, C. L. Redman (ed), 47–53. New York, Wiley, 1973.

FOX, CYRIL, *The Archaeology of the Cambridge Region*. Cambridge, Cambridge University Press, 1923.

——'A Bronze Age Barrow on Kilpaison Burrows', *Archaeologia Cambriensis*, vol. 81: 1–35. 1926.

——*The Personality of Britain*. Cardiff, National Museum of Wales, 1932.

FRANKFORT, HENRI, *The Birth of Civilization in the Near East*. New York, Doubleday. 1956.

FRASER, A. D., 'A Review of *The Dawn of European Civilization*', *American Journal of Archaeology*, vol. 30: 196–97. 1926.

FRIED, MORTON, *The Notion of Tribe*. Menlo Park, Cummings, 1975.

GATHERCOLE, PETER, 'Patterns in Prehistory: An Examination of the Later Thinking of V. Gordon Childe', *World Archaeology*, vol. 3: 225–32. 1971.

——'Childe, Empiricism and Marxism', Ms. 1974.

——'Gordon Childe and the Prehistory of Europe', Ms. 1975.

——'Childe the "Outsider"', *RAIN*, no. 17: 5–6. 1976.

GRADMANN, ROBERT, 'Beziehungen zwischen Pflanzengeographie und Siedlungsgeschichte', *Geographische Zeitschrift*, vol. 12: 305–25. 1906.

GREEN, SALLY, *A Biography of Vere Gordon Childe*. Ms. 1976.

HALL, H. R., 'Review of V. G. Childe, *The Most Ancient East*', *Antiquity*, vol. 4: 247–49. 1930.

HARRIS, MARVIN, *The Rise of Anthropological Theory*. New York, Crowell, 1968.

——*Cannibals and Kings: The Origins of Cultures*. New York, Random House, 1977.

HAURY, E. W., 'The Greater American Southwest', *Courses Toward Urban Life*, R. J. Braidwood and G. R. Willey (eds), 106–31. Chicago, Aldine, 1962.

HAWKES, C. F. C., *The Prehistoric Foundations of Europe to the Mycenaean Age*. London, Methuen, 1940.

——'Archaeological Theory and Method: Some Suggestions from the Old World', *American Anthropologist*, vol. 56: 155–68. 1954.

HEICHELHEIM, F. M., *An Ancient Economic History*, vol. I. Leiden, Sijthoff's, 1958.

HOBHOUSE, L. T., G. C. WHEELER and M. GINSBERG, *The Material Culture and Social Institutions of Simpler Peoples*. London, Chapman and Hall, 1915.

HOMO, L., *Primitive Italy and the Beginings of Roman Imperialism*. London, Kegan Paul, 1926.

KLEJN, L. S., 'Marxism, the Systemic Approach and Archaeology', In *The Explanation of Culture Change*, C. Renfrew (ed.), 691–710. London, Duckworth, 1973.

——'Kossinna im Abstand von vierzig Jahren', *Jahresshrift für mitteldeutsche Vorgeschichte*, vol. 58: 7–55. 1974.

KLINDT-JENSEN, OLE, *A History of Scandinavian Archaeology*. London, Thames and Hudson, 1975.

KOSSINNA, GUSTAF, *Die Herkunft der Germanen*. Leipzig, Kabitzsch, 1911.

——*Ursprung und Verbreitung der Germanen in vor- und frühgeschichtlicher Zeit*. Berlin, Germanen-Verlag, 1926.

KROEBER, A. L., 'On the Principle of Order in Civilization as Exemplified by Changes of Fashion', *American Anthropologist*, vol. 21: 235–63. 1919.

KROEBER, A. L. and J. RICHARDSON, 'Three Centuries of Women's Dress Fashions: A Quantitative Analysis', *University of California Anthropological Records*, vol. 5: 111–54. 1940.

KUHN, T. S., *The Structure of Scientific Revolutions*. Chicago, University of Chicago Press, 1970.

LEACOCK, E. B., 'Introduction', to *The Origin of the Family, Private Property and the State*, by Frederick Engels. 7–67. New York, International Publishers, 1972.

LEONE, M. P., 'Views of Traditional Archaeology', *Reviews in Anthropology*, vol. 2: 191–99. 1975.

LINDSAY, JACK, *Life Rarely Tells*. London, Bodley Head, 1958.

LUBBOCK, JOHN, *The Origin of Civilization*. 4th edition. London, Longmans, Green, 1882.

——*Prehistoric Times as Illustrated by Ancient Remains and the Manners and Customs of Modern Savages*. 7th edition. New York, Holt, 1913.

MCKERN, W. C., 'The Midwestern Taxonomic Method as an Aid to Archaeological Culture Study', *American Antiquity*, vol. 4: 301–13. 1939.

MCLELLAN, DAVID, *Marx*. London, Fontana, 1975.

MALLOWAN, MAX, *Mallowan's Memoirs*. London, Collins, 1977.

MARWICK, H., 'Review of V. G. Childe, *Skara Brae*', *Antiquity*, vol. 6: 104–5. 1932.

MILLER, MIKHAIL, *Archaeology in the U.S.S.R.*

London, Atlantic Press, 1956.

MILLS, W. C., 'Excavations of the Adena Mound', *Ohio Archaeological and Historical Quarterly*, vol. 10: 452–79. 1903.

MONTELIUS, OSCAR, *Der Orient und Europa*. Stockholm, Königl. Akademie der schönen Wissenschaften, Geschichte und Alter-thumskunde, 1899.

MORET, A. and G. DAVY, *From Tribe to Empire: Social Organization among Primitives and in the Near East*. London, Kegan Paul, 1926.

MORRIS, JOHN, 'Gordon Childe', *Past and Present*, vol. 12: 2. 1957.

MOSELEY, M. E., *The Maritime Foundations of Andean Civilization*. Menlo Park, Cummings, 1975.

MOVIUS, H. L., 'Review of J. G. D. Clark *et al.* (eds). *Contributions to Prehistoric Archaeology Offered to Professor V. Gordon Childe*', *Man*, vol. 57: 42–43. 1957.

MULVANEY, D. J., 'V. G. Childe, 1892–1957', *Historical Studies; Australia and New Zealand*, vol. 8: 93–94. 1957.

MYRES, JOHN L., *The Dawn of History*. London, Williams and Norgate, 1911.

——'Primitive Man in Geological Time', *Cambridge Ancient History*, J. B. Bury, S. A. Cook and F. E. Adcock (eds). 1–56. Cambridge, Cambridge University Press, 1923a.

——'Neolithic and Bronze Age Cultures', *Cambridge Ancient History* (*op. cit.*), 57–111. 1923b.

——'The Cretan Labyrinth: A Retrospect of Aegean Research', *Journal of the Royal Anthropological Institute*, vol. 63: 269–312. 1933.

NILSSON, SVEN, *The Primitive Inhabitants of Scandinavia*. London, Longmans, Green. 1868.

PEAKE, HAROLD J., *The Bronze Age and the Celtic World*. London, Benn, 1922.

——'The Beginning of Civilization', *Journal of the Royal Anthropological Institute*, vol. 57: 19–38. 1927.

PEAKE, HAROLD and HERBERT J. FLEURE, *The Corridors of Time*, vol. I. *Apes and Men*; vol. II. *Hunters and Artists*; vol. III. *Peasants and Potters*; vol. IV. *Priests and Kings*. Oxford, Oxford University Press, 1927.

PERRY, W. J., *The Children of the Sun*. London, Methuen, 1923.

——*The Growth of Civilization*. London, Methuen, 1924.

PETRIE, W. M. F., *The Making of Egypt*. London, Sheldon, 1939.

PIGGOTT, STUART, 'Vere Gordon Childe, 1892–1957', *Proceedings of the British Academy*, vol. 44: 305–12. 1958a.

——'The Dawn: and an Epilogue', *Antiquity*, vol. 32: 75–79. 1958b.

——'Childe, Vere Gordon', *Dictionary of National Biography 1951–1960*, E. T. Williams and H. M. Palmer (eds). 218–19. Oxford, Oxford University Press, 1971.

PIGGOTT, STUART *et al.*, 'Archaeology of the

Submerged Land-surface of the Essex Coast', *Proceedings of the Prehistoric Society*, vol. 2: 178–210. 1936.

PIGGOTT, STUART and MARJORIE ROBERTSON, *Three Centuries of Scottish Archaeology*. Edinburgh, Edinburgh University Press, 1977.

PITT-RIVERS, A., *The Evolution of Culture and Other Essays*. Oxford, Oxford University Press, 1906.

PUMPELLY, R. (ed.), *Explorations in Turkestan*. 2 vols. Washington, Carnegie Institution, 1908.

RATZEL, FRIEDRICH, *Anthropogeographie*. 2 vols. Stuttgart, Engelhorn, 1882–91.

RAVETZ, ALISON, 'Notes on the Work of V. Gordon Childe', *The New Reasoner*, vol. 10: 56–66. 1959.

REISNER, G. A., *Archaeological Survey of Nubia, Bulletin No. 3*. Cairo, National Printing Department, 1909.

RENFREW, A. C., 'Trade and Culture Process in European Prehistory', *Current Anthropology*, vol. 10: 151–69. 1969.

——*Before Civilization: The Radiocarbon Revolution and Prehistoric Europe*. London, Cape, 1973a.

——*Social Archaeology*. Southampton, The University, 1973b.

——'Trajectory Discontinuity and Morphogenesis: The Implications of Catastrophe Theory for Archaeology', *American Antiquity*, vol. 43: 203–22. 1978.

RENFREW, A. C., D. HARKNESS and R. SWITSUR, 'Quanterness, Radiocarbon and the Orkney Cairns', *Antiquity*, vol. 50: 194–204. 1976.

ROUSE, IRVING, 'Vere Gordon Childe, 1892–1957', *American Antiquity*, vol. 24: 82–84. 1958.

——*Introduction to Prehistory: A Systematic Approach*. New York, McGraw-Hill, 1972.

ROWLANDS, M. J. 'The Archaeological Interpretation of Prehistoric Metalworking', *World Archaeology*, vol. 3: 210–24. 1971.

SIEVEKING, G. 'Progress in Economic and Social Archaeology', In *Problems in Economic and Social Archaeology*, G. de G. Sieveking et al. (eds), xv–xxvi. London, Duckworth, 1976.

SMITH, F. B., 'Foreword,' *How Labour Governs*, by V. G. Childe. 2nd ed., v–x. Victoria, Melbourne University Press, 1964.

SMITH, G. ELLIOT, *The Ancient Egyptians and the Origin of Civilization*. London, Harper, 1923.

——*The Diffusion of Culture*. London, Watts, 1933.

SMITH, I. F., 'Bibliography of the Publications of Professor V. Gordon Childe', *Proceedings of the Prehistoric Society*, vol. 21: 295–304. 1956.

SPAULDING, A. C., 'Review of V. G. Childe, *Piecing Together the Past*', *American Anthropologist*, vol. 59: 564–65. 1957.

——'Explanation in Archaeology', in *New Perspectives in Archaeology*, S. and L. Binford (eds), 33–39. Chicago, Aldine, 1968.

SPRIGGS, MATTHEW, 'Where the Hell are We? (or a Young Man's Quest)', in *Archaeology and Anthropology*, M. Spriggs (ed.). *British Archaeological Reports, Supplementary Series*, No. 19, 3–17. 1977.

STEWARD, J. H., 'Evolution and Process', in *Anthropology Today*, A. L. Kroeber (ed.), 313–26. Chicago, University of Chicago Press, 1953a.

——'Review of V. G. Childe, *Social Evolution*', *American Anthropologist*, vol. 55: 240–41. 1953b.

——*Theory of Culture Change*. Urbana, University of Illinois Press. 1955.

TALLGREN, A. M., 'Archaeological Studies in Soviet Russia', *Eurasia Septentrionalis Antiqua*, vol. 10: 129–70. 1936.

TAYLOR, W. W., *A Study of Archaeology*. Washington, American Anthropological Association, Memoir 69. 1948.

THOMSON, GEORGE, 'Review of V. G. Childe, *History*', *The Modern Quarterly*, N.S. vol. 4: 266–69. 1949.

TIMES OBITUARY, 'Prof. V. Gordon Childe: An Eminent Prehistorian', *The Times*, 12. 21 October, 1957.

TREVELYAN, G. M., *Illustrated English Social History*. 4 vols. London, Longmans, Green, 1949.

TRIGGER, B. G., *Time and Traditions: Essays in Archaeological Interpretation*. Edinburgh, Edinburgh University Press, 1978.

WHEATLEY, O. K., *Vere Gordon Childe – A Study of the Concepts He Employed for an Historical Interpretation of Archaeological Data*. Ms, 1972.

WHEELER, R. E. MORTIMER, 'Prof. V. Gordon Childe: Robust Influence in Study of the Past', *The Times*, 13. 23 October, 1957.

WILLEY, G. R., *Prehistoric Settlement Patterns in the Viru Valley, Peru*. Washington, Bureau of American Ethnology, Bulletin 135, 1953.

WILLEY, G. R. and P. PHILLIPS, Method and Theory in American Archaeology. Chicago, University of Chicago Press, 1958.

WILSON, DANIEL, *The Archaeology and Prehistoric Annals of Scotland*. London, Macmillan, 1851.

WINTERS, H. D., 'Value Systems and Trade Cycles of the Late Archaic in the Midwest', in *New Perspectives in Archaeology*, S. R. and L. R. Binford (eds), 175–221. Chicago, Aldine, 1968.

WOBST, H. M., 'The Archaeo-ethnology of Hunter-Gatherers or the Tyranny of the Ethnographic Record in Archaeology', *American Antiquity* 43: 303–9. 1978.

ILLUSTRATION ACKNOWLEDGMENTS

Courtesy R. J. Braidwood 19

Edinburgh University Library 2

Institute of Archaeology, London, Photo Lyvia Morgan Brown 33

Photo courtesy Institute of Archaeology, London 11, 16, 17, 21, 23, 26, 29, 30, 31

The Journal of the Royal Anthropological Institute (Vol. 74) 8, 9

Photo Jaroslav Malina 22

National Portrait Gallery, London 5

Photo S. P. O'Riordain, courtesy Department of Archaeology, University College, Dublin 32

Photo courtesy Stuart Piggott 1, 20, 24, 25, 27

Photo courtesy Colin Renfrew 28

Riksantikvarieämbetet, Stockholm, Photo ATA 3

Reprinted by permission of Routledge & Kegan Paul Ltd 7

Photo Crown copyright, Royal Commission on Ancient Monuments, Scotland 13, 14, 15

Photo Crown copyright, reproduced by permission of the Scottish Development Department 12

Diagram on page 46 and map on page 78 were drawn by Peter Bridgewater

INDEX

A figure 2 or 3 in brackets immediately following a page reference means
that there are two or three separate references to the subject on that page.
References in *italic* type indicate illustrations. These are plate numbers,
not page numbers.
The following abbreviations are used: Amer. – American; anthrop. –
anthropologist; arch. – archaeologist; Aust. – Australian; Br. – British.